SURVIVE
AND
THRIVE

SURVIVE AND THRIVE

HOW TO PREPARE FOR ANY DISASTER WITHOUT AMMO, CAMO, OR EATING YOUR NEIGHBOR

BILL FULTON AND **JEANNE CHILTON DEVON**

HARPER HORIZON

ISBN 978-1-4003-3424-7 (eBook)

ISBN 978-1-4003-3423-0 (SC)

Library of Congress Control Number: 2023933208

Printed in India

23 24 25 26 27 28 29 30 31 32 /REP/ 15 14 13 12 11 10 9 8 7 6 5 4 3 2 1

CONTENTS

INTRODUCTION

You probably never even thought about it. Not *really*. It's okay, neither did anyone else who wasn't sitting in a subterranean bunker with an AR-15 defending a stash of canned beans and powdered milk. *That* guy is the one that the vast majority of today's prepping books have been written for. You are not that guy.

If someone had asked you a few years ago (in the BeforeTimes™), "What if there's a global pandemic or a deadly virus—are you prepared?" you would have wondered what cheesy Hollywood plague movie they'd been watching or silently judged their tinfoil hat. But then 2020 happened, and . . . *surprise!* Overnight, a weird microscopic Nerf ball became the most infamous pathogen since the 1918 Spanish flu.

COVID-19 made people realize that, without much notice, life can go ass-over-teakettle, and that a microbe one five hundredth the width of a human hair can make you forsake civilization like a Himalayan mountain hermit for weeks or even months on end. When hunker-down orders, quarantines, and lockdowns came, a huge swath of regular, confused, freaked-out America was left to either pore over mind-numbing websites ending in *.gov*, figure out which talking head to listen to on cable news, or just go with their gut instinct . . . that turned out to be hoarding toilet paper. The early days of catastrophic shortages of masks, hand sanitizer, and bleach wipes, and the Armageddon-style grocery store shelves proved that being unprepared has a cost and that we can't always depend on some magical supply chain to cover our asses.

It's been years of calamity—a deadly worldwide pandemic, devastating forest fires, hurricanes, floods, unprecedented deadly heat waves, blizzards, and freezing temperatures that have left millions of people without power and water for days on end. Now there are new reports that say climate change will be even worse than we thought.

And here you are. You don't have 100 acres, or a bunker, or a stockpile of weapons, and eighty million rounds of ammo, and you don't want to. But suddenly all those only-happens-in-the-movies scenarios have turned out to be not-so-fictional.

That's where we come in. This handbook is for you. It's a reasonable, comprehensive, basic guide on how to get prepared for . . . anything. We can't stop the bad stuff from happening, but we *can* help you make it a whole lot less stressful for you and your family—and at the same time get you excited about living, step-by-step, in a new way that is good for you, your community, and the world you leave for future generations.

Contrary to what you've learned by watching fake reality shows, *prepping* doesn't mean heading into the woods to eat bugs and drink tree sap to survive. At its best, prepping is collaborative and societal, it's green, it's sustainable, it's family-friendly, it's educational and functional, and it makes your community and the planet a better place. It's not, nor should it be, scary. It should be empowering and even fun. Ultimately, it's a model for twenty-first-century living. Really.

Up until now, the material written on *prepping* for disasters has been littered with creepy Armageddon porn written by paranoids who are afraid that inner city looters are coming for their guns, their daughters, and their pocket Constitutions. But here's the reality: you don't need vast acreage surrounded by trip wires and pitfall traps to make it through the next disaster. And you don't need a garage full of paper towels either (we're looking at *you*, Walmart shoppers, throat-punching each other in aisle five). What you need is a reasonable, commonsense plan that works for your life, and a guide to get you there.

This is that guide. We're here to answer your questions; provide tips, tricks and work-arounds; deliver *aha!* moments and everyday hacks; provide handy checklists; and alleviate your anxiety about what to do in case of fire, flood, earthquake, hurricane, blizzard, power outage, pandemic, or Florida meth gators. Okay, if it's that last one, just *run*.

The Aztecs may have been a couple of decades off with their prophecy, but it doesn't mean you can't start right now to get ready for whatever fresh hell awaits us in the rest of the *Terrible '20s*. Unfortunately, most of us are only one earthquake, hurricane, or wildfire away from real trouble. And not to rain on anyone's parade, but COVID-25 or 28 or 30 is chilling out there in the rain forest, just waiting for someone to eat a sloth. There's no way any of us can *predict* the future—but we can *prepare* for it. So let's do this!

Spoiler Alert: You—yes, *you*—are about to become a prepper.

YOUR GUIDES

So who are these people anyway? you may be asking yourself.

Bill Fulton is an Army vet turned FBI undercover operative who infiltrated a right-wing extremist group determined to overthrow the government and start the next Revolution. (You weren't expecting that, were you?) He owned a military surplus store catering to the Beard 'n Bunker set, and now homesteads his own sustainable organic farm in Vermont where he also bakes, knits, distills essential oils, raises critters, and has been known to drink home-brewed beer with a chicken. He's prepared for it all, and he's living the self-sufficient, sustainable lifestyle with his wife and two kids.

Jeanne Devon is a Seven Sisters graduate who took that fancy degree, moved four thousand miles from the east coast to Alaska, and became a writer and adventurer. (Sorry, Mom and Dad). She forages and preserves wild plants, subsistence gardens, and fishes Alaska's wild seafood. She cooks, camps, and travels across the Last Frontier with her husband. She's also a national award-winning blogger and *New York Times* bestselling author. She's spent years in the rural subarctic, 150 miles from a movie theater, over two thousand miles from the nearest professional sports franchise, and at least 70°F from any sane people. She's survived earthquakes, volcanoes, -60°F, power outages, and being stranded on a boat in the Gulf of Alaska.

We'll be your guides to tackle the basics—and then some. Stick with us and you'll become a pro at this stuff! In this one volume you'll learn about:

- **WATER:** Basic water requirements to stay alive and healthy, safety and storage, and some science-y ways to find water in unlikely places and purify it when you need it.
- **FOOD:** What foods are the best for long-term storage across a spectrum of special dietary requirements, how much you need of what, and how to grow, harvest, preserve, and utilize your own food even if you're gardenless in Manhattan!
- **SHELTER:** An introduction to how to prepare your home, including how to turn off utilities and find unseen hazards, weak spots, and safety zones.
- **SAFETY:** Simple tricks and methods to secure yourself and your shelter to ensure safety from the wrath of nature and bad guys.
- **EMERGENCY EVACUATION BAGS:** Easy itemized lists for your emergency first aid kit and what clothing and gear are must-haves depending on where you live, plus specialized add-ons for specific disasters you're likely to encounter in your area.
- **WELLNESS:** Things you can do to keep your mind and body in great shape so you can take care of yourself and others. There really are keys to happiness!
- **HACKS:** Handy hacks and survival tips you never knew that just might save your bacon (or your homemade vegan breakfast strips).
- **LISTS, LISTS, LISTS!** Basic essentials, checklists, and to-dos at the end of every chapter so you never have to wonder if you're prepared.

But first things first. What's your starting point? And don't worry if it's square one. That's where everyone starts!

You'll have to do a hard self-assessment on questions one through nineteen, but we'll give you the answer to question twenty. It's your own brain and stress. If there are a few, or more than a few, of the other questions that you can't answer, or if you know that your answer isn't going to cut it in an emergency, don't despair. This book is in your hands and we've got you covered!

Self-Assessment (Twenty Questions)

1. How long could you survive on the food you have if something happened right this very minute that kept you from the grocery store?
2. How much emergency water do you have and is it properly stored?
3. How full is your gas tank right now and how far would you get if there were no functioning gas stations?
4. Do you have any survival supplies at work like food, water, or clothing?
5. Do you know what wild forageable foods grow in your area and which plants are dangerous?
6. Do you know how to preserve food? (canning, salting, fermenting, pickling, or drying)
7. Do you know the best way to escape from your apartment or place of work?
8. Do you have a fire extinguisher on every floor of your home?
9. If you were separated from your loved ones in a disaster, do you have an official plan to reconnect that everyone knows? Do you have photos of your family in your wallet, not just on your cell phone?
10. How long could you survive if your car went off a rural road in a snowstorm?
11. Do you have a secondary source of heat in your home?
12. Is anyone who doesn't live with you likely to end up in your home during an emergency and are you prepared for their needs?
13. How much prescription medication do you have on hand right now?
14. How much pet food and pet meds do you have on hand?
15. What is your secondary source of power if there's a blackout?
16. Where are all your critical documents located right now and are they safe from a storm, flood, fire, or other disaster? Are they accessible on paper and digitally? (will, insurance, identification, medical information, photos, contact information)
17. Do you know how to shut off water, power, and gas to your home? Do you have the tools to do it?
18. Do you have the ingredients and know-how to cook simple basic meals with shelf-stable pantry staples?
19. How quickly could you and everyone you live with be ready to evacuate your home with all the critical items and supplies you need?
20. What's the one big obstacle to successfully navigating a disaster that you may not have been thinking about?

Before you commit to doing anything or start squirreling away emergency rations, you'll first need to take a pause and assess the strengths and limitations of your current living environment—and the people living in it. Everyone will have different skills, levels of preparedness, and needs. Your job is to think through where you are, what will be available to you, and what areas you want to work on to make sure that everyone feels comfortable in their ability to handle the emergencies or natural disasters that are most likely to come your way.

ASSESS YOUR SITUATION

WHERE DO YOU LIVE? How close are you to town? What is within walking distance: grocery store, police station, emergency shelter, pharmacy, school, gas station, emergency clinic or hospital? How far away are these resources and do you know alternate routes to get there if you're driving?

WHAT KIND OF DWELLING DO YOU HAVE? Your preparation is going to be different if you live in a fifth-floor urban apartment, a house in the suburbs, or somewhere even more rural. Do you have easy access to the outside? Are you on the ground floor? Does your home have more than one floor? What are the escape routes and is there access to the roof?

HOW MUCH SPACE DO YOU HAVE? Do you live in a postage-stamp-sized apartment, or do you have acreage? If you have outdoor space, is it a huge yard, or just a balcony? Do you have a garage, a basement, or a storage shed, or are you going to have to make sure every square inch is Tetris-ed to maximum advantage? What about outside? Could you put in a garden, or would growing food require containers on the balcony or maybe microgreens in your kitchen?

HOW MANY PEOPLE LIVE WITH YOU? Do you have a spouse? Kids? Elderly parents? How many pets do you have? (Yes, they're people too!) And is there anyone who may come to your home for support during an emergency like neighbors, friends, or relatives? You have to think of more than just you and figure out how you'll be able to help those around you too.

WHAT TRANSPORTATION DO YOU HAVE ACCESS TO? Do you have a car or two? A bicycle? An ATV? Is public transportation available? Are you near an airport, train station, or bus stop? Is everyone in your home able-bodied?

Would you be able to leave your area safely if you had to, or will you be hunkering down, come what may?

WHAT ABOUT YOUR UTILITIES? Do you cook with gas or electricity? Do you have city water or a well? How is your home heated? How is your water heated? Do you have a landline phone?

WHAT COULD GO WRONG? What types of natural disasters are most likely to occur where you live? Fire, flood, tornado, earthquake, hurricane, blizzard, mudslide, nuclear accident, avalanche? Do you live near a military base or major infrastructure that could be targeted in a hostile attack?

WHO'S GOT THE MAD SKILLZ? Assess the skills of all those in your household. Maybe it's just you, or maybe you've got a whole brigade. Either way, go down this list of basic and important survival skills and figure out who knows what. Are there any gaping holes? Are there any skills you or others would be willing or excited to learn about? Ideally, someone in your household should know how to do or learn how to do all these things. Write their initials next to each of these skills:

_____ Basic first aid including wound care and CPR

_____ Starting a fire with or without a lighter or matches

_____ Cooking with fire (s'mores do not count!)

_____ Canning/preserving food

_____ Filtering water

_____ Foraging and knowing what toxic or poisonous plants and mushrooms grow near you

_____ Fishing/hunting: knowing regulations and locations for your area, and understanding the basics and safety

_____ Growing food: microgreens, container gardens, hydroponics, or garden plots

_____ Making hardtack and other long-term portable survival food

_____ Cooking: understanding the basics of food safety and how to prepare simple meals with pantry staples that people will want to eat

_____ Making yeast and baking bread

_____ Signaling for help

_____ Map reading and navigation

_____ How to turn off utilities safely: gas, electric, and water.

_____ Basic car maintenance: checking fluids, checking air pressure and changing tires, using jumper cables, changing fuses and lights, basic troubleshooting

_____ Tying simple utilitarian knots

_____ Safely using an axe, hatchet, and knife

_____ Being an organized leader: checking, updating, and replacing survival supplies; making sure there's an emergency plan and everyone knows their part; organizing practices or teaching/learning sessions for all of the above skills.

Now that you're in the right headspace, it's time to survive and thrive!

CHAPTER 1

WATER

Y ou can survive without food for a couple of weeks but you'll only last about 100 hours (that's a little over four days) without water—less if the temperature is hot. Not to be a buzzkill right off the bat, but without water you're dead in a long weekend. That's why we start with water and why you should too.

After oxygen and basic shelter, this is as fundamental as it gets. Having a sufficient supply of drinkable water is essential, but there are some very important steps you must take, or you could ruin the most important survival stash you have!

And don't think you're covered just because you have running water right now. Water lines can burst from age, earthquake, or freezing; water can become contaminated; lack of electricity can knock out your pump; or the whole water utility can go down. As a matter of fact, the first things likely to be impacted by a natural disaster are water and electricity. And with that 100-hour death clock ticking, you want to make sure you've got a ready supply of clean water, no matter what's going on in the outside world.

HOW MUCH WATER DO I NEED?

The magic number for drinking and hygiene is one gallon per person, per day. You'll drink about half of that, and use the other half for hygiene needs. The Federal Emergency Management Agency (FEMA) recommends you have three days' supply of water on hand. *Days?* Sorry, FEMA, we beg to differ. If space allows, try to have enough water to last your household for two weeks or longer.

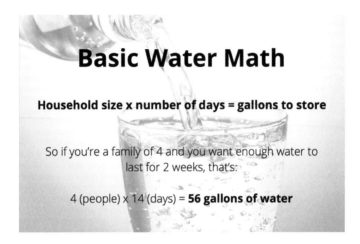

Basic Water Math

Household size x number of days = gallons to store

So if you're a family of 4 and you want enough water to last for 2 weeks, that's:

4 (people) x 14 (days) = **56 gallons of water**

Why so much water? Because finding, transporting, filtering, and disinfecting water is a ginormous pain in the ass, and the longer you can go before having to deal with it, the happier you will be. Bad water (even if it looks crystal clear) can lead to illness, dysentery, weakness, fatigue, inability to eat, and a host of other problems that can make you worse off than the actual disaster. We hope you'll never have to thank us, but if you end up needing water for more than three days, you definitely will.

Dogs will drink about one ounce per pound of body weight per day, and cats will drink a total of five to ten ounces per day, depending on their size. So factor them into the equation too!

HOW THE HECK DO I STORE THAT MUCH WATER?

If you're trying right now to imagine fifty-six gallon milk jugs full of water and wondering where you're going to keep them all, stop right there. There is a best way to store water safely, but it involves some critical dos and don'ts.

- **DO NOT** store water in anything but *food-grade water storage containers.* You'll be able to tell if the container is safe in a couple of ways. Plastic containers marked with 1, 2, 4, or 7 on the bottom are all acceptable and food-grade for water storage. A food-grade container will also have some kind of marking or indication saying it's *"refrigerator safe"* or *"freezer safe."*

- **DO NOT** store water in any container (even food-grade) if it has *ever* been used to hold anything else—even food. Make sure your containers are brand new and designated for water storage only. So no rinsed-out milk jugs, Gatorade bottles, or used Tupperware. You will never get all those chocolate milk molecules out of the pores in your plastic—and bacteria love chocolate milk as much as you do.

- **DO NOT** store water in anything that cannot be sealed. An open container is easily contaminated and provides a breeding ground for microbes. Your rain barrel may be full, but you don't even want to know what's living in there, never mind actually dipping a cup in there and drinking it.

- **DO NOT** store water in a warm place or where it is exposed to direct sunlight. Basements, pantries, closets, and garages away from windows are all good locations. Think cool and temperature controlled. Crazy temperature fluctuations and heat will make your water spoil faster. Nope, water doesn't last forever. We'll get to that.

- **DO** make sure you rinse and sanitize your containers before you fill them with the water you plan to drink. This will ensure that your water doesn't taste *funny* and will get rid of any residual bacteria or plastic chemical residue on the inside of the container. Just put one teaspoon of regular bleach in a quart of water, pour it into your container, and swish it around for thirty seconds so all inner surfaces are covered. Then dump the water out, fill it up, and you're good to go!

THE BEST WAY TO STORE WATER

It all depends on:

- How much space you have
- Your budget
- The size of your household
- How much water you want to store

The good news is that there are a few options if you have limited space.

Water Bricks

These ingenious tough little storage units are incredibly efficient, safely stackable, easy to move and handle, and can be configured to fit into almost any space. If your objective is to fit as much water as possible into as little space as possible, or into an awkward space (like closets or under a bed or desk), these are for you. They come in 1.6-gallon and 3.5-gallon sizes. They can be stacked up to five levels high, and each brick has a handle, so it's easy for most adults to move them around. You can also get one with a special lid with a spigot so you can dispense water straight out of the brick.

Water bricks have a fill line that can be used to make ice. Just fill to the indicated mark and freeze it for use in a cooler, to extend the life of food in your fridge if the power goes out, or to help keep medications that require refrigeration from spoiling. (See *products* in Appendix B for more.)

Five- and Seven-Gallon Plastic Water Containers

There are many different cost options when choosing a slightly larger container. Cost depends on how tough and how leak-proof you want your container to be.

The most rigorously tested, toughest, most leak-proof five-gallon water cans come from exactly where you'd expect—the military. These containers have been put through multiple stress tests and they survive it all. They are easy to fill, easy to pour from, and easily transported. You can pick up a semi-stackable military water container from LCI for about forty-five dollars with the knowledge that it will survive being dropped from a low-flying helicopter, getting run over by a Jeep, and all the other stuff the military could think up. And they'll last almost forever. (See Appendix B for more.)

Budget Buys

If cost is your top concern, and you know you'll be treating your water supply more gently than the US Army, you can find good food-grade plastic water storage containers that are easier on the budget and will still get the job done. Our suggestion is Aqua-tainer from Reliance Products—check out Appendix B for more!

Water Barrels

If you've got the space and the budget, and don't anticipate having to move your water supply around, consider one big water barrel that holds fifty-five gallons, or more than one barrel if you have the desire and the room. If you have a basement, this is an ideal option but may not be realistic if you're in an apartment or small space.

Fifty-five gallons should take care of a family of four for two weeks. But for convenience, it's always a good idea to have smaller, more portable containers around in addition to the big barrel. If you've got all your eggs in one basket (or all your water in one barrel), make sure it stays in perfect condition and out of the sun.

Bathtub Bladders

No, these are not as gross as they sound, and come in handy. You don't always know when an emergency will hit. But when you have advanced notice that a hurricane or weather event is coming, it never hurts to save up some extra tap water just in case. We recommend the WaterBOB bathtub storage emergency drinking water bladder. (See Appendix B.)

You don't want to hear this, but once you've prepared your water supply, and stored it properly, you'll still need to replace it every six months to be sure it's free from bacteria that may have developed. Changing out your supply twice a year is *still* less of a pain in the ass than trying to make undrinkable water drinkable. So when you're planning, be sure you can move your containers around for emptying and refilling, or that there's a ground drain you can use to empty that big fifty-five-gallon tank. And best of all,

think about ways you can use the water you're recycling so it isn't wasted: wash the car or water the lawn, the garden, or indoor plants! Make sure you add a calendar entry to remind yourself to swap out the water every six months.

Can't I just buy cases and cases of bottled water? you ask. Technically, yes, but that's a *lot* of cases of bottled water, and if you do that, we will judge you and so will the Earth. A twenty-four-pack of bottled water contains about three gallons. That's three days for one person. So, if a family of four used nothing but bottled water, that's about 450

plastic water bottles you've put out into the world in *just two weeks*. Not cool, water prepper—not cool.

What if I run out or didn't prepare? We've tried to avoid it, but here we are. Hurricanes, floods, or water pipe breakage may cause local authorities to recommend you use only bottled, boiled, or disinfected water. Nobody's perfect. If you didn't anticipate your water needs, there are still things you can do without driving through your neighborhood going full *Mad Max*. But you *must be* diligent and prepare carefully. Anyone who grew up playing the Oregon Trail has died of dysentery enough. You remember the trauma; don't relive it.

SNEAKY SOURCES OF POTABLE WATER YOU HAVE RIGHT IN YOUR HOUSE:

- **THE RESERVE IN YOUR HOT WATER HEATER.** Water heaters with tanks store fifty gallons or more of drinkable water. *Turn off the gas or electricity to the water heater first* to avoid damaging your water heater or potentially causing a fire. It will take at least twelve hours for the water to cool once the power has been turned off. After the water has cooled, open the drain valve which is located at the bottom of the hot water heater to retrieve the water. You can attach a garden hose to the drain valve to easily fill your container.
- **THE WATER IN YOUR TOILET TANK.** (Not the bowl—we repeat, *not* the bowl!) As long as it doesn't have any chemical tablets or cleaners in it, it will give you three to five gallons.
- **ICE CUBES IN THE FREEZER.**
- **LIQUID IN CANNED VEGETABLES.** (Eau de green beans *will* keep you hydrated!)
- **WATER FROM POOLS OR SPAS** is fine for washing or bathing.

FIND YOUR OWN WATER SOURCE

Rain

Collecting rainwater from your balcony or yard may make you feel like a wild badass, but don't get carried away just yet. It's sad but true that water falling from clouds and through the air picks up all the toxic crap humanity is pumping into the atmosphere, so it actually isn't good to drink unless you disinfect and filter it first. Most rainwater collection systems gather water after it's run off the roof, which means bugs, and bird poop, and well . . . you get the idea.

That said, rainwater collection is an age-old method for gathering a renewable supply of water, which is a great option if you don't want to worry about your stored water running out. Ancient Romans had neighborhoods with large cisterns, and paved courtyards to help capture runoff. And don't even get us started on the aqueducts!

Self-replenishing rainwater collecting is commonplace in countries like Australia and Germany. The US has been slower to catch up, but the burgeoning green-building movement will make rooftop catchment and other forms of urban water harvesting more popular. There are now even some cities, like Tucson and Seattle, that *require* rainwater collection systems in new housing developments.

Some states and cities require permits for rainwater collection or greywater use. (Greywater is water that comes from any sinks, showers, and drains that aren't in contact with fecal matter. Blackwater is the term used for that.) For individual users, it's usually a simple process and is there just to be sure everyone's on the same page and you're not going to inadvertently contaminate groundwater. People get touchy about groundwater for good reason!

Don't wait for disaster to strike to start thinking about what kind of rainwater collection system you want. You should have whatever system you'll use set up well beforehand so you can be all smug like the wild, badass nature god/goddess that you are.

So if you want to set up a rainwater collection system, go for it. Just make sure you have what you need to properly disinfect and filter it if you want to drink it.

Drinking aside, there are still plenty of uses for rainwater, like washing vehicles and pets, flushing toilets, watering plants and gardens, washing clothes, and bathing.

How practical and productive a rainwater collection system is depends a lot on where you live and how large of an area (like a roof) you can collect from. But there's no question that harvesting and utilizing rainwater is a net sum gain for the planet. In many areas it lessens the burden on increased water demand from dwindling aquifers and other water sources.

Government regulation at multiple levels and the manufacturers of appliances have been making water efficiency a top priority over the years, but efficiency can only take us so far. You'll never be able to effectively flush a toilet with a tablespoon of water, so it falls to us to pick up the mantle and find ways to contribute. This is good not only in an emergency, but to develop a greener and more sustainable lifestyle, which in turn makes you a better human, *and* more able to handle an emergency. See how that works?

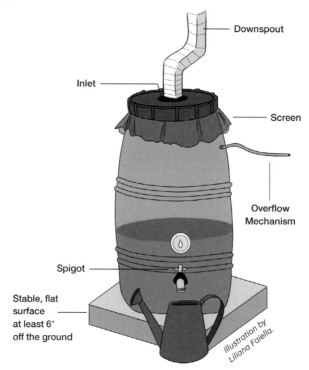

You can take rainwater collection as far as you want—from leaving a bucket under a downspout and using what you collect to water houseplants (they'll love the non-chlorinated treat), to a DIY garbage can system for non-drinking use, to using a simple food-grade polyethylene rain barrel you can convert to drinking water if necessary (using the methods discussed in this chapter), to complex containment systems with metal cisterns, or to underwater tanks costing tens of thousands of dollars that would make you the toast of ancient Rome. It's easy to find a system that works within your budget, your space, your needs, and the availability and importance of having an extra water supply.

A rain barrel is a great way to start your rainwater collecting adventure. The average size of a home-use rain barrel is between forty and sixty gallons and fits under a downspout that diverts the runoff from your roof. The best roofs for rainwater collecting are metal, but any type of roof will work.

Let's say your roof is 50 feet x 30 feet, making it 1,500 square feet. That's slightly smaller than average. If you live in a fairly rainy state like Tennessee, that means your own roof can provide you with 44,715 gallons of rainwater a year! In a dry state like Arizona, (where arguably you need it most), it can provide almost 10,000 gallons a year, which is 10,000 gallons better than nothing. In areas where the water bill is high and the water supply is low, it can really start to make sense to invest in rainwater collection. (See Appendix B for what we consider the gold standard rainwater collection system.)

MAKE YOUR OWN WATER SOURCE

Dehumidifiers and Atmospheric Water Generators

A great emergency drinking-water hack (presuming you've got electricity) is to use a dehumidifier, which takes water molecules right out of the air. Keep the reservoir clean and disinfected, boil the water, and run it through a coffee filter before drinking. Or if you want to be fancy you can buy an atmospheric water generator (AWG) that is specifically designed to create potable water and leaves you with pure drinkable water right in the reservoir. It turns out to be less expensive than bottled water, and as long as you have electricity and it's over 35°F (3°C) you should be good to go. AWGs produce anywhere from one to seven gallons a day and cost anywhere from eight hundred to a few thousand dollars.

The High School Science Class Magic of the Solar Still

If you're really in a jam, there's a DIY water hack that costs almost nothing and can produce clean drinkable water even in the desert.

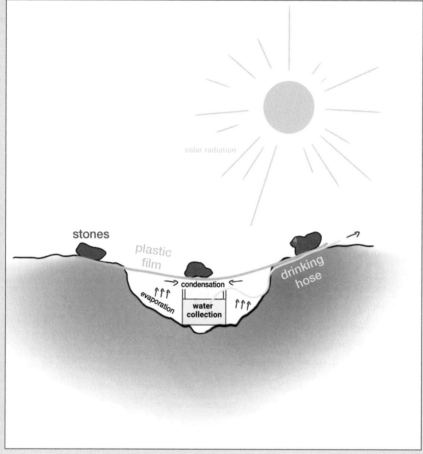

Illustration by Liliana Faiella.

MATERIALS

- A wide-mouth container (a clean bucket, or glass jar)
- Heavy clean plastic sheeting (approximately 4'x 4' for one still)
- A shovel or trowel
- Some rocks
- Vegetation (if possible, and especially if your soil is dry)

CONSTRUCTION

1. Dig a hole. Find a fairly level spot with loose soil that gets sunshine for most of the day, if you can. Make the hole about two feet across and deep enough that your container can rest at the bottom, with the top of the hole eight to twelve inches above the rim of the container.
2. Place the container in the center of the hole. Choose a container with a wide mouth and with a base wide enough so it doesn't tip over.
3. If you have moist vegetation, like grass, weeds, or leaves, pack it around the container at the bottom of the hole.
4. Lay the plastic sheeting over the top of the hole.
5. Place rocks and/or dirt around the edge of the plastic sheeting to hold it in place over the hole, and to seal the hole as best you can.
6. Place one rock in the center of the plastic sheeting, directly over the container. Make sure you allow the rock to make a depression in the plastic and that it is located over the mouth of the container.
7. When everything is in place, leave the still for twenty-four to forty-eight hours. Don't keep checking the still or you will let out all the moisture and slow down the process.
8. As the sun penetrates the plastic it will warm the air inside the hole, like a greenhouse. The moisture from the trapped air, the soil, and the vegetation will evaporate and condense on the bottom side of the plastic sheet and run down to the center, where it will drip into your container!
9. After twenty-four to forty-eight hours, enjoy your pure, potable water!

The amount of water you get depends on several factors: the moisture in the air, the amount of vegetation you use, the weather conditions, and the moisture in the soil. If you don't get enough water quickly enough, you can always make more than one solar still.

Natural Water Collection

The same principle of *don't drink it unless you have to* goes for water from ponds, creeks, and rivers. Save this kind of water for plants or washing dishes or clothes if you can. But if you need to, you can drink outside water *if* you disinfect and filter it first.

1. Choose moving water (river/stream) over stagnant water (pond/lake).
2. Start with the clearest water you can find.
3. Do not collect water that is visibly dark, smells like chemicals, or has an oily sheen.
4. Allow the water to sit until solids and cloudiness settle to the bottom.
5. Pour the top portion of clear water through a coffee filter and dump out the sediments at the end. Then disinfect your filtered water using one of the methods below.

Use Google Maps to look at satellite views of your area, and scan for water sources near you so you know where they are. Print the locations on paper or write them down in the notes section at the end of this chapter in case you don't have power.

DON'T FORGET TO DISINFECT!

Boiling

If you end up, for some reason, with naturally found water as your only drinking source, bringing it to a rolling boil for two full minutes will kill off the microbial nasties, and running it through a coffee filter once or twice will take care of most of the rest. But even if you kill and filter out every little microbe, if water is chemically contaminated or has heavy metals, you can't make it safe to drink no matter what you do. So, don't go boiling up petroleum-contaminated flood water and thinking you're good to go, because it won't turn out well. Disinfectants will only work on organic contaminants.

Boiling water takes a lot of heat and energy too, so if you don't have electric power or gas, you will want to use a different method—like bleach.

Bleach

If you can't boil water, bleach is a good alternative. (Do not drink or inject bleach, no matter what someone tells you.) Use the chart below to calculate how much you need. Don't use color-safe bleach or Tuscan Breeze bleach, just regular, plain old Clorox bleach. You don't need much, and you want to be very sure you use the right amount, so have a dropper to measure it.

This is also a good way to disinfect your own stored supply of water if you suspect it's been sitting too long or been in a warm location where bacteria might breed.

EMERGENCY DISINFECTION OF DRINKING WATER

Volume of Water	6% Bleach Additive	8.25% Bleach Additive
1 gallon	8 drops	6 drops
2 gallons	16 drops ($^1/_4$ tsp)	12 drops ($^1/_8$ teaspoon)
4 gallons	$^1/_3$ teaspoon	$^1/_4$ teaspoon
8 gallons	$^2/_3$ teaspoon	$^1/_2$ teaspoon

Once you've added the bleach, let it sit for a few hours or pour it back and forth from container to container to get rid of the chlorine smell and so it doesn't taste like you're drinking pool water.

Iodine

Add five drops of 2 percent tincture of iodine to each quart of water you want to disinfect. If the water is cloudy, you can double the amount. After you add the iodine, let the water sit for at least thirty minutes before drinking.

Disinfectant Tablets

You can disinfect water with purification tablets that contain chlorine, iodine, chlorine dioxide, or other disinfecting agents. They may make the water taste a little funny, and some people experience irritation of the mouth or throat when they drink a lot of this kind of water. So these are great for an emergency but not really meant for long-term use.

You can buy tablets like Potable Aqua and MicroPur online or at pharmacies or camping and outdoor supply stores. Strengths vary but generally fifty tablets would last an adult for a week.

HOW TO FILTER WATER

Most water filtration systems you can buy are not designed for high-volume use, but their effectiveness and portability make them a great second choice in addition to your own stored water supply. And for anywhere from a hundred to a couple thousand dollars, larger-capacity filtration systems can rid your water of all manner of plagues, parasites, and sediment. There are lots of great products mentioned in Appendix B—but you can always make your own!

BYOB (Build Your Own Bucket filtration system)

For those who love a good DIY project and want to purify larger volumes of water, you can even build your own bucket bio-filtration system using, you guessed it, a stack of buckets. It's easy to make, cheap, and effective. The bucket system essentially does what water treatment plants do to purify water, but on a much smaller scale. A bucket bio-filter will remove solids and waterborne pathogens. A three-bucket system should last you for about 5,000 gallons. Using our handy water math, that means it will last one person more than thirteen years! The setup requires lots of rinsing, so you will have to create and prep your bucket system *before* you need it, so it's ready to go.

The High School Science Class Magic of the Bucket Bio-Filtration System

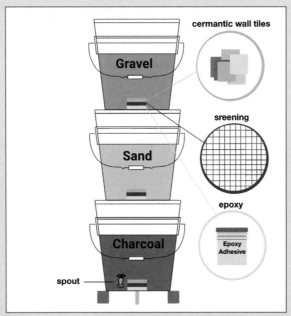

Illustration by Liliana Faiella.

ITEMS YOU'LL NEED (YOU CAN FIND THESE AT ANY HARDWARE STORE):

- Three five-gallon buckets with lids to use for filtering media
- One extra five-gallon bucket to rinse the media
- Drill with 1" and 2" drill bit/hole saws
- Fifty-pound bag of pea gravel
- Fifty-pound bag of sand
- Twenty-five pounds of activated charcoal (small diameter if possible)
- About two feet of window screening
- Three square ceramic bathroom tiles
- Scissors
- Two cinder blocks or something to use as a sturdy stand that the bucket can straddle

FIFTEEN STEPS TO CLEAN, DRINKABLE WATER

1. Drill a 1-inch hole in the center of the bottom of all three buckets.
2. Change over to the 2-inch hole saw and drill a hole in the center of the lid of two of the three buckets. Don't drill the final lid.
3. Cut two 3-inch squares of screen for each bucket. Epoxy the two pieces of screen on top of each other on the inside of the buckets so they cover the 1-inch holes.
4. Let the epoxy cure.
5. After the epoxy has cured, place a ceramic tile over the screening with its shiny side up. Use a small amount of epoxy in the corners of the tile to hold it in place.
6. Choose a location for your bucket stack so you won't have to move it. If you are in an earthquake zone, make sure it won't fall on your car or essential utility infrastructure in your home. Consider leaving the three buckets side by side under a tarp until you need them.
7. Make sure the activated charcoal is smashed fine. It should be .08-inch to .1-inch (2 mm) in diameter. You can buy it that way (recommended) or smash it yourself (not recommended unless you need to smash something).
8. Rinse all the media separately in five- to ten-pound batches by placing it in the fourth bucket, adding water, sloshing it around, and pouring the water out. Repeat this process until the water runs clear. It may take a few times, but it will increase the efficiency of the system.
9. Put the rinsed media in their designated buckets: one for gravel, one for sand, one for charcoal.
10. Snap the two lids with the holes on to the charcoal and sand buckets.
11. Place the two cinder blocks (or whatever you're using) at a distance so the edges of the bucket can be stable on each side but leaving space in between.
12. Place the charcoal bucket across the cinder blocks. Make sure it is stable.
13. Center the sand bucket on top of the charcoal bucket and check for stability again.
14. Put the gravel bucket on top of the sand bucket to top off the stack. Once again make sure it is stable. Place the lid with no hole loosely on top to keep out dust and dirt while you're not using your filter.
15. You can pour up to three gallons of water at a time into the top bucket for filtration. Place a container on the ground under the hole, between the cinder blocks, to collect your filtered water. If the water is cloudy, it just means you didn't rinse quite well enough. Put water through until it runs clear and enjoy your drinkable clean water, master prepper!

BUT I DON'T LIKE WATER!

You are so not alone. There are many people, despite being 65 percent water themselves, who just aren't fans of the H²O. And even though plain clean water is the best way to stay hydrated, let's face it—it tastes like . . . water. If you have to boil it or add bleach or iodine it can be even worse. There's no reason to be miserable if you don't have to be, so have a stash of water enhancers like Stur or Mio, or alternative beverages like 100 percent fruit juices, shelf-stable boxed milk, unsweetened iced tea mix, or sports drinks with electrolytes (in moderation). Just avoid high-fructose corn syrup and beware of drinks that can actually dehydrate you like the ones containing caffeine and alcohol that act as diuretics. That means they make you pee more than you drink. Beer, anyone?

Do what you need to do to make sure your body is hydrated, because becoming dehydrated is the last thing you want.

If you're stressed, it's easy to miss the signs of dehydration. Also, if you're over sixty-five, you're more likely to miss indicators of dehydration because you actually *feel* less thirsty as you age. Normally, the body's first indicators that you're dehydrated are feeling thirsty (go figure), dark urine, or infrequent urination. After that, you'll notice dry mouth, dry eyes, lack of sweating, muscle cramps, nausea or vomiting, heart palpitations, light-headedness, headache, brain fog, irritability, and weakness.

Here are some easy ways to tell if you're dehydrated:

1. Check the color of your urine, which should be clear to very light.
2. When you squeeze your fingernail bed, it whitens. It's true, try it! This happens because you are forcing blood out of the capillaries. Hold your hand above your heart and press/pinch the nail until it turns white; release the pressure and count how many seconds it takes for color to return. If you're hydrated, blood returns in two seconds or less. If you're dehydrated, it may take longer than that for your nail to return to its original color.

Water should be a priority because after severe dehydration comes coma, organ failure, and death. So let's not go there. Here's a list of everything you will ever need to handle a water emergency. Go through the list and decide which combination of items best fits your requirements and ability. Then get to it, make a plan, and take care of one of the most critical preparations for any emergency.

WATER PREPAREDNESS LIST:

- Fourteen gallons or more of potable water stored per person and two per pet.
- Five-gallon opaque water containers or stackable water bricks.
- Rainwater collector.
- Pocket filter/straw, French press purifier, or other filtration system.
- Home water filtration system if space allows.
- Water enhancers (like Mio or Stur, for electrolytes and flavor).
- Eye dropper for bleach or iodine.
- Chlorine bleach, tincture of iodine, or disinfectant tablets.
- Large coffee filters or water filtration fabric.
- Atmospheric water generator or home dehumidifier (and white vinegar or hydrogen peroxide for cleaning).
- Solar still construction material: shovel or trowel, 4' x 4' plastic sheeting, wide-mouth container, rocks.
- Bucket filtration system construction material: four five-gallon buckets, fifty pounds of pea gravel, fifty pounds of sand, twenty-five pounds of activated charcoal, six 4" squares of window screen, three ceramic tiles, two cinder blocks, drill with 1" and 2" hole saw attachments.

ARE YOU READY?

_____ Do you know how much water you want to store for an emergency?

_____ Do you know how you will store it and have the proper containers?

_____ Do you know how to purify and filter water if you run out, and do you have the supplies to do so?

_____ Do you know the location of the nearest natural uncontaminated water source?

_____ Do you know how to check for dehydration and its warning symptoms?

_____ Is your water actually stored and ready to go? Because reading about it and knowing how doesn't make a difference if it's not there to drink!

CHAPTER 2

FOOD

There are a few things you can do to extend your time on earth without food. One is, drink a lot of water. This is another good reason to be a water hoarder if the last chapter didn't already convince you. Second, you can limit your physical activity. The fewer calories you burn, the fewer you need to take in. Having supplies on hand and being ready for an emergency situation will help with that. Third, keep your surroundings warm and dry enough so you're not burning up fuel just to maintain your body temperature. We'll get to that one soon. Finally, you can be a woman. Yep, the British Nutrition Foundation in a study called *The Biology of Human Starvation* shows that women are better able to withstand starvation due to the naturally greater amount of *adipose tissue* (fat) in their bodies. This is the time when having a few extra pounds pays off! Your body will know enough to burn that fat first and save your precious muscles and organs for later. Score one for survival of the species!

Let's maximize your total potential for staying well-nourished and healthy during times of physical and emotional stress!

Rule #1: Always make sure your pantry is well-stocked. You don't want to be left with nothing but an ancient jar of relish and a half-empty quart of sour milk in the fridge because tonight you were really counting on takeout Thai food—not an earthquake. And as convenient as your local grocery store and DoorDash may be, the modern food supply chain is a house of cards. The better you prepare ahead of time, the more you can just *Pandemic and Chill* instead of running around with your hair on fire looking for bread and milk. This chapter will tell you how much and what to have, where to keep it, plus some handy recipes, so you're fueled up and ready to go when there's an emergency or lockdown. And lists. Lots of lists!

HOW MUCH IS ENOUGH?

The Department of Homeland Security says you should stock enough food for seventy-two hours. We're not sure what planet the Department of Homeland Security is making recommendations for, but clearly, it's not Earth.

First, the human body is *designed* for short periods of fasting and you'd last fine without *any* food for seventy-two hours if it came down to it. Early homo sapiens couldn't just run to the Quik Stop or open the fridge for a snack. Food was unpredictable and not always readily available, so that's what we are built for.

And as long as you've got water you could potentially survive a couple months without food. But *nobody* wants to be on an involuntary hunger strike, eyeing that fat little squirrel out there in the tree . . .

Second, the average person already *has* about a week's worth of food in the kitchen on a given day. Ideally, you'll want to have two weeks to a month's supply for everyone in your household, but your personal plan will depend on available space, what you can afford to spend, and your own goal. If you have no idea what that goal should be, here's a good place to start:

- One to two weeks' worth of produce and refrigerated goods
- Two weeks' worth of semi-perishable groceries that don't need refrigeration (bread, crackers, and long-lasting produce like apples, potatoes, onions, winter squash, etc.)
- Two to four weeks' worth of frozen foods like vegetables, fruits, meat and fish, and a few convenience meals that you prepared ahead of time and froze, or prepared frozen foods from the store.
- Four weeks' worth of long-lasting bulk items such as dried beans, rice, and canned/jarred things like tomatoes, marinara sauce, and peanut butter, as well as non-grocery items such as medicine and toilet paper. We'll get to the details in a minute.

- Are you working with very limited space? Shoot for two weeks' worth of everything.

Bottom line: Everyone's needs are slightly different, but if you plan for 2,000 calories a day for every household member (even kids) for the time period you want, you won't come up short. And make sure you don't forget to store emergency food for pets! Some have special dietary needs and particular foods, but even if your dog is perfectly content eating dog-friendly table scraps, a sudden change in diet can have (how shall we put this?) unintended digestive consequences.

Depending on your size, or if you are in a cold environment without adequate heat, your needs will vary; but here are some sample menus to give you an idea of what 2,000 calories a day actually looks like in a few different circumstances. Just like you need to plan fuel for your car or your house, you need to plan fuel for your body!

BASIC EMERGENCY NUTRITION

This is no time for the *How to Melt Pounds on the Catastrophe Diet* plan, because in a situation where you'll be in the house for a while, or navigating tough situations, there are certain things more pressing than fitting into your skinny jeans. You will want to focus on foods that fit these criteria:

1. Shelf-stable
2. Calorie-dense
3. Easy to prepare
4. Delicious

You may not get all of those things in every bite you eat, but those are your goals.

Shelf-Stable Foods

It's never been easier to buy a variety of tasty, easy to prepare, shelf-stable foods. Not only can you buy the old-fashioned standbys like rice, beans, pasta, and canned food; technology now offers you vacuum sealing, boil in bag meals, powdered soups and sauces, pouches of precooked grains, jarred sauces, bottled beverages, dried spices of every description, military MREs (meals ready to eat), gourmet backpacker foods that come to life with boiled water (and have lots of calories!), and a whole lot of other pretty delicious pantry foods our grandparents couldn't have imagined.

So next time you're in the grocery store, grab a few things to experiment with. And who knows, you may try out that powdered hollandaise sauce mix and decide to incorporate it into your pantry from now on!

Calorie-Dense Foods

Don't get too excited about the *calorie-dense* part—it doesn't mean Doritos and Rocky Road. Although, don't toss your Doritos if you have them already because (drumroll) they happen to make great fire starters! Who knew?

Carbohydrates and proteins have only four calories per gram—but fat has nine! It's efficient fuel, packs the most amount of energy in the least amount of space, and it will keep you feeling full longer so you won't need to eat as much. Fat can literally be a lifesaver. If you've ever watched the television series *Alone,* you'll know that the real game changer for which participants survive the longest isn't beach greens, it's porcupine fat. And no, we're not going to make you do that.

Emergency situations require not only *high* calories but *good* calories. You've heard the phrase, "*garbage in, garbage out*"? When your body and mind are stressed, this is doubly true. So, let's talk *fat*—the good kind—because not all fats are created equal.

Avocados

Avocados are powerhouses of nutrition and delicious, good-for-you fat. A whopping 80 percent of an avocado is good fat, and it's full of anti-oxidants, cholesterol fighters, and fiber. Did you also know you can peel, slice, and freeze avocados and they turn out just fine when you're ready to use them? It's true! Freeze some up for sandwiches, smoothies, or the coveted emergency guacamole!

Nuts

Nuts are tasty bundles of nutrition and healthy fats, and they can be added to salads or other dishes, or just enjoyed as a crunchy snack.

Walnuts are the king of healthy nuts, followed by macadamias, pecans, peanuts, hazelnuts, Brazil nuts, and pistachios. Their oils will spoil eventually so keep them vacuum sealed if you're going to store them for a long time. Otherwise, enjoy them as a healthy snack regularly, and you'll always have fresh ones on hand.

Low or no-sugar nut butters are great emergency food too. Go for smaller jars unless you know you'll eat the giant tub. This ensures you've got fresh, non-rancid peanut butter when you need it!

Canned meats and fish

If you haven't yet discovered the joy of a can of sardines, this is the time, my friend! Buying sardines by the six-pack and enjoying them on avocado toast for a small, quick, and decadent meal can keep you full *all day*. Canned fish, in general, is a great healthy staple, especially small, oily, cold-water fish like sardines, salmon, herring, mackerel, and anchovies, which are all loaded with good fat. Your old friend tuna is good too, but as a large fish that lives a long time and is high on the food chain, it tends to accumulate mercury and other bad stuff in its meat, so limit intake to once every week or two and try canned pink salmon as a substitute!

Canned chicken breast or turkey with no sodium added are good choices too. Pork, beef, and of course ham, also come in cans. Always go for low-sodium and no-sugar-added options and limit your consumption of canned processed red meat like bacon or corned beef hash.

Eggs

Eggs are another source of healthy fat and protein, and store-bought eggs can last in the refrigerator for four to five weeks or longer. Keep them in their original container for longest life and best protection. Powdered eggs are also an option. They're not as tasty as fresh, but they'll last five to ten years in their original packaging.

Chia seeds

Fat is probably not the first thing that comes to mind when you think of chia seeds, but one ounce of this magical little superfood contains eleven grams of healthy fat, the majority of which is heart-healthy omega-3 fatty acids. They are also loaded with fiber, are really good for you, and have the strange quality of expanding when wet which means they fill you up, and they are delightful in puddings, stews, smoothies, soups, yogurt, you name it!

Powdered fat

Yep, powdered fat is a thing. While any liquid fats like oils or shortening must be consumed and replaced so they don't go rancid, powdered fat will last indefinitely. Everyone knows about powdered milk, but did you know you can buy a can of powdered butter? It's true!

CARBS: THE GOOD AND THE BAD

Carbohydrates are a good form of quick energy, but not all carbs are the same. Your emergency carbs should come in the form of whole-grain cereals, breads, and pasta. They should be mostly *complex* like the carbs found in fruits and vegetables. Eating lots of *simple* carbs like refined sugars in the form of cupcakes, sugared soft drinks, and white breads and pastas can make your blood sugar peak and crash, and peak and crash, and that means . . . feelin' hangry. This includes kids, so bear that in mind when you're deciding what they're going to eat when you're all hunkered down together. What they like and what they need are likely not the same.

Good ways to handle the sweet craving without candy, soda, cookies, or ice cream? Try sweetening with honey, stevia, or monk fruit which is amazingly good and doesn't spike your blood sugar. Put a splash of 100 percent fruit juice in carbonated water instead of drinking sugary or artificially sweetened soda. Or try Zevia brand sodas which are sweetened with stevia. Have some dark chocolate instead of milk chocolate. Have a frozen banana mashed up with a little peanut butter!

All that being said, there's always an exception to the rule. It's a good idea to keep a small stash of sugared hard candies like Werther's or Jolly Ranchers around. But don't think of them as a snack food; think of them as little packets of emergency energy if you need it.

THE EIGHT INDESTRUCTIBLE FOODS YOU MUST HAVE

Not much lasts forever, and you can't eat diamonds or true love, *but* there are some super-prepper foods that last *almost* forever so you can create your own TEOWAWKI pantry. Yes, this acronym actually exists in the prepper world and means *the end of the world as we know it*. We promise never to use it again.

Those eight indestructible must-haves are:

1. **OATS.** If stored in an airtight container in a cool, dry place, oats will last indefinitely. They're also good in their original packaging for two to three years and are a powerhouse of nutrition and a source of good fat.
2. **POWDERED MILK.** You can also use shelf-stable milk in cartons, but it will only last six to twelve months. An unopened package of powdered milk is still good two to ten years after the printed *best by* date.
3. **HONEY.** Try to get real local honey from a trusted source because honey is the third-most faked food! Yes, counterfeit honey is a real problem. Over half of the honey for sale in the United States is fraudulently adulterated with high fructose corn syrup, which is *not* what you want. Do your research and find the real stuff!
4. **DRIED BEANS, LENTILS, PEAS.** When stored sealed in a cool, dry place they can last pretty much forever. Keep in mind though, that they start to lose vitamin content after two or three years and by five years, most of the nutritional value is depleted even though they are still safe to eat.
5. **RICE.** Store white rice in a sealed container in a cool location and it will be usable for many years.
6. **PEANUT BUTTER.** Unopened commercial peanut butter will last for years, and if it's opened, for several months. Even if your peanut butter goes rancid and smells bad you can still eat it and it won't make you sick.
7. **DRIED PASTA.** Dried pasta will never really go bad if stored sealed in a cool, dry place. But like beans and rice, it will lose some of its flavor and nutritional value over time.
8. **SALT.** Salt, believe it or not, is an essential nutrient, which means you need it to live. Most of us get *plenty* of salt, but it's good to always have salt on hand. A healthy, active adult needs between 200 and 500 mg of sodium per day and should aim for no more than 1,500 mg a day. You tend to lose a lot of salt when you sweat, so in hot weather, or when you are working hard, make sure you get enough.

Yes, those eight ingredients sound like *the* most boring ingredient basket ever seen on *Chopped*, but if the goal is to keep everyone alive and fed, they can't be beat. Just the combination of beans and rice is a global staple that makes a *perfect protein*. And if you really are in a long-term survival situation, boring basics will do the job, so be sure your kitchen always has a good stock of these. Better yet, if you incorporate them into your normal eating routine (and why wouldn't you?), just eat what's getting older and replace it with newer products. That's preparation you hardly have to think about!

SUPPLEMENTAL SHELF-STABLE FOODS

In addition to the eight survival superfoods *and* your high-calorie staples, think about adding the following items to your emergency larder:

- Whole-grain crackers or matzah
- Power bars—watch the sugar!
- Trail mix—heavy on nuts, seeds, and fruit, and use dark chocolate chips instead of M&Ms.
- Dried seaweed snacks
- Dried fruit like apricots, raisins, cherries, prunes, blueberries, apples
- Cereal, granola, cream of wheat
- Canned fruit in water or natural juice
- Canned vegetables—in our opinion green beans, tomatoes, and olives are the best.
- Canned soups, stews, and chili
- Bone broth—a super nutritious and delicious warm beverage on its own, or to use in cooking
- Potato flakes—add water and *bam!* Mashed potatoes!
- Vitamins and supplements including electrolyte packets or capsules
- Coffee and tea
- Juices, no sugar added
- Spices like black pepper, garlic, cumin, chili powder, onion powder, pepper flakes, and Italian seasoning
- Whole-grain bread
- Bread flour

- Jarred or canned pasta sauce
- Simmer sauces for rice, veggies, and meat
- Dry packets of sauce and gravy mixes
- Dry yeast
- Shelf-stable milk
- Powdered eggs
- Flours and whole grains

Take a walk down the canned food aisle in the grocery store and see what's there. Familiarize yourself with your options and stock up accordingly. Picking up a few cans on each shopping trip adds up quickly.

FOODS TO BUY IF YOU KNOW WHAT'S COMING

If you've got time to prepare for a likely lockdown or approaching storm, make the most of it! Pick up some fresh produce and meats that will last more than a couple of days. You may not have power, but you'll still be able to enjoy fresh food for a little while if you think ahead! Here are some suggestions:

- Unripe avocados
- Green bananas
- Sweet and white potatoes
- Onions
- Iceberg lettuce
- Watermelon, cantaloupe, or other melons
- Winter squashes like acorn or butternut
- Apples, oranges, hard pears
- Hard unsliced salami or pepperoni
- Hard cheese
- Grab a meal you can cook right away using fresh meat, salad, and whatever else may be in short supply later if you don't already have food like that in your fridge.

Don't forget to stock up for *all* the members of your household, including family members with special dietary requirements, babies, and pets!

Always keep enough baby food and formula on hand so you can go for several weeks without a resupply. The same goes for pet food.

And when assembling your pantry, don't forget your favorite Ethiopian coffee or Stonewall Kitchen vodka sauce, because happiness matters too. You don't have to start off with powdered milk, beans, and rice on day one! Have foods that will give you comfort and a sense of normalcy during stressful times.

PREMADE EMERGENCY FOOD PACKS

Believe it or not, you are not the only person concerned about having enough food on hand if something bad should happen. As a matter of fact, there are enough of us out there that a whole industry of freeze-dried emergency food suppliers has sprung up offering everything from a single meal to a year's supply of food. Backpackers have been enjoying freeze-dried meals for a long time because they are simple to prepare, leave minimal waste, cleanup is easy, and they are lightweight. You name it, it's been freeze-dried in a pouch—lasagna, scrambled eggs and sausage, beef stroganoff, pasta primavera, pad Thai, and even ice cream. The good news is someone else has done all the work. All you do is add water, and there are no pots or pans to wash! The bad news is that no matter how good it sounds, it's not as good as if you made it yourself, and a thirty-day supply for a family of four will set you back about (have a seat and don't choke on your freeze-dried mac and cheese) $3,200. And it may not even contain 2,000 daily calories per person!

Even if you're not going all in, it's probably not a bad idea to keep at least a few meals or a couple of days' worth of meals for a time when food prep seems overwhelming, no matter how simple. There are many brands to choose from and you can try experimenting with different meals to decide which ones you like best.

STORAGE

Now that you know what kinds of things you should be stocking up on, where are you supposed to keep all that food, and how are you supposed to store it safely?

Short-Term Storage

The easiest way to prepare for a disaster that might last a few days or even a few weeks is to buy food that you will use normally in your day-to-day life, buy in bulk, and rotate it so you always have the newer food on hand. Let's take pasta, for instance. If you buy a ten-pack of spaghetti from Costco, just incorporate it into your normal food routine and when you're down to three or four bags, get a new supply to start on when the old stuff is gone. Or buy rice in a large bulk bag and do the same thing if you have room.

If you don't have space or won't use it relatively quickly, consider repackaging that bulk rice or other food in sealed Mason jars, or split the bag with a friend or two. You can store jars or ziplockk bags or canned food inside a sturdy opaque tote, Tupperware container, five-gallon bucket, or just on a high shelf. You can even use that ridiculous little cabinet over the refrigerator. Just taking these simple steps will ensure your food will last for at least a year. And that's all most people will need.

Long-Term Storage

We promised you no Armageddon bunker stuff, but if you are serious about storing large amounts of food, or storing food for years or decades, you'll have a few challenges, but it's completely doable. There are several factors that will be conspiring against you as you prepare your long-term emergency pantry, and we'll get to them one by one. The main objective is to keep your food protected from all types of outside influences, and the best way to do *that* is to repackage and store your pantry staples. If you just throw a big ol' bag of beans in the basement or under the bed, after a while, you're asking for trouble. So, here's your plan.

Illustration by Liliana Faiella.

Your Enemies and How to Beat Them
Moisture

First, the only bulk dry foods you should be preparing for extreme long-term storage are foods with a moisture content of less than 10 percent.

That means foods like white (not brown or wild) rice, dried beans, dried pasta, powdered milk, dried corn, wheat berries, sugar, powdered eggs, and dehydrated potato flakes. Moisture in your food will encourage spoilage over time.

You know those little bags of silica that come with a new pair of shoes or in a vitamin bottle? Those are called desiccants, and they remove excess moisture from the air inside packaging. They are your friend for food storage. Buy new sealed packets that aren't already full of moisture and bury them in your dry food before you seal it up.

And never ever leave your food on the floor, especially in a basement. Make sure it's high and dry and in waterproof containers. Boxes of pasta sitting on a shelf are a no-go. If you have room, you can also utilize heavy-duty (preferably metal) shelving to store lots of food and supplies. Make sure you don't overload the capacity of the shelves because food can be heavy!

Oxygen

Oxygen will encourage not only spoilage, but bugs. Make sure that the container you're using seals tight like a Mason jar or use a five-gallon bucket with a gasket. Use oxygen-absorbing packets (which just contain iron powder) like you would use desiccants for moisture.

Light

It's always best to store food in a dark place, or in an opaque container that doesn't let light in.

Heat

Shoot for somewhere that's a constant 40–60°F if possible. Basements are ideal, if you have one. Garages are not good because temperature fluctuation is intense. A closet in the middle of your home, away from windows and doors to the outside, will work too.

Pests

Store all your food in heavy plastic containers, or even a metal garbage can if you have rodents in the neighborhood. Also, check your food containers periodically to be sure they are looking like you left them and nobody's trying to bust in for a midnight snack.

Time

Even if you manage to create an ideal food storage environment, and your rice is still edible after years, chances are it may taste a little *off* and it will definitely have lost a lot of its nutritional value. So if you can use up your emergency food and replace it with new food every year or two, that's the best way to go.

Long, Long-Term Storage

If you're serious about long-term food storage, invest in food-safe mylar bags for repackaging your food into a low-oxygen, dark, moisture-proof environment.

Then you can store the mylar bags inside a sturdier container like a five-gallon bucket. If you're going to open and close the bucket with some frequency, a screw lid or *Seal* lid is great. If you're going to store for extended periods, get a good solid food-grade bucket with a snap-on lid and a gasket.

When packaging your food, keep in mind that depending on what you're storing, a five-gallon bucket can get mighty heavy. Keep heavier buckets on the bottom shelf or on the bottom of the stack. You can also mix up your bagged food to distribute weight. No need to fill a whole bucket with nothing but rice. Put your mylar bags of rice and beans on the bottom, and lighter weight foods on the top.

If you're going total hard-core survivalist (or if you simply don't have room in a basement or closet) you can bury a cache of food inside a five-gallon bucket in your yard or other location to retrieve later in a true emergency. Just be sure you use desiccants and mylar bags.

All the Hacks to Extend the Life of Your Food

You don't need to be in a food emergency to use these tips and tricks. Americans throw away a full one-third of all the food they buy because it went bad. You'll save money and resources, and be kinder to the planet, if you use what you buy. But especially in an emergency situation when you only have so much fresh food, these tips can be invaluable in making that food stay edible longer.

Dairy

Always store milk and yogurt on the bottom shelf all the way in the back of the refrigerator, which is the most consistently cold section for longest usability. Cheese should ideally have its own drawer so it doesn't interact with other foods that can affect taste.

Eggs

For everyday storage, keep eggs in their original packaging, and never store any dairy items in the door of the refrigerator, which is the least cold spot with the most temperature fluctuation. Store-bought eggs are often treated with food-grade mineral oil to keep them fresh for months. If you love fresh eggs (and who doesn't?) you can coat them with mineral oil and then keep them at room temperature for up to nine months! Just flip them over once a month. You can also use avocado oil or coconut oil; they don't go rancid as quickly as other oils. And are you ready to have your mind blown? If you've had eggs for a long time and want to make sure they stay usable, you can freeze them! Just crack the eggs in a bowl, mix them with a fork (not too much) and put them in freezer bags or containers. Mark them with how many eggs are in the bag, and thaw when you're ready to use them. Ice cube trays work as well. Mix the eggs and pour into the ice cube tray. Each cube is about one egg, which makes measuring easy.

Meat

Keep meat in its original packaging, and on the bottom shelf in the back of the refrigerator where it's coldest. Also make sure you put meat and fish on a plate so you don't have inadvertent leakage all over the place.

Apples

If they came in a plastic bag, remove it and put them in a bowl on the countertop. Refrigerate or store them in a root cellar or cool basement and they'll last for a couple of months, but keep them away from other produce (see below)!

Avocados

Refrigeration slows down ripening. Or you can wait for ripeness, then slice and freeze them for use later.

Bananas

Wrap the stems with plastic wrap or foil to delay ripening. You can also peel and freeze bananas to use in smoothies.

Berries

All tend to go bad quickly, so consider freezing some for use later in baking or smoothies. To keep strawberries fresh, give them a dunk in a solution of three parts water and one part distilled white vinegar, then dry them on a paper towel. Give blackberries and raspberries a dunk in water without the vinegar. Blueberries can be washed just before eating. Always go through berries and pull out any that are starting to mold. That stuff spreads.

Cruciferous veggies (broccoli, cauliflower, brussels sprouts)

Store in a loose, open plastic, or produce bag in the crisper. Add a paper towel to absorb extra moisture, and ditch that tight plastic wrap on your cauliflower.

Carrots

Cut the greens off immediately to keep your carrots hydrated. They'll stay crisp for a month or more if you store them in water in your refrigerator! If you have wilted carrots, they're still great cooked. And keep them away from apples, which can make carrots taste bitter.

Celery

Take it out of the plastic bag, keep the whole head of celery intact, wrap it in foil, and put it in the crisper. It will stay fresh for a month!

Citrus fruit

Lemons, limes, grapefruits, and oranges will keep for a few days to a week at room temperature. After that, put them in a single layer in the crisper of the refrigerator.

Cucumbers

They like things a little warmer than your refrigerator so store them in the fridge door where temperatures don't get as cold. Remove any tight plastic wrapping and store them in a loose plastic or produce bag.

Eggplant

Keep these divas out of the refrigerator, out of direct sunlight, and away from bananas. A shaded countertop or pantry is where they are happiest.

Flour

As stable as flour may appear to be, it does have a shelf life. White flour will keep for about a year in a sealed container in the pantry and two years in the fridge. Whole grain flour will only last about three to four months at room temperature and six to eight months in the fridge. For a staple with so many uses, that doesn't seem like much shelf life. But there is a way to have flour available indefinitely—namely wheat berries! Wheat berries are not berries at all, but the edible kernel of wheat with the inedible outside husk removed. And if you store them with desiccants and oxygen absorbers inside mylar bags, they will last for more than thirty years!

The *CHARD GM*-150 manual grain mills are simple to use and don't require electricity. You'll be able to grind about a pound a minute and adjust the setting from coarse to fine. Just clamp it onto a table or other solid surface and you can use your preserved wheat berries whenever you like!

Illustration by Liliana Faiella.

GRAIN MILL

You can cook wheat berries like you would rice, simmering for an hour or so on the stovetop, or you can grind them up to make flour. About two-thirds of a cup of wheat berries will give you a cup of flour. All you'll need is a small grain mill, and some practice baking with your home-ground flour.

Garlic

Store with plenty of ventilation and out of sunlight. You can also roast a whole head of garlic, wrap it in foil, and freeze it for later use. They even make special *garlic driers.*

Greens

Prewashed greens in a plastic tub won't need any special handling. For other greens, fill the sink with cold water and soak them until all residual dirt is gone. Then use a salad spinner or dry them on dish towels or paper towels. You can chop kale, collard greens, or any greens you plan to cook, and put them in a plastic container with a couple of paper towels.

Herbs

You can treat a bunch of fresh herbs like the bouquet that they are. Put the stems in a glass of water! Then cover the tops with loose plastic and keep them in the refrigerator.

Melons

Melons are their sweet, delicious best when left to ripen at room temperature away from sunlight. Ripening in the fridge gives them a weird rubbery consistency. If you're looking for ice-cold watermelon on a summer day, refrigerate it for a couple of hours before serving. Once melon is cut, you can store it in a sealed plastic container in the fridge for a few days.

Mushrooms

Always keep mushrooms in a paper bag with a paper towel inside. Ditch the plastic wrap they came in and don't seal them in an airtight container or they will go slimy. Keep them dry and unwashed until right before you're ready to eat them.

Onions and shallots

Keep them out of the fridge and store in a hanging wire basket or mesh bag in a cool, dry place with plenty of air circulation.

Peppers

All kinds of peppers can be stored in a plastic bag with a paper towel in the crisper.

Tomatoes

Tomatoes do not like the cold at all, not when growing and not when sitting in your kitchen. Keep them out of the fridge or they'll become mealy and tasteless. Find a cool, dry spot out of the sun. And wait until right before you eat them to wash them.

Potatoes

These are the ultimate root cellar veggie. Store them in a cool, dark, dry place and they'll last for months. And if you want to extend their life even more, store them with apples! But never store them with onions or you'll make the potatoes sprout faster! Vegetable storage is all about the science of gaseous emissions.

Stone fruit

Peaches, mangoes, apricots, nectarines, and plums do best in a mesh basket out of the sun to ripen. Once they start to feel a little soft, you can prolong their life and delay the end stages of ripening by refrigerating them.

Big Ethylene Producers	Very Ethylene Sensitive
Apples. As much as we love them, apples do not play nicely with others. They are one of the biggest ethylene producers and should basically be kept in solitary confinement away from other produce, unless you want to use apples to speed up the ripening of other things, like avocados!	Asparagus
Avocados	Broccoli

Big Ethylene Producers	Very Ethylene Sensitive
Bananas	Brussels sprouts
Honeydew melon	Carrots
Mangoes	Cauliflower
Pears	Cucumbers
Peaches	Leafy greens
Plums	Onions
Potatoes	Pumpkins and squashes
Strawberries	
Tomatoes	

Speaking of gaseous emissions, there's a reason you shouldn't store all your fruits and vegetables together in one big happy basket. Why can't they all just get along? Most produce gives off a gas called ethylene as it ripens—and some gives off more than others. And all this ethylene gas can wreak havoc on other produce, causing it to ripen or rot more quickly, depending on the sensitivity of the victim. So here's your cheat sheet. To extend the life of your produce, never keep foods in the first column next to foods in the second. Why has nobody ever told you this? We don't know, but you're welcome!

FOOD PRESERVATION

Before the invention of refrigeration, the global supply chain, and a bunch of impossible-to-pronounce chemical preservatives, people still had to eat. If our forefathers and foremothers hadn't figured out how to preserve food for times of drought, famine, and warfare, you wouldn't be reading this right now. Food preservation was literally a matter of life and death, and it was all learned the hard way, by trial and error. But we've managed to forget most of that incredible knowledge in just a few generations thanks to modern conveniences and unhealthy additives. Pop-Tarts and Twinkies are semi-immortal *not* because of the wisdom of grandmothers, but because of a team of scientists in lab coats.

If you've ever been confronted by a great deal on bulk produce and you think to yourself, *Unless there's a vampire invasion, I can't possibly use twenty heads of garlic*, think again! Berries, vegetables, meat, fish, and garlic are all fair game in bulk quantities if you know the art of preserving them to use later.

Here are seven basic food preservation techniques brought to you by your ancestors. These are some great skills to resurrect in your own life, not only because they're healthier than eating preservative-laden food, but because if something happens and you can't count on a grocery store, you *can* count on delicious food you love that you preserved yourself. #winning

And if you find yourself in a situation like a hurricane warning when you think you may lose power, or if you overbuy food, you can implement some of these techniques on the fly to preserve food you already have in your refrigerator or on the counter that you're worried might spoil.

Dehydrating

Let's begin at the beginning. The very earliest form of food preservation was dehydration using sun and wind which naturally preserve meats, grains, fruits, and vegetables. Dehydration was happening in the Middle East and Asia as early as 14,000 years ago. In the Middle Ages, in areas that didn't have enough sunlight or wind, people built structures called *still houses*, inside which a low fire was made and the heat was used to dry plant-based foods. People in cold regions like Scandinavia and Alaska used freeze-drying instead. All these methods remove moisture and, therefore, the conditions required for mold or bacteria to grow.

Today, it's relatively cheap and easy to buy a food dehydrator that provides heat and ventilation. Small beginner models made of plastic run about forty dollars and larger professional models with doors and multiple metal trays can cost hundreds. Dehydrators utilize trays, ventilation, and low heat to create dried foods that will last.

FOODS THAT DEHYDRATE WELL INCLUDE:
- Beef and other lean meats
- Fish
- Fruits of all kinds
- Eggs

- Yogurt
- Vegetables

- Herbs
- Jam—fruit leather, anyone?

FOODS THAT DON'T DEHYDRATE WELL INCLUDE:
- Avocados
- Olives
- Fatty meats

- Butter, milk, and cheese
- Nuts and nut butters
- Juices

Freeze-Drying

If you want to go top-of-the-line and get fancy, freeze-dryers are incredibly good at preserving food. We're talking food that lasts twenty-five years without refrigeration or preservatives. But like anything that's the gold standard, it has a price tag to match. Freeze-dryers commonly cost thousands of dollars depending on the size and model you choose, so be sure it's something you will use enough to make it worth the investment. They can also be large, and the vacuum cycle makes noise, so be sure you have space for the model you're thinking about and that it's somewhere the noise won't bug you.

Freeze-drying relies on a process called sublimation. Evaporation is the transition of a liquid, like water, to a gas, like water vapor. Sublimation is similar but the water goes from a solid (ice) directly to vapor without passing through the liquid stage. Turns out this is an unbelievably effective way to preserve any kind of food that isn't either mostly sugar or mostly fat. After freeze-drying a batch of food, you must make sure you package it in moisture-proof air-tight containers like mylar bags or Mason jars and add an oxygen absorber packet. After that your food should be good to go for decades!

Having freeze-dried meals that you know you love and that are ready to go at a moment's notice (with just a little rehydration and heat) is a great feeling. Once you get the hang of freeze-drying and make it a habit, you'll be well on your way to never worrying about having enough food.

Salt-Curing

As another way to vanquish food-spoiling moisture, early cultures discovered that salt would do the trick by drawing moisture out of the meat and creating an environment inhospitable to bacteria. The salt-curing of meats and seafood not only preserves or enhances the taste, but also prevents the growth of pathogens that could taint meat and make people sick.

Super-Simple Salt Pork Recipe

INGREDIENTS:

Pork belly

Sea salt

Brown sugar (optional but delicious)

DIRECTIONS:

Cut the pork belly into squares about 1–1.5" thick. This will speed up the curing time since you are creating more surface area on the pork, but you can use a whole pork belly if you like, which you may find easier to store for a long time.

Create your curing mixture which is one part brown sugar to five parts sea salt. You can leave out the brown sugar if you like, but it adds a nice flavor.

Spread a thick layer of curing mixture on an oven tray or flat-bottomed container. Lay the pork on top and cover it completely. Make sure all surfaces are covered. Use a nice thick layer for best results.

Let the pork rest for two to three days.

You'll see a lot of liquid come off the pork as the salt draws out the moisture. Remove the pork and then cover it again with fresh salt or the salt/sugar mix.

Let the pork rest for another two to three days.

After the curing process is done, rinse the pork well, and blot dry with paper towels.

If you have room in the refrigerator, store it there for maximum usefulness. If you have another cold place to store it, like an unheated basement or garage in the winter, you can hang it there to make sure rodents can't get at it.

When you are ready to use your salt pork for cooking, soak the amount you need in warm water for about an hour to get rid of the excess saltiness. You can cook up a little piece for a taste test and determine if you need to change the water and continue soaking.

Salt-curing has been around for thousands of years too, and *salt pork* was a staple on old-world sailing ships and carried by travelers and warriors as a high-fat, high-protein food. Well-cured salt pork can last up to a year without refrigeration. If you find yourself wanting to preserve a lot of pork for an emergency or a sea voyage, or if you just want to try it for fun, here's how to do it:

Freezing

For people in the northern tier, freezing was an obvious choice for food preservation. After the harvest, food was buried underground or in the snow to keep it edible throughout the winter. The Chinese were freezing food in underground cellars since at least 3000 BC. And in the West, *iceboxes* or *iceboxes* were common for storing food before modern refrigeration was available. Today freezing remains a practical and useful way to preserve food—as long as you have electricity available from the grid or a backup energy source. And if you're living in a below-freezing environment, you can utilize the great outdoors if your power goes out. Just be sure to keep your freezer goods off the ground and out of reach of animals.

Vacuum Sealing

To really extend the life of your frozen food, invest in a vacuum sealer. If you just toss a steak in a freezer bag and stick it in the freezer, you can expect it to be edible for about six to eight months. If you vacuum-seal it first, you've extended the life of your meat to one to two years! You'll also be sure to avoid freezer burn, funny tastes picked up from other foods, and that feeling when you discover a lump of mystery fish covered in ice crystals that's destined for the trash.

Vacuum sealing and freezing also helps you maximize the room in your freezer by creating neatly portioned, stackable food that you can easily label with a Sharpie and date. And it creates less waste by allowing you to freeze leftovers you wouldn't have been able to get to before they spoiled.

A vacuum sealer will set you back from fifty dollars to a couple hundred dollars for a home model, but it's completely worth it if you use it and make it a normal part of your food storage routine.

Freezing

Chances are good you had no idea you could freeze these foods:

EGGS. If you're planning on using them for cooking, you can crack eggs, mix them, and freeze them in a Ziplock bag or airtight container.

MILK. Freezing milk will change its texture a little bit, but if you want to use it for cooking, freeze it instead of letting it go bad and dumping it down the sink.

NUTS. Vacuum seal them or wrap them in plastic wrap. Freezing will keep the oils from going rancid and drastically increase their life.

FRESH VEGETABLES. Most vegetables can be frozen after blanching. To blanch, simply slice or chop the vegetables in sizes you'd want them for eating, then put them in rapidly boiling water for two minutes, pour them into a colander, and submerge in a sink full of cold water to stop the cooking process. Then vacuum seal or freeze in plastic bags, label, and cook the rest of the way when you're ready to eat them.

HERBS. Put a teaspoon of chopped fresh herbs into each section of an ice cube tray. Fill with water, freeze, and save the magical herb cubes in a plastic bag for later use.

CHEESE. The texture may get a little crumbly, but if you're using cheese for cooking you can freeze it.

GARLIC. Garlic can be frozen either peeled and chopped, peeled as whole cloves, or (the best!) roasted as a whole head, left in the skin, and wrapped in foil.

AVOCADO. Slice and lay the slices flat in a freezer bag.

BREAD. Toss in the freezer as it comes from the store, or wrap in an additional plastic bag to keep fresh longer.

ONIONS. Chop and store in freezer bags. Every time a recipe calls for half an onion, I always chop the other half and freeze it. It's a great time-saver for a future recipe and you'd never know the difference.

Sugaring

When it comes to long-term food storage, nobody has it down to a science like the humble honeybee. In fact, honey is so resistant to microorganisms that foods submerged in honey will last for centuries.

Sugared Lemons Recipe

Sugared lemons are a delight! And this preservation method works for all citrus fruit. If you have extra citrus, don't let it spoil in the bowl. Grab it while it's still in good shape and try out this simple recipe that will keep for a month or more. And use organic citrus if you can, since you'll be able to eat the rind.

INGREDIENTS:

Granulated sugar
6 lemons (or the equivalent amount in oranges, limes, or other citrus fruit)
Tools
Mason jars with lids

DIRECTIONS:

Wash and dry the lemons.

Cut off the ends of each lemon and slice thinly, removing seeds.

Place a thin layer of granulated sugar on the bottom of the jar.

Add a layer of sliced lemons.

Sprinkle sugar on top and continue layering lemon slices and sugar until you fill the jar. Make sure all the lemons are sugar-covered as you go.

The lemons will start to release their juice and should be ready to enjoy in about 48 hours.

You can enjoy sugared lemons in all kinds of baking, on salads, with roasted vegetables, on salmon, chopped up on buttered toast (lemon marmalade anyone?), or as a cocktail garnish.

For this reason, honey was used in many ancient cultures medicinally, to treat burns and wounds.

Until 2003, the oldest honey ever found was in King Tut's tomb, but another tomb discovery, of a noblewoman near Tblisi, Georgia, turned out to be two thousand years older than that—about fifty-five hundred years old! And evidence of humans keeping bees was discovered in a cave painting in Valencia, Spain, which may be as much as fifteen thousand years old.

The process of sugaring utilizes honey or sugar to preserve foods. Sugars not only sweeten but draw out water from pathogens, which dehydrates and kills them. The ancient Greeks and Romans used heated sugar and fruit pectin to create jams, jellies, and preserves. Medieval methods included storing fruits and meats in honey for use later in the year.

Fermenting and Pickling

In general, the goal of food preservation is all about doing away with microorganisms that can spoil food and cause illness. But in some cases, those little micro-buggers can be beneficial—and even tasty! Some bacteria and fungi have unique properties which allow them to break down sugars and destroy harmful pathogens. The result is either acid or alcohol—think yogurt, wine, beer, or vinegar. Fermented foods have the added benefit of being extremely good for you and they help create a healthy gut! Those are some microbes we can definitely get behind.

One form of fermentation is pickling, which preserves foods in vinegar. Little did the ancient Mesopotamians know that when they figured out how to make cucumbers last a long time by storing them in vinegar brine, they had created a gastronomical delight that would last for thousands of year—the humble pickle! And like many other preserved foods, the pickle was not only used on long sea voyages to deter scurvy, but also as a valuable military snack. Mark Antony, after hearing from Cleopatra that she believed pickles were the key to her health and beauty, gave pickles to his troops to keep them strong.

Illustration by Liliana Faiella.

"Quickle" Recipe

This recipe is for quick pickles which should last in your refrigerator for a month. For longer preservation, can your pickles using the water bath canning method detailed in the canning section.

INGREDIENTS:

Cucumbers
Distilled white vinegar
Granulated sugar
Kosher salt
Water

TOOLS:

Jars with lids
Wide funnel

DIRECTIONS:

Make sure you start with clean, dry jars.

Wash the cucumbers and cut into spears or slices.

Optional: flavor your pickles by adding sliced garlic cloves, peppercorns, rosemary, mustard seeds, or the classic dill. You can experiment with your favorite seasonings if you want to add a little zing and interest to your pickles.

Mix up your brine by combining:

1 cup water
1 $\frac{1}{3}$ cups distilled white vinegar
$\frac{1}{3}$ cup granulated sugar
2 tablespoons kosher salt

Bring your brine to a boil in a saucepan until the salt and sugar dissolve.

Remove from heat and allow your brine to cool for 10–15 minutes.

Place cucumbers in jar allowing enough room to completely cover with vinegar, leaving about $\frac{1}{2}$ inch of space at the top.

Pour the brine over the cucumbers; stir, and tap the jar on the countertop to remove any air bubbles.

Seal the jars with the lids and refrigerate for two to three days. Voilà! Pickles!

DIY Sauerkraut

Sauerkraut is another great place to start if you are interested in trying your hand at fermenting! Not only is it easy and tang-a-licious, it provides your body with twenty-eight distinct strains of probiotics (good gut bacteria that aid in digestion, weight control, and all-around good health). That's better than you'll get from any expensive probiotic supplement you can buy in the store.

Stored in a dark, cool place, your homemade sauerkraut will keep for many months. The cooler the temperature, assuming it's above freezing, the longer it will last. It will continue to ferment over time, but more slowly at cooler temperatures. The refrigerator, a root cellar, or a cool basement are all ideal.

It's incredibly easy to make your own sauerkraut. All it takes is two ingredients and a lot of . . . smashing!

INGREDIENTS:

Cabbage

Salt (2 tsp. per pound of cabbage)

TOOLS:

Sharp knife

Large bowl

Tamper (or a small jar full of rocks)

Mason jar(s) with lid(s)

DIRECTIONS:

Peel off any old or discolored leaves from the cabbage.

With a large, sharp knife, cut the cabbage in half from top to bottom, through the core.

Remove the core from the cabbage.

Slice the cabbage into thin strips about $1/8$" wide. Leave long strands or chop as you like.

Put the cabbage in the bowl and add the salt.

Mix it up with your hands and walk away.

Come back in 20–25 minutes, and you'll see that the cabbage has begun to give up the goods—the goods being cabbage juice!

Squeeze fistfuls of cabbage tightly in your hands or use a tamper to crush the cabbage until it is wilted. It will release even more juice. This will take 3–5 minutes.

Put cabbage and juice into the Mason jar(s), filling no more than two-thirds of the jar.

Push down on the cabbage until it is covered with brine and make sure there are no trapped pockets of air. You can put a small weighted jar of rocks on top to keep the cabbage under the liquid.

Over time your cabbage will *relax* and fermentation will begin.

Wait about two weeks, if your jar is at 65–70°F.

Put the lid loosely on the jar, and check it every day or so to release any built-up pressure.

Taste your sauerkraut. If you like the taste as it is, great! But you can wait, and your patience will be rewarded with more tang as time goes on. When your sauerkraut is pale yellow or beige, and reaches the desired tanginess, screw the cap on tight and put it in the refrigerator. It should keep for many months.

If you began the fermentation process in the fridge, sauerkraut will still happen but it will take more time. Remember, each batch will be different, so experiment with location and time, and enjoy!

And the fair queen was at least partially correct; the health benefits of pickle juice have been confirmed. Pickle juice will relieve muscle cramps, helps keep you hydrated, controls blood sugar levels, contains powerful antioxidants, and boosts your gut health. With a resume like that, and an easy recipe, think about giving pickling a try to extend the life of your garden or supermarket veggies.

Don't limit your pickling to just cucumbers. You can use this recipe to pickle onions, cherry tomatoes, carrots, and other veggies for use in salads, on sandwiches, or as the perfect garnish for a Bloody Mary.

You can pickle cauliflower, green beans, and asparagus but add the extra step of blanching them to help retain color. That means you'll need to drop them in boiling water for two minutes and then immediately plunge them into a sink of ice water to stop the cooking process before you put them in the jar.

And if this simple version of pickling turns your crank, you'll want to try out our next method of food preservation and take it to a whole other level.

Canning

Canning food is something most of us think of as old-fashioned and may remember our grandparents doing. But canning, which dates back to the 1790s, is actually one of humanity's newest methods of food preservation. It came about, believe it or not, because Napoleon offered a cash prize to whomever could come up with a way to preserve food for use in military campaigns, and a guy named Nicholas Appert won with pretty much the method we use today. Canning uses heat to destroy harmful pathogens and then utilizes cooling to create a vacuum seal on a can or a jar that prevents contamination and degradation of the food inside. It's all about thermodynamics, but doing it isn't nearly as complicated as it seems.

And you don't have to be a grandma in an apron or a French imperialist invader to get in on the joys of canning. Our great grandparents often *had* to can in order to preserve food that would last throughout the year. And today, many people are reviving the lost art. In the modern industrial age, people like knowing where their food came from and how it was grown. The good news is that learning to can food is pretty simple, and it will allow you to preserve the bounty from your garden or Costco!

Water Bath Canning 101

Water bath canning is a simple way to dip your toe in the water and decide if you want to explore the magical universe of canning your own food. This method works for acidic foods like fruits and berries, tomatoes and salsa, pickles and relishes, chutneys, pie fillings, and fruit sauces. For other foods with lower acidity, you'll need to use the pressure canning method detailed after this section.

TOOLS:

Mason jars with lids and rings

Tongs or a jar lifter

Measuring cup

Wide-mouth funnel

Dish towels

A large vessel like a deep stock pot

A wire rack that fits inside the pot (or a dish cloth)

DIRECTIONS:

First, find a recipe you want to try, and gather your ingredients. Always choose fresh produce in good condition. You can prepare your recipe before or during the rest of the process.

Put the wire rack or a dish towel at the bottom of your stock pot to make sure water and heat completely surround the jars; place the empty Mason jars on the rack and fill the pot with water to submerge the jars.

Put a lid on the pot and bring the water to a boil. Add the lids and seals to the pot and boil for 3–5 minutes to sterilize them. Sterilization is what will allow you to keep your goodies edible for at least a year after canning.

Using the tongs, carefully lift the jars, lids, and rings from the stock pot; empty the jars and set them, along with the lids

Illustration by Liliana Faiella.

and rings, on a clean kitchen towel on the countertop to dry. Be very careful you don't burn yourself.

Use the funnel to fill the jars with your delicious jam (or whatever you've chosen) and leave about $1/2$ inch of room at the top of the jar. Be sure your mixture is warm when you put it in the jar.

Using a damp cloth or paper towel, wipe the rims of the jars so they are clean. Don't touch the rims with your fingers.

Center the warm lid on the jar, and screw the ring securely, but not super tightly around the lid to hold it in place.

Using the tongs or jar lifter, return the sealed jars to the stock pot. Now your jars will be full so they will displace more water, and you may need to remove some of the water from the pot so it doesn't overflow. You can use a measuring cup for this. The jars should be submerged about an inch under the water.

Illustration by Liliana Faiella.

Allow to boil, following your recipe for the specified amount of time.

Remove pot from heat, and carefully remove your jars from the water and place them back on the towel. As the jars cool, you should hear a lovely popping noise which tells you that the jar has sealed properly.

Test your seals! After the jars have cooled, remove the ring and lift the jars from the edge of the lid a few inches off the counter. Do the lids feel firmly affixed to the jar? Congratulations! You did it!

Now, in January you can enjoy the scrumptiousness of a tomato sauce from your garden, or strawberry jam, or crunchy pickles.

If you love water bath canning after you try it out, you can take it a step further. Invest in tools like a jar lifter, or a canning pot with a rack if you don't have them, or even explore pressure canning for less acidic foods.

Should you go with water bath or pressure canning? Pressure canning (different than pressure cooking) requires a piece of equipment called a pressure canner. This method utilizes the buildup of steam in a locked device to create intense pressure and heat that will completely sterilize and preserve any cannable food. However, delicate sweet fruits and tender vegetables can become compromised with the intense heat and pressure, and are better left to the gentler water bath method. Nobody wants rubber jelly or mushy pickles, amirite? But for tougher foods, pressure canning works very well and is *required* to safely preserve them.

Here are some foods that require pressure canning: most unpickled vegetables, including green beans, carrots, corn, potatoes, asparagus, spinach, peas, beets, and peppers; all meats and fish; low-fat stock. Always make sure you follow the USDA guidelines for canning, and be especially careful with meat and fish which require high temperatures.

And sadly, no amount of cash prize from Napoleon makes these veggies palatable after the canning process: cabbage (unless it's sauerkraut!), broccoli, cauliflower, lettuce, eggplant, or squash. Also, never can anything containing milk, butter, or cheese.

Safety First!

Before you start pressure canning food, be sure you follow all the best practices in the *USDA Complete Guide to Home Canning* to avoid food poisoning.* And regardless of what pressure canner you decide to get, *always make sure you have a couple of extra pressure gauges.* They will corrode over time and need to be replaced. And never ever try to use a pressure canner unless you are sure everything, including the gauge, is working properly. You'll be dealing with lots of pressure and lots of heat, so always use an abundance of caution. A pressure canner is no good to you without a gauge.

---

* You can download it free at: https://nchfp.uga.edu/publications/publications_usda.html or order a printed copy at: https://mdc.itap.purdue.edu/item.asp?Item_Number=AIG-539.

ARE YOU READY?

_____ Have you obtained the eight Armageddon foods?

_____ Do you have a system in place to store your shelf-stable pantry staples (such as using desiccants, oxygen removers, and mylar bags inside five-gallon buckets)? Or maybe your plan is to just have extra staples on hand and rotate through them?

_____ Have you gone down the list of supplemental foods and made sure you have an adequate supply for 2,000 calories per day for everyone in your family for at least two weeks? Or are you making a plan to obtain these foods over time?

_____ Have you factored in the special dietary needs of pets, babies, elders, or anyone with food allergies or special dietary requirements?

_____ Have you marked Prep Day on your calendar twice a year to check your food and water stores to rotate out what needs to be used, and replace it with new?

_____ Have you taken your time to peruse the canned food section of the supermarket to see what kinds of shelf-stable foods are available canned?

_____ Are you practicing best produce-extending tricks and food storage techniques to extend the life of your perishable food?

_____ Do you have paper copies of favorite recipes that will be easy to make from your pantry staples?

_____ Have you tried at least one type of food preservation technique like dehydrating, pickling, canning, or fermenting?

_____ Do you have a few favorite books of easy recipes or printed copies of recipes to use in case you lose the internet or electricity?

_____ After evaluating your food preparedness, have you thought of investing in:

- a food dehydrator
- a vacuum sealer and bags
- a canning pot
- a pressure canner
- a grain mill

CHAPTER 3

FORAGE, FARM, AND MICROGARDEN

FORAGING

The world is full of food if you know where to look. Foraging may sound like the last desperate attempt of a starving person wandering through the woods to find some calories, but the truth is that foraging is becoming a very popular pastime, with elite dining establishments featuring local wild-gathered foods as a healthy, organic, and environmentally friendly alternative to crops grown on commercial farms.

There's something empowering about heading outside and coming home with a basket of wild edibles that just makes you feel good. It's like a treasure hunt with an edible reward at the end. And many foraged foods can be preserved and used later utilizing the food preservation techniques we talked about in the last chapter. Wild strawberry jam anyone? Frozen cranberries for your next smoothie? Dandelion wine? Dried wild mushrooms for a hearty soup or stew! The possibilities are limitless, delicious, and can help fill your pantry for good times and uh-oh times alike.

Foraging is also a fun activity to do with a partner, friends, and kids. Seeking, finding, and eating run deep within our human history. We were designed to live as hunter/gatherers, and while hunting in the modern world can be a bigger and more complicated undertaking, gathering is pretty darn easy!

With high grocery costs and unreliable or fragile supply chains, the knowledge that you gain from foraging can be a step toward living a more sustainable life that withstands the influence of changing outside forces.

And don't despair if you don't live in a wild rural environment. Even in megacities like New York and L.A. you can find and utilize local urban wild foods found in city parks and trail systems. In New York City, an unbelievable 66 percent of plants have some human food use! But the more urban your foraging is, the more you will need to wash your treasures with a good produce wash, and then do it again, to remove any unwanted residue.

Shaggy mane mushrooms, pineapple weed, and cranberries from an evening walk in Interior Alaska.

Before you take the plunge into the delicious and addictive hobby of wild foraging, there are a few things you need to know so that you don't inadvertently act like a jerk or suffer any ill effects from your bounty.

THE FIVE RULES FOR BEGINNER FORAGERS

Rule #1: Be Careful!

Know your plants! You must feel absolutely comfortable identifying any plant before you touch or consume it. Plants are full of chemical compounds—some beneficial, some inert, but others that can cause adverse reactions in humans and animals through ingestion or even skin contact. Some can even cause death. Mushroom soup you're only *pretty sure* about could be a literal recipe for disaster.

In North America, watch out for poison ivy, poison oak, poison sumac, cow parsnip, and devil's club, which you know, if you've been unlucky enough to encounter any of them, can cause major skin irritation. Other dangerous plants to watch out for include giant hogweed, monkshood, water hemlock, and nightshade. There are far too many to list them all here, but if you are ever unsure about a plant, err on the side of caution and leave it be.

That said, there are also many wild plants that are widespread, plentiful, great for foraging, and have no nasty poisonous look-alikes to worry about, like the humble but mighty dandelion!

Rule #2: Understand Your Land

Study up on the area you plan to forage, or better yet find an experienced foraging guide. Learn what poisonous plants grow there, and which edibles you can safely harvest. Your local Cooperative Extension Service is a trove of information about all things plant and may offer classes or demonstrations on foraging local wild foods.

Try to avoid foraging near industrial areas or factories; golf courses or parks where herbicides and pesticides are used; roads, parking lots, or places where water and soil could be contaminated by exhaust or run-off. Areas that are off the trail and away from human activity are generally safer. Don't stray too far, though. Always make sure you know where you are, stay in sight of the trail, and know how to get back to where you started!

Rule #3: Harvest Responsibly

Always check local land management rules for harvesting limits or restrictions on what you are allowed to harvest, and follow these guidelines.

Take only what you need, and only what you know you will use. Never wipe out all the plants or berries in one area. Leaving enough edible plants for wildlife and for the plants themselves to regrow means you are preserving a sustainable resource for the future. That usually means leaving 10–20 percent of what you see where it is. Always be mindful of the impact you could have on habitats like deserts, wetlands, tundra, and other sensitive ecosystems. And make sure if you want to forage on private land that you get permission from the property owner.

Rule #4: Leave No Trace

Pay attention to your impact when venturing off-trail in search of plants. When you can, walk on surfaces like logs, rocks, gravel, or bare earth. Be careful of trampling on plants as you go. Some areas, like tundra, can take years to recover from a single footprint.

Remember to pack out all wrappers, bottles, cans, and garbage you bring.

Rule #5: Go for the Weeds!

When in doubt, or first starting out, go for weeds! As long as they are in a clean and uncontaminated area, edible weeds are easy and fun to harvest. Dandelions, pineapple weed, plantain, nettle, and other weeds are delicious, good for you, and you are unlikely to cause harm to the population. Weeds are tough, resilient, plentiful, easy to find, and they grow like weeds!

INTO THE WEEDS!

It's time to polish up that rusty hunter-gatherer DNA, grab a basket, and go weed hunting! The good news is, you can start your foray into foraging right near where you are, maybe even in your own yard or neighborhood! If you're not quite ready to jump into foraging groups on Facebook or march into the woods for the day, here's a great way to get your feet wet and get a feel for eating food that you find. It may seem strange at first, but it gets addictive quickly!

Dandelions

You may have yanked them out of your lawn, cursed them out loud, or burned them with fire. But remember, one person's nuisance weed is another person's salad! Dandelions may be almost universally hated, but the truth is that the humble and maligned dandelion is a forager's best friend, and a great place to start enjoying the many benefits of wild food. Technically, they aren't even weeds; they are perennial herbs! Every single part of the plant is edible, and it can be easily found in all fifty states and most of Canada. Dandelions are native to Europe and Asia but were actually brought to North America to be used for . . . wait for it . . . *food!* We did this to ourselves, so we may as well reap all the benefits!

When dandelions start to grow in the spring and before they flower, take advantage of the new baby leaves. They are tender and delicious raw, so throw them in a salad or steep them to make a delicate dandelion tea!

As the leaves get bigger, they can be enjoyed sautéed, and they taste kind of like mustard greens. The small unopened buds can also be tossed in a salad, and the opened flower heads can be fried whole, plucked for salad toppers, or used to make dandelion jelly or wine. A medicinal tea made by boiling the flowers is sweet and honey-like and acts as a diuretic. Leaves and flowers can also be used to make fritters! Even the deep tap-root can be eaten roasted or sautéed.

This is my own chemical-free yard/ dandelion harvesting ground! It's easy to enjoy the young leaves, early blossoms, and roots! And my family weren't the only ones who got to feast!

If grocery stores are closed, or you've been eating rice and beans for a while, the idea of fresh greens right outside the door will sound pretty nice. And they are an excellent source of vitamins and minerals like vitamins A, C, E, and K, folate, calcium, and iron.

There's only one thing you need to be careful about. Don't harvest dandelions that have been sprayed with herbicide or pesticide. Travel off the beaten path or use your own unsprayed yard/lawn to enjoy dandelion *everything*. See Appendix A for a delicious dandelion recipe. (Yes, really!)

Plantain

This is another amazing gem in the world of edible plants that has disguised itself as an annoying weed in your backyard. It was brought to North America from Europe and has naturalized itself into the ecosystem. It isn't even considered an invasive species because it made itself at home without displacing other native species or disrupting the ecosystem. Plantain is awesome like that!

If greens are hard to find during or after a disaster, young new leaves of plantain make a great addition to that dandelion salad and are full of protein, fiber, and vitamins. And if you catch the tender young flowering shoots before they start to produce flowers and seeds, you're in for a treat. Just snap off the shoots (they should come off easily if they are tender and sweet) and sauté them just like you did with the dandelion greens (Appendix B) until they are tender. They taste a bit like asparagus and are a really tasty and very nutritious side dish.

The medicinal value of plantain can't be overstated. If you find yourself with insect bites, skin irritation, or the dreaded "I can feel a splinter in my finger, but I can't find it," plantain will come to the rescue. Simply chew up a leaf or two, spit it out, and place it on the affected area. Bites, burns, and rashes will be soothed, and it will draw out that little sliver! You can also dry plantain, crumble it, and put it in a little muslin bag or even a sock, toss it in the tub, and run a bath. Give it a few squeezes and let it sit in the tub while you soak. Add oatmeal for sensitive skin, or lavender for additional healing and soothing. Ahhhh . . .

Chickweed

Meet another yard nemesis waiting to adorn your table with nutritional greens! Chickweed is easy to identify and can be found almost everywhere in the United States. Harvesting is a breeze because chickweed is prolific and often will grow in large clumps that form a large mat over the soil. It loves shady damp places. You can often find chickweed in your garden or growing next to the side of buildings. Just be sure it's pesticide and herbicide free. You can eat all parts of the plant, but most people will just grab a bunch and cut it off mid-stem. Rinse it well and remove any other grasses or weeds that may be mixed in. Drop it in boiling water for thirty seconds and then fry it up in a pan just like dandelion greens and plantain shoots for a nutritious side dish. People also make delicious pesto from chickweed, and you can even add it to a smoothie! If you hate weeds, eating them is the best revenge!

Berries

Another food that's fairly easy and safe to forage (as long as you follow the rules) is berries! Even if you weren't lucky enough to experience the pure joy of eating summer-ripened berries right off the bush as a kid, it's not too late. Here are three foolproof berries that make great foraged fruit! When you find a great berry patch, save the GPS coordinates, and make sure to leave enough berries for wildlife and to grow more plants. Then you can return year after year to enjoy the fruits of your labor. It's kind of like having a special secret fishing hole!

Blueberries

There are more than a dozen species of wild blueberries for you to enjoy. From the low-bush tiny wild berries of Maine and Alaska, to larger high-bush species further south, they are a great source of vitamins and nutrients and can be preserved by freezing or drying, or as jam or syrup. Blueberries grow in acidic soils. Look for them on roadsides, areas with lots of fallen trees, fields, and mountainsides.

Blackberries

The perfect berry for beginning foragers, there is no mistaking blackberries for anything else and they often produce enormous crops of large and delicious berries in late summer. The dense, prickly brambles are the only downside to this harvest so be sure to wear long sleeves and pick with care.

Blackberries can be enjoyed as you pick them, used in salads, in oatmeal, for jams and jellies, in muffins and pies, for syrups, and many other uses.

The Himalayan blackberry species, introduced to North America in the 1880s, is considered a noxious weed. So, if you come across them feel free to pick with impunity. Never has eradicating an invasive species been so delicious!

Raspberries

Most people can spot a raspberry right away. The wild version is just as tasty sweet, but probably slightly smaller than store-bought and with an intense flavor. These too are great right off the bush, in baked desserts, on pancakes, or in jams and jellies. You can also freeze or dry them.

The world of forageable berries is huge! Find out which edible berries grow near you (and if they have any dangerous look-alikes), how to identify them, and when the peak picking season is. Berry picking is a great reason to get outside and get kids interested in nature and wild foods. Depending on your location, you can harvest and preserve cranberries, lingonberries, huckleberries, salmonberries, nagoonberries, cloudberries, black raspberries, strawberries, gooseberries, paw paw, and dozens more.

Wild Mushrooms

Did your heart just seize up with fear? The idea of foraging for mushrooms is a hard *no* for many people. Their brain starts imagining poisoning everyone at a dinner party or hallucinating from a batch of risotto. These are good instincts because mushrooms, if you are careless or reckless, can mess you up, big time. But knowledge is power, and if you want to be confident about harvesting all the goodness of wild mushrooms, connect with an experienced forager or group who will take you under their wing and show you where and how to harvest good mushrooms safely.

Mushroom identification and foraging classes are often offered through colleges and mycology clubs like the North American Mycological Association. There are also Facebook groups available to assist you in identification, but be sure to take several clear photos of the mushroom to include the top, the underside, a side view, and a picture that shows what the mushroom is growing on and what other plants are nearby.

It's a good idea, when trying a new edible mushroom, to sample a little bite and wait 24–48 hours to make sure you don't have a personal sensitivity to it, even if it isn't poisonous. And remember, wild mushrooms always need to be cooked before eating!

That said, there are four types of mushrooms—known as "the foolproof four"—that are great for beginning foragers. They have no dangerous look-alikes so if you are careful and prudent, it's a great place to start.

Chicken of the Woods

Sounds tasty already, right? Chicken of the Woods mushrooms have a distinctive look that makes them easy to identify—and yes, they kind of taste like chicken!

They are usually found on dead or dying trees, on or near the base; they grow in a cluster or shelf; and they have pores underneath, not gills. Depending on where you live, you may find them any time between spring and fall. There's no mistaking their yellow or orange tops, making them among the easiest mushrooms to find in wooded areas. They aren't hiding! Look for young mushrooms without damage or dry or brittle edges. Don't soak mushrooms because they tend to absorb water. Just brush them off or wipe with a damp cloth to preserve their amazing meaty texture. Store fresh mushrooms in a paper bag (no plastic, or they will slime!), cut them into strips to freeze, or dehydrate them for later use.

Porcini

Porcini means *piglets* in Italian, and these adorable plump mushrooms with fat stems and thick caps are beloved by pigs (because pigs are not stupid!). Their tops look kind of like a hamburger bun,

and they have pores on the underside of the cap, not gills. Porcinis, also known as King Bolete mushrooms, are sublime, but they aren't easy to cultivate. That means that those who forage are the ones who get to enjoy this rare and coveted mushroom.

Porcinis can be found in the fall on the edges of wooded areas where forest gives way to open space. You can find them growing near the roots of spruce and pine trees, as well as beech, hemlock, birch, and chestnut trees. Pigs and people aren't the only ones who love porcinis; unfortunately, insects do too. Larger, older mushrooms are more likely to have already been discovered by bugs. Check for bore holes. Sometimes you can just cut away infested areas and eat the rest, but it's best to go for younger untouched porcinis. And always try to forage mushrooms with a good knife, cutting them off at the base rather than pulling them up by the roots.

Porcinis are nutty, robust, and delicious. You can use them in stews, soups, gravy, risotto, or ragu. Sauté and add them to any dish that would benefit from an extra dose of deliciousness. They are also great dried for later use.

A surprise trove of foraged bolete mushrooms and blueberries. This is why you should always carry a knife!

Bolete

The edges of hiking trails are great places to find bolete mushrooms. We got a great harvest, which I chopped, cooked up in a massive batch of mushroom gravy, and then froze in portioned out ziplock bags. We enjoyed that gravy on burgers, steaks, and potatoes all year long.

Chanterelles

There are several mushrooms in this family, and they are abundant in many areas of the world. They range in color between yellow and white, and can be easily recognized by the prominent, strange-looking folds (not technically gills) that extend from the cap all the way down the stem. They are hard to cultivate,

so foraging is your best source of this earthy and slightly peppery fungal delight. They have been coveted by humans around the world for centuries, but they found a royal following in France where the revered chanterelle made a prominent showing in palace kitchens in the eighteenth century and became more widely known. The chemical composition of the chanterelle makes it perfect for use in recipes with cream, oil, butter, eggs, and wine. No wonder the French declared them officially *magnifique!*

Chanterelles can be found in both deciduous and coniferous forests and sometimes grasslands, and range in size from an inch to several inches across. When you find one, there are sure to be more because they come in clusters.

Morels

Morels are the holy grail of foodie foraging, because they are almost impossible to cultivate and have an intense and unforgettable flavor that makes them the standout ingredient in any dish, but particularly in mushroom soups, sauces, and entrées where they can shine as the star of the meal.

Morels have an unforgettable look too, with a textured cap that resembles a honeycomb or peach pit. There's only one other mushroom that resembles a morel on the outside, but they are easy to distinguish from

one another because when a true morel is sliced in half, it will be hollow on the inside while the "false morel" will not.

Morels can be found in the Northern Hemisphere in North and Central America, Europe, and Asia when the weather starts to warm up in late spring. They especially like areas where there has recently been a moderate-intensity fire and ash has made the soil more alkaline. Morels are so highly prized that there is a growing industry of commercial wild morel harvesting, and good morel locations can be a guarded secret because of their culinary and monetary value.

When you find morels, be sure to collect them in a mesh sack so the spores spread as you continue the hunt, ensuring more to be found the following year!

CREATE YOUR OWN FORAGING SPACE

If you are fortunate enough to have a yard or green space, create your own foraging opportunities! Don't use herbicides and see what naturally grows in your yard—you may be surprised! After foraging for mushrooms, shake the spores out in a shady corner. Plant hostas, daylilies, berries, and other ornamental edible plants you can forage if you need to. You can even plant trees with edible leaves, just in case! Chinese elm, mulberry, hawthorn, sassafras, linden, beech, and birch trees all have edible leaves. Plant nut and fruit trees that will grow in your area and learn how to preserve the harvest. You can create a beautiful and interesting foraging space right outside your door.

GET FORAGING!

Wild foods are fresh, delicious, and rich in many nutrients. One California study that tested wild foraged greens found, with the exception of vitamin C, the wild greens tested were generally *more nutritious than kale*! Mother Nature knows what she's doing and the closer we can get to her, and the farther away from processed, factory-farmed foods, the happier and healthier we will be, and the less reliant we will be on the modern supply chain with all its hazards and unpredictability.

Mind you, we've just touched the tip of the iceberg here. There are hundreds of forageable greens, fruits, mushrooms, roots, berries, flowers, seeds, and nuts. Think rosehips, cattails, kelp and other seaweeds, dock, ramps, hazelnuts, fireweed, fiddlehead ferns, wild leeks and onions, sorrel, sunchoke, pine needles, yarrow, elderberry, stinging nettle, watercress, and more! It's a banquet out there! Find out what's around you, connect with experienced foragers, and start filling your basket!

Learn foraging skills and where to forage before it becomes a necessity. And don't expect foraging to become your primary food supply. You won't be the only one hitting the berry patches, and you may not be able to get too far from home.

GYOF (GROW YOUR OWN FOOD)

You have a life, and statistically you're probably not going to quit your day job to go off and buy yourself forty acres in the countryside, hop on a tractor, and try to figure out how to become a sustainable farmer so you can grow all your own food. Most of us have, at best, a big yard and, at least, a small city apartment with no green space at all. Most of us also don't have a whole lot of time to spend digging, and hoeing, and weeding, and all that. But the good news is that none of that means you can't supplement your diet with food you grow yourself, or you can't be prepared to do it if you need to.

Why bother growing your own food when the bodega is right down the block or you live a five-minute drive from Costco? By now you've probably figured out that relying on the magical invisible supply chain to come to the rescue may make you feel good, but it's a risky game. Food ingredients are often trucked from one location to a central warehouse kitchen where they are combined. Packaging comes from yet another location and is shipped to where the food is made. Then the food must be packaged and delivered across the country to a location near you. Local disasters, severe-weather events like floods or earthquakes, economic instability, energy shortages, worker shortages, climate change, pandemics, road closures—all these things can interrupt the supply chain and your ability to get food and vital supplies.

Food manufacturing that relies on one or two major manufacturers (think baby formula) is vulnerable to collapse. And what about agricultural products like fertilizers, or parts for farm equipment, or agricultural workers, or truckers, or truck parts? If you really stop and think about it, you'll realize how much there is that could possibly go wrong. And even if there is food on the shelf, all the things above and more could make it extremely or even prohibitively expensive.

Even if you've paid attention so far and have a good supply of rice, beans, and all the other must-have survival foods, there's really no substitute for fresh food, especially if you are affected long-term.

You've now learned some basic techniques to store and preserve food, so you're just a few steps away from canning homegrown tomato sauce, pickling some homegrown onions, or storing a big bucket of potatoes that came from containers in your yard.

And finally, growing your own produce has a much lower carbon footprint and cost! Your veggies don't have to migrate halfway around the world on trucks, barges, or airplanes to get to you. There's your lettuce, right on the porch!

Starting Small

What if we told you that you could grow powerhouse superfoods with more nutritional value by weight than vegetables, that tasted great, jazzed up your food, gave you a dose of chlorophyll energy, and could be grown right on your windowsill with minimal effort, cost, and sunlight?

Maybe we sound like an infomercial but if that sounds good to you, then you should start growing sprouts and microgreens immediately!

Sprouts

Sprouts are the easiest greens you'll ever grow. All you need is enough space for a Mason jar. You don't even need soil or sun! You can sprout legumes, grains, or seeds, and consuming those sprouts is often easier on the digestive system than eating the plant itself.

Great seeds for beginning sprouters are: broccoli, alfalfa, millet, clover, radishes, mung beans, chickpeas, lentils, and peas. You can even buy a bag of premixed seeds for variety.

You should always buy seeds packaged and sold for sprouting rather than just buying peas or lentils at the store and hoping for the best. Seeds packaged for sprouting have not been irradiated to stop them from sprouting as some supermarket seeds are. Also, they are tested for E. coli and other pathogens because sprouting seeds aren't boiled or cooked before consumption. There are many great online resources for sprouting seeds and you can also sometimes find them in health food stores or greengrocers.

You should find directions on sprouting from wherever you buy your seeds, but here's how to do it with our favorite blend of broccoli, clover, radish, and alfalfa from *Sprout House*. You can use a Mason jar with a special screened lid for sprouting, but you can also use a square of muslin or cheesecloth held over the mouth of the jar with a rubber band.

- Soak 2 tbsp. of seeds overnight in a jar or bowl of water for about 8 to 10 hours. Don't soak too long or you risk drowning your seeds!
- After the initial soak, drain the water and rinse the seeds with fresh water.
- Drain out *that* water making certain there are only wet seeds in the jar and no standing water.
- To ensure proper drainage, tilt the jar upside down in a bowl so the jar is at an angle and you aren't cutting off air flow to the seeds.
- Twice each day, once in the morning and once in the evening, rinse and drain well, making certain there are only wet seeds or sprouts in the jar, and no standing water. Put the jar back in the bowl after each rinse.

- Sprouts are ready to eat in about five to seven days!
- After the sprouts are the size you want, give them a final rinse and lay them out on paper towels to dry for about an hour before storing in the fridge in a ventilated container.

That's all there is to it! Remember, your sprouts may have different soaking times so be sure to check.

Microgreens

Microgreens are just sprouts with a little more commitment. Generally, you will sow your seeds into *seed starter soil* (not regular potting soil) and harvest the greens by cutting the stems above the level of the soil, rather than eating roots and all like you do with sprouts. There are dozens of varieties of microgreens you can grow for use in salads, sautés, smoothies, sandwiches, burgers, garnishes, side dishes, and more.

Not everything is suitable for microgreens though. Plants of the nightshade family are definite no-nos, so *do not eat microgreens of eggplant, tomato, peppers, or potatoes because they are poisonous!*

Some of the best varieties for beginners are lettuce mixes, peas, sunflowers, broccoli, cauliflower, turnips, and wheat grass (which most people use for juicing). When you buy seeds make sure they are organic and buy in bulk because you'll be using a lot of seeds! Trying to keep yourself in microgreens by buying those teeny packets at the garden store will break the bank. But bulk buying means you'll be flush with fresh crispy greens any time you want, even when you've been in lockdown for three weeks and your neighbors are eating Spam and saltines and getting really cranky.

How to Grow Lettuce Microgreens

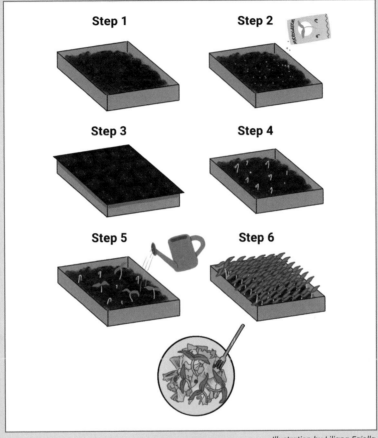

Step 1
Step 2
Step 3
Step 4
Step 5
Step 6

Illustration by Liliana Faiella.

Unlike sprouts, microgreens will need some sunlight or a grow light to develop the dark green chlorophyll in their leaves, so pick a sunny window or set up a small grow light. Then decide what size of tray or pot you can fit in that space. Let's say you can fit a standard-size seed-starting tray which is about 10" x 20" x 2.5".

- Pour 2 cups of water in the bottom of the tray.
- Fill the tray with fine seed-starting mix leaving about one-half to two-thirds of an inch of space at the top lip of the tray.

- Lightly compact the soil and make sure it's flat on the surface.
- Take about an ounce and a half of lettuce-mix seeds and sprinkle them evenly over the top of the soil. They will be very densely spread on the surface.
- Spray the top of the soil with enough water to make the surface wet but not soggy.
- Set another empty tray right on top of the seeds. They won't need light to sprout.
- Check back in a few days and you should see that sprouting has begun!
- A few days after sprouting, remove the tray, then water (without water-logging) and put the tray in the sun or about 8 inches under a grow light.
- Continue to water and check the progress of your microgreens.
- They should be ready to harvest about two to three weeks from planting, once true leaves have appeared.
- Harvest with scissors and enjoy!

You can grow microgreens in almost anything. Each type of microgreen will have slightly different needs, and for some you'll need to soak the seeds like you do with sprouts. But here are the general instructions for growing mixed lettuce microgreens so you can get a feel for what it takes and decide if you want to jump into the exciting world of growing your own!

REGROWING KITCHEN SCRAPS

You may have seen videos pop up on social media that make it look simple to grow a lemon grove in your living room, or tell you to put kitchen scraps in a glass of water and they will regrow so you never have to buy green onions again. Don't believe everything you see on Instagram, but there's a shred of truth in there.

First, unless you're just a botany/plant nerd (and there's nothing wrong with that!), give up the idea of a fruit grove or a producing avocado tree started from seed. For our purposes here it takes way too much time and effort to see the fruits of your labor. (See what we did there?)

But you definitely can make your grocery order stretch out or prolong your supply of fresh produce by giving some of your kitchen scraps a second life. To maximize your bonus harvest it will take more than a glass of water, but it's worth it. You're not guaranteed results with this method because successful propagation of plants and gardening are dependent on many factors. But here is a list of produce that might just surprise you with an unexpected second harvest!

Potatoes

Best for your first try! Have you ever had a potato that starts to sprout, or turns green? Before you toss it in the trash or the compost, try planting it! Potatoes are prolific, and burying your little green reject could result in a big ol' pile of perfectly good potatoes in four to six weeks! You can plant it in a bed or in a container. A five-gallon bucket will even do! Nothing to lose, and a bunch of free potatoes to gain!

Onion/Garlic

If you have an onion or garlic that has started to sprout, listen to it!

It wants to grow and it just can't wait! Don't chuck it, plant it. If you're lucky, it will eventually divide and give you a cluster of new bulbs.

Lettuce, Cabbage, Celery, Leeks, Bok Choy

Anything you prepare by chopping off the top and discarding the bottom part of the plant is a good candidate for replanting. Take your lettuce stump (or whatever you're using) and plant it so the root end is in the soil and the top cut part is above the soil. If you're lucky, you'll notice leaves start to appear and regrow. Multiple small heads of lettuce (or cabbage) may even show up.

Beets, Carrots, Turnips

Sadly, once you've eaten the sweet, calorie-dense roots of carrot, beet, and turnip, there's no growing it back. *But* that's not to say that these little stumps won't give you something else—greens! You can plant the chopped-off tops of these root vegetables and they'll continue to push up nutritious green leaves for you to harvest and enjoy. Beet and turnip greens can be boiled, sautéed, and used just like any other greens. But carrot greens? You may be wondering to yourself if they are even edible. Oh, yes, they are! Carrot greens are healthy and delicious and taste like if carrots and parsley had a baby. You can use carrot greens in pesto, soups, fritters, salads, and more.

Herbs

You're not going to fill your caloric needs by eating a bunch of herbs, but you can improve your quality of life (and your quality of food) by learning how to propagate them. You'll also save a pantload of money because if you've ever bought fresh herbs in the grocery store you know how fast it can add up!

Here's a method that will work for most common herbs like oregano, basil, cilantro, mint, marjoram, and the famous four—parsley, sage, rosemary, and thyme.

Practice your kitchen propagation skills, enjoy the extra bounty, and use these skills to extend your produce and create food from scraps! This will be important knowledge and experience to have if you ever really need to use it. And if you have kids, get them in on the act.

Propagating Herbs from Scraps

- Start by cutting off the top three or four inches of the herb stem.
- Leave the first two sets of leaves on the top of the stem and remove everything below that.
- Then place the freshly cut stem in a glass of water. Use bottled spring water if your tap water is treated with chlorine or water softener.
- Make the water deep enough that it covers where you plucked off the lower set or two of leaves.
- Then place the herbs on a sunny windowsill.
- Change the water every few days.
- Be patient because it might take a few weeks to see new roots emerge.
- Once the roots are an inch long and begin to send off side roots, you can carefully plant in fine seedling soil mix in a pot with good drainage.

It's easy to propagate store-bought basil!
This took about two weeks.

They love this kind of stuff and it's a valuable lesson in biology, kitchen economics, and sustainability they will carry with them.

TAKE STOCK

If growing food from scraps is not your jam, or if you just plain don't have time, there's still no reason any of your vegetable leavings should go to waste. Nor should your meat bones either. Keep a gallon-sized ziplock freezer bag in the freezer, and put all your discarded veggie leaves, stalks, ends, and peels in it—herb scraps too! Then when it's full, throw it in a pot of simmering water all day and you will be rewarded with delicious, nutritious vegetable stock! You can use it for soups, stews, sauces, or to boil rice—any recipe calling for water or stock.

You can also break chicken or other poultry bones or use leftovers from other cuts of meat and throw them in there too. It's all fair game when you're making stock. After six to eight hours (and you can add more water if you need to) pour through a strainer lined with cheesecloth into a large bowl and let it cool. You can freeze it in containers or in ice cube trays for later use!

SURVIVAL GARDENING

There have been hundreds and hundreds of books written about gardening. People have dedicated their lives to perfecting gardening skills, learning their own particular region, what grows, what pests there are and how to deal with them, what soil they have and how to remediate it, learning how to time plantings for maximum benefit and yield, and learning which varieties of plants will perform best in their unique environment. The bottom line is that gardening can consume as much time as you want to give it. That doesn't mean it should be intimidating.

Let's get down and dirty. What if you're not an avid gardener and don't want to be, but you've been thinking it might be a good idea to know how to grow some of your own food. If you want an easy, efficient survival garden, you will need to find crops that are:

1. easy to grow and are reliable producers
2. nutritious and calorie dense

3. able to produce a lot of food per square foot
4. able to be kept, stored, or preserved easily

There's no one-size-fits-all food crop, so you'll have to do a little research about your particular area—its temperature range, USDA Hardiness Zone, precipitation, type of soil, elevation, and so on. Again, your local cooperative extension service or gardening club will be a wealth of information and help about what plants thrive, how to encourage them, and the optimal time to plant. Remember, other people have already figured this stuff out, so now all you have to do is *find those people!* You'll also discover that gardeners and plant people love to share knowledge and help newbies.

Here are some good crops to start researching. They will grow in many areas, and they meet all four criteria above. You can investigate whether they are good for your region and plant accordingly!

In addition, for suburban or urban gardeners who don't have the luxury of a giant garden plot or who don't even have room for raised beds, all these vegetables can be grown in containers. This allows you to use small spaces and to reconfigure your garden for maximum sunlight. You can start small and add containers as you become more knowledgeable and confident in your green thumb.

Another bonus is that you'll never need to do any backbreaking shoveling or tilling, which makes container gardening much more manageable for kids, elders, and those who find in-ground gardening physically challenging.

If you are container gardening, make sure you start with a potting mix designed specifically for growing in containers.

THE DOOMSDAY DOZEN FOR YOUR SURVIVAL GARDEN

1. POTATOES

White potatoes are the king of survival crops. There's no single food that fulfills all of a human's nutritional needs, and you should never eat just one thing. *But,* if you did, you could survive for a long time on just potatoes. Throughout history the humble spud has been a food staple in many different cultures. It's incredibly easy to grow, it's prolific, and it's versatile. You can grow potatoes in the ground, a raised bed, or a container. Boil 'em, bake 'em, fry 'em, stuff 'em—the mighty potato should be one of the first things you learn to grow and enjoy.

After you harvest, let your potatoes dry in the sun for a little while, but don't wash them. Brush off any big dirt clumps but don't expose them to water until you are ready to eat them. Store them in a cool, dry place in paper bags or boxes and they'll keep for months! Never store them in plastic (they will turn slimy), in the fridge (they will mush), or anywhere near onions, apples, or bananas (they will sprout).

2. BEETS

Beets are a great early season/cold season crop. They can germinate even when it's still freezing at night. Like most deeply colored vegetables, they are full of healthy phytochemicals and nutrients. They've also been a pantry staple of cultures from Northern and Eastern Europe to the Middle East for thousands of years. Even early Egyptians, Romans, and Greeks loved beets, primarily for the greens, which can be eaten raw when young, or boiled/steamed when older. They taste a bit like spinach! Beet roots have a long shelf life and can also be preserved by pickling. Or try them thinly sliced and dehydrated as beet chips! Store the roots in a sealed plastic bag in the crisper drawer of the fridge or in a cool, dry place and they should last several weeks. Remember you can leave beets in the ground even when it gets cold which is a great way to extend their lifespan.

Important note: If you've never eaten beets before, don't be alarmed if you start to pee pink! Pink pee panic is a thing, but there's no need to call 911. You aren't dying, you are just experiencing a harmless condition called *beeturia* which is what happens when all those lovely pigments get filtered out by your kidneys.

3. TURNIPS

Turnips, like beets, are cold-hardy and can be sown early in the spring and harvested late in the fall. They store well in cool, dry places too. You can roast the root with other root veggies, boil and mash them with butter and salt, use them in soups and stews, and they also make excellent chips. Turnip greens are delicious too, making those little white globes with the pink tops a great addition to your survival garden.

4. KALE

You had to know this dark green nutritional heavyweight would make the list. Kale is mocked mercilessly but it fits all the criteria for the food you want in supply during the apocalypse. It's hardy, easy to grow, gets really big, produces a lot of leaves, is good for you, and you can enjoy it in a variety of ways.

Pro tip: Never pull your plant up by the roots if you think it's time to harvest. You can pluck leaves here and there as you need them, and the plant will just continue to make more. Some species of kale can get leaves that are well over a foot long! Little leaves can be chopped and enjoyed in salad, but bigger leaves are more suitable for chopping and boiling, steaming, or making kale chips! Or try blanching, draining, vacuum sealing, and freezing to save for after the harvest is over. And don't forget to save those kale spines from the center of the leaf for your veggie stock!

5. SPINACH

Spinach is another great green to have on hand. It also grows quickly and can withstand some cold. You can plant seeds in the ground, raised beds, or well-draining containers as soon as you can work the soil. With just forty-five days until maturity, you'll have a crop of spinach before you know it. Try to plant in full sun, or plan out how you can move containers around to take advantage of the sunshine throughout the day. Just be sure to harvest before it starts to get hot or your spinach may bolt and go to seed. You can plant a second crop in late summer when temperatures start to cool.

6. CABBAGE

Chopped into slaws, stir-fried, boiled, baked, or stewed, the versatile and hardy cabbage should always be part of your vegetable plot or container garden. If you plan carefully, you can take advantage of the many types of cabbages that mature from spring to late fall, and have cabbage almost all year long, depending on where you live. They love sunshine and rich, compact soil. They are also suitable for container growing but they need space, so one head will be enough to fill a five-gallon bucket.

7. PEAS

Peas and lentils are fun and satisfying to grow. You can densely sow the seeds directly into the soil. They don't mind being close to each other, so take advantage of that and you'll get a big harvest! Peas are perfect for along walls or garden edges. They can also grow in containers. Make sure you know how high your peas will grow because peas climb! You'll need to provide a trellis or netting of the proper height. Try to keep them out of the wind or secure them to the trellis if you can't. If you time it right, you can get two bumper pea crops, early and late.

Peas, pods, and shoots can be eaten fresh, but peas are also suited well to freezing and drying for future use. If you like snow peas, you can even ferment the young pods!

8. CORN

If you thought you needed a yard like the one in *Field of Dreams* to grow corn, think again! Corn, yes even corn, can be grown in a container! Make sure it's about twenty inches wide and at least twelve inches deep with drainage holes on the bottom. Soak your seeds and sow directly into the soil. Each container should be able to grow four corn plants. Of course, you can sow directly into the ground too, or start your corn in a seed starting tray and transplant it. If you have room, plant corn in groups to help with pollination.

Corn requires warm temperatures and consistently moist soil. It will take about ninety days to mature. You can tell it's ready when the silks at the top of the ear turn brown. You can enjoy your corn fresh or frozen, or dry it out to save for replanting.

9. SQUASH

You want a prolific, high-yield, fast-growing plant? Nothing beats zucchini!

Zucchini is delicious and versatile. You can eat it raw in salads, boil it with butter and salt, bake it with tomato sauce and mozzarella, or make zucchini bread or muffins. Use it as a thickening agent for sauces and soups (you'll never even notice it!). You can also preserve it by freezing or pickling.

To make sure your plants keep producing all season, be sure to prune back old leaves, especially the ones touching a neighboring plant. Pruning will stimulate new growth, keep air flow between plants to cut down on powdery mildew, and will allow insects to find and pollinate all the flowers!

And don't forget winter squashes. They get their name not because that's when they are ready to harvest but because they will last into the winter, which is a great feature for your survival garden. Acorn squash, butternut squash, and spaghetti squash are all popular and can be grown in containers, but there are many other varieties of winter squash with dense, sweet flesh that you can enjoy fresh for months after harvest. Squash plants tend to grow big so only plant one per five-gallon bucket size. If you want to make sure you get a very robust plant, you can plant three per container and then be ruthless and pluck the smaller two after they've had a few weeks of growth.

10. TOMATOES

Who doesn't love homegrown tomatoes? To take on the most coveted crop around, you'll need a five-gallon container for each full-sized tomato plant because it's got a big root system. Use loose potting soil specifically for containers. You'll also need to fertilize every few weeks with a high nitrogen/phosphorous fertilizer.

Tomatoes are a little needy, but they give as good as they get. So, start schmoozing that plant by giving it what it needs, and it will love you back with sweeter, more delicious tomatoes than you could ever find in the store. Make sure the soil stays damp and water a couple of times a week if needed. They will also need five to eight hours of sunlight or bright indoor light a day. Make sure to bury the stem up to the first true pair of leaves. The tomato plant will put out stabilizing roots right from the stem that will keep it stable in the soil and less likely to fall over! You'll still probably need to stake your tomatoes just to be sure.

For your best chance of success, plant cherry tomatoes! You can grow them in a basket like a hanging plant and if you start them in great soil, fertilize them, and keep them from drying out, you'll be amazed at how many cherry tomatoes can come from one little plant!

Whatever tomatoes you decide to plant, make sure you choose the right variety for your conditions. When your harvest comes, enjoy it fresh, and then can, freeze, or dry what you want for later.

11. BEANS

There are dozens of kinds of beans, but for our purposes here, we want beans that will produce the highest yield in the smallest space. And frankly, if you're looking for beans you can dry and store, you're better off just buying a bulk bag of dried beans ahead of time than going through all the time and effort of trying to do it yourself. Save that garden space for a different kind of bean—the green bean!

Green beans come in two growing varieties—bush beans and pole beans. Bush beans may sound easier, but pole beans are the ones you want. They take up less square footage and produce a higher yield per plant. The only thing you'll need are poles! You can get eight-foot wooden stakes at Lowe's or Home Depot for a couple of dollars. Configure them like a triangle about twelve to sixteen inches apart, push them down in the soil, and tie them at the top. Then plant three or four pole bean seeds right in the ground underneath and let them do their thing. You'll get a big harvest of beans you can eat fresh, freeze, dry, or pickle—all in a couple of square feet of soil.

And if you want to, you can even grow pole beans in containers. If you can't find or transport big, long poles, you can get shorter ones, overlap them, and attach them together with duct tape. You can plant three plants in a one-gallon container or four plants in a twelve-gallon container.

As you can imagine, plants growing more than eight feet tall will require a steady supply of water so make sure you are checking regularly to ensure they don't dry out. When your pole beans start getting too high to harvest from, you can nip the tops and the plant will become slightly bushier and produce beans where you can reach them. Keep harvesting your beans as they become the right size, and the plants will continue to make more flowers and more beans.

12. CARROTS

If you are growing carrots in containers, either choose a carrot variety that doesn't get super long or make sure your container is deep. You don't want the carrots bumping against the bottom of the pot or grow bag, or they'll start growing sideways into weird shapes. They'll still taste good, but they'll be harder to clean and peel. Always use the freshest carrot seed you can find, and use more than you need. You can thin out as you go until you have about two inches between plants. If you delay your thinning you can even enjoy baby carrots and carrot greens along the way! You can also grow carrots in raised beds as long as you take their depth and the length of the carrot into consideration. In some ways, growing carrots is easier in containers because you can control moisture and drainage, and make sure there are no rocks or other obstacles in the soil that make carrots turn out deformed.

Fertilize when you sow with an all-purpose fertilizer, and then again in four weeks, and make sure you give them lots of sun—six to eight hours a day. In sixty days you'll be crunching away on a fresh carrot harvest!

If you are growing carrots in the ground, you can expand your harvest by growing carrots one or two plants at a time here or there, or around the edges of beds. They don't take much room so you may as well take advantage of that! You can also leave carrots in the ground late into the season to preserve them. If you leave them for a long time, they can develop a woody texture raw, but you'll never know the difference once you cook them. Once your carrots are peeking out over the top of the soil and are about an inch wide, they are ready to pull!

HOW TO GROW AN INDOOR VEGETABLE GARDEN

Technically if you have enough space, soil, water, light, money, and TLC to give, you should be able to grow anything you grow outdoors indoors too. But most people don't have the resources, cash, or space it would take to have a productive cornfield or a watermelon patch in the basement, so manage those expectations. But you can start small and, taking a few things into consideration, create a garden that will give you greens and vegetables all year round.

LOCATION. Do you have a bunch of south-facing windows? Do you have some space to dedicate to indoor plants in trays or pots? How many hours of sunlight will you have in the winter? What temperature do you keep your house? Would you be able to rig up a system to supplement sunlight with adjustable grow lights?

TEMPERATURE. This is one area where indoor gardening can have an advantage. Your house or apartment is probably going to have a more comfortable and steady temperature than the great outdoors, both for germinating and sustaining many plants.

LIGHT. If you live in the South, you may be able to grow right on the windowsill with no artificial light. The less light you have, the more likely you'll need to supplement that light with artificial lights. No worries, though, you won't need a super-expensive setup or special pricey grow lights. Just get regular inexpensive shop lights and make sure the bulb is 5,000–6,500 Kelvin with an output of 2,500 lumens or more. Get a timer system too, because while twelve hours of light is optimal for growing conditions, you won't have to run the lights that whole time if you have sunlight as well. You can set the lights to run only in the early morning, and again in the evening, and let the sun handle the rest.

SOIL AND DRAINAGE. Always make sure to use (and we cannot stress this enough) sterile potting mix designed for indoor use. Do not just dig up dirt from the yard, and don't get random *topsoil* from the garden store. Invest in the proper soil and you will be rewarded with a home that is not infested with bugs. You're welcome. When you plant, always use containers with good drainage. You don't have to be fancy; you can plant in sawed-off milk jugs, or Tupperware, but just make sure if there aren't drainage holes in the bottom that you put them there yourself with a drill.

WATER. You're going to have to be a little bit anal about watering. Mother Nature is not going to bail you out either by providing rain or by retaining moisture in a whole yard full of soil. These little plants are going to be 100 percent dependent on you for water, and the containers are going to be small and will dry out fairly quickly. So set timers, or reminders, or whatever you need to do, but you'll need to check almost daily to make sure the soil is moist and happy. Mulch is your friend. When you are planting seeds, put a thin layer of straw mulch over the top. It will make it much easier to water without disturbing the seeds or new sprouts, and it will also help retain moisture.

HEAT AND AIR. Your grow lights will provide some additional heat which can be very helpful in the germination phase and beyond. You can also find small indoor greenhouses with soft sides and shelves that allow you to keep pots and trays in a warmer, more humid environment if that's what your particular plant will like. Just be sure to ventilate from time to time to avoid mold issues and keep good air flow. Plants also like a bit of wind. Think of an intermittent fan as sending your little green friends to the gym for a workout. A breeze will help them stay strong and upright, and will also keep mold away.

FERTILIZER. After the first few weeks you'll need to start fertilizing your plants. Make sure that the fertilizer you are using is made for indoor plants and does not stink up your house to high heaven.

Which Veggies to Plant Indoors?

Choosing plants is going to be as big a factor as anything in the success of your indoor garden. Just to put it out there right now, butternut squash is not going to happen. Its space requirements are just too great to be a practical candidate for your indoor survival garden.

When choosing edible plants to grow indoors, you want plants that have:

1. successful germination rates,
2. a shallow root system,
3. temperature needs that match your house,
4. light needs that you will be able to accommodate,
5. an uncomplicated life cycle that doesn't require either insects to pollinate or male and female plants. You want no muss, no fuss as much as possible.

Here are some plants that fit all those criteria to get you started and set you up for success:

Growing Tomatoes

The first time I tried growing tomatoes indoors, I used a great fertilizer for *outdoor* tomatoes, and as a result I came home from a weekend away and it smelled like a large farm animal had died in my house. The smell was there for *days* . . . which felt like weeks. Save yourself and do not do this!

Come on, little fella!

The good news was that I managed to grow actual tomatoes inside in Alaska and they ripened when it was below zero outside. No grow lights either, just an indoor greenhouse and a lot of patience. It was not a bumper crop by any means, but it goes to show that you never know until you try! And every failure or less-than-anticipated crop teaches you what to do next time.

Jeanne

LETTUCE. Romaine and loose-leaf lettuces grow quickly and vigorously. Try to give them at least four hours of full-spectrum light. You can harvest what you need and just let them keep sending up new leaves!

SPINACH. This is another super-fast-growing plant that will be ready to reward you in less than fifty days! Unlike lettuce, it's more likely to give you a single harvest before it bolts, but you can stagger plantings so there's always something ready. Keep this one in a cooler spot—about 65 degrees.

ARUGULA/ROCKET. A delicious zesty, peppery green that can be harvested in as early as four to six weeks! It's very easy, prolific, and delicious.

PEAS. They've got a shallow root system and can grow densely. You'll just need to make sure they have two to three feet to grow up and give them a net or trellis to climb. The flowers are self-pollinating too, so you won't need to bring a beehive into the kitchen to make things happen.

HERBS. Basil, oregano, thyme, cilantro, chives, dill, green onion, mint, and rosemary will all produce in small containers, and nothing is more lovely in the winter than jazzing up a soup, sauce, or stew with fresh herbs!

You can experiment and be successful with other veggies too, like radishes, tomatoes, potatoes, and even carrots!

CONTAINER GARDENING OUTDOORS

What if your heart wants a sustainable hobby farm, but your reality is an apartment or condo where a small balcony or a concrete patio are your only available growing spaces? Container gardening may be for you, especially if you have a spot that receives six to eight hours of sunlight daily.

The Container

Which container you use is up to your imagination, but always make sure it has drainage holes, and that if you use plastic, it's *food-grade* so you don't have nasty chemicals leaching into your soil. Fabric grow bags are worth checking out too. They store flat and have big handles which makes moving them around a breeze.

It always pays to check with your garden center, farm supply store, or nursery to see if they are getting rid of any plastic containers. Often, you'll be able to find them there for free, which is great because you're reusing material and saving money. Check freecycle pages too, if you have them in your community.

For most of what you'll grow, you can probably get away with a three-gallon container, but if you're growing plants with large root systems like eggplants, potatoes, peppers, cucumbers, broccoli, cabbage, beans, okra, or tomatoes, go with a five-gallon bucket instead.

Water

And remember, smaller containers may be less expensive and easier to handle, but you'll need to water and fertilize more often because you're using less soil and it will dry out faster. A tried-and-true method to determine whether your plant needs water is to stick your finger down into the soil up to or a little past your middle knuckle. If the soil feels moist, you should be good.

If you're not confident you'll remember to check frequently to see if your plants have enough water, get an *oya* for each pot. An oya is a clay vessel you bury in the soil before you plant that releases moisture and keeps roots happy. When you water, just refill and cap the oya. If you've already planted, you can find watering attachments for plastic bottles that will drip-water your plants. Also, an inch or so of mulch will help keep moisture from evaporating. But there's no substitution for a daily check-in.

Illustration by Liliana Faiella.

When you do water, use a gentle attachment on your hose or a watering can with many small holes. Also, be sure to give a good soak when you water so you encourage roots to grow large and deep, helping your plant and its produce thrive.

Fertilization

After the first several weeks, your containers are going to need to be fertilized—more often than a garden bed would need. Choose a good organic fertilizer like fish emulsion or seaweed and follow the instructions on the package.

Soil and Seeds

Don't just dig up soil from the ground or use a generic topsoil. Your soil is just as important as your seeds, if not more so. Soil is an investment and you'll want a good organic soil sold specifically for containers or raised beds.

When choosing seeds or starts, select smaller varieties of the vegetables you want to grow. You can find cucumbers, tomatoes, beans, and all kinds of veggies that are quite compact and suitable for small-space gardening.

Sunlight

Try to make sure your plants get at least six to eight hours of sunlight a day. The good thing about containers is that you can move them around to maximize sunlight and shift their location as the sun changes its position in the sky and with the changing of the seasons. If you have a patio or deck you can even put them on a platform with casters so you're not breaking your back every time you want to change things up.

RAISED BEDS

If you have enough room and a good sunny location, you can quickly and easily construct a raised garden bed. You'll often get a bigger and longer harvest from a raised bed than from a bed in the ground because your soil will be less compacted, better able to drain, better quality, and will warm up earlier in the spring so you can get planting earlier.

You will need four boards you can screw together to make a square or rectangle. You can use 2x4s, 2x8s, scrap pieces—whatever you can attach to create a bed the size you are looking for. A typical size for a garden bed is 8' x 4', but you can easily make one 4' x 4' to utilize a smaller space. You'll also need a few smaller pieces of wood to act as braces on the inside corners so your boards don't pull away from each other. Don't make your garden bed wider than four feet, to allow you to reach in and pull weeds, water, and harvest without breaking your back or having to climb into the bed.

We suggest using untreated lumber since you'll be growing things you'll want to eat, and you don't need wood leaching all kinds of noxious chemicals into your soil. Once you've chosen your boards, see if the lumber yard or box store will cut them for you, and if they have any scrap material you can use for the bracing blocks.

Soft fir and pine are the cheapest woods, but will need to be replaced in three to eight years depending on your climate. Woods like redwood and cedar cost more but will last up to three times longer than untreated softer woods. (If you are using a naturally pest- and rot-resistant wood like redwood, always choose wood that is certified by an organization such as the Forest Stewardship Council that promotes responsible forest management.)

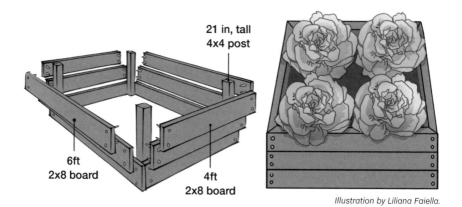

21 in, tall
4x4 post

6ft
2x8 board

4ft
2x8 board

Illustration by Liliana Faiella.

The basic frame design can be stacked and braced to the height you desire. Eight inches will work just fine. You may want a higher bed for your own convenience, for deep-rooted plants, to create a garden for someone in a wheelchair (2.5 feet high), or for a senior or anyone who would benefit from a garden that doesn't make them bend over (3 feet high).

If all this still sounds like too much, no worries! You can buy a premade raised garden bed and forget all the fuss and power tools. They come in vinyl, metal, or even fabric, and they'll have you planting in no time with little or no assembly required.

COMPOSTING: HOW TO MAKE YOUR OWN BLACK GOLD

If you've decided to try your hand at growing your own food and have never given composting a try, you should! It helps create rich soil, assists with aeration and water retention, stops erosion, saves landfill space, recycles nutrients from your plants, allows you to control what is in your soil, suppresses plant diseases and pests, and is much less expensive than buying compost. It will always be available to you and increases your harvest. That's a [counts on fingers] twelve-win situation! How often do you find that?

So what exactly is compost? It's an organic material created by combining carbon-rich material with nitrogen-rich material and adding water. All you have to do is combine these three ingredients and let Mother Nature do the rest.

Then beneficial microbes get to work breaking down materials like dead leaves, newspaper, eggshells, vegetable scraps, and coffee grounds to create a feast for your plants.

Three Basic Ingredients

BROWN (carbon-rich things): Dead leaves, twigs, shredded newspaper and cardboard, sawdust, wood chips, hair and fur, hay or straw, fireplace ashes

GREEN (nitrogen-rich things): Vegetable and fruit scraps, coffee grounds and filters, eggshells, grass clippings, tea bags, nut shells, houseplant trimmings

WATER: To make the magic happen

Things to never compost

Meat or bones, fat/grease/oil/lard, pet waste, dairy products, coal or charcoal ash, diseased or insect-infested plant material, clippings that have been treated with chemical pesticides, black walnut leaves or clippings. All these things either attract rodents or other animals, stink, or contain chemicals or pathogens that can harm you, so leave them out.

How to Compost

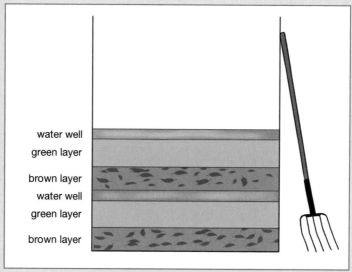

water well
green layer
brown layer
water well
green layer
brown layer

Illustration by Liliana Faiella.

- Add your brown and green materials as you collect them from your yard or green space. If you have large twigs or branches they will need to be shredded or chipped to a small size.
- When you add something new, moisten the pile. You can also use a tarp to cover the pile to help retain moisture.
- Add roughly equal amounts of browns and greens, and once your pile is established you can start putting food scraps in it, about eight to ten inches under the top of the compost.
- Every few weeks you should "turn" your compost, which means using a pitchfork or shovel to move your compost around so what's in the middle ends up on the edges, and what's on the edges ends up in the middle. This is to aerate the compost and make sure your microbes are getting enough oxygen, and to adjust your brown/green ratio in case you had too much of one in the same place.
- If everything is going well, and your little microbe community is thriving, your compost will get warm! Do not be alarmed because this is a good sign. If you want to get fancy, you can buy a compost thermometer and take its temperature. If you want to speed up the process, turn the compost

when it gets below 120 degrees. That way your super-oxygenated critters will break down that material in record time.

Composting is an art and a science. As a survival skill, this is one to consider long-term. If a hurricane strikes, you won't be trying to make a compost pile. But if you've already got one going and are using it to help increase your supply of DIY food, then you are on the way to becoming a little more sustainable and less affected by supply chain interruptions.

Location

Try to select a dry, shady spot close to your water source for your compost bin or pile, and don't put it against your house.

INDOOR COMPOSTING

Yep, it's possible. If you are composting properly, your compost should not smell or attract unwanted guests. You can make your own indoor bin by drilling holes in the bottom of a three-gallon bucket and setting it on a plant saucer. Or you can buy a specially made bin designed for indoor composting. Keep the size small and manageable if you're composting indoors. Your mini-compost should be ready in two to five weeks!

ARE YOU READY?

- Foraging
  What you need to bring will depend on where you are foraging, and what you are foraging for, but here's a good comprehensive list.
  _____ Rain poncho or lightweight raincoat
  _____ Comfortable waterproof shoes/boots
  _____ Tall socks with lightweight long pants tucked in to prevent ticks
  _____ Lightweight long-sleeved shirt
  _____ Field guide (or any printed resource with good illustrations or photos)
  _____ Snacks
  _____ Water
  _____ Hand sanitizer
  _____ Fully charged cell phone
  _____ Printed map of the area/GPS device/compass or whatever gets you back to where you started
  _____ Ziplock bags, small Tupperware containers, or cloth bags for your harvest
  _____ Sunscreen
  _____ Hat
  _____ Insect repellant

_____ Scissors

_____ Benadryl, in case of insect stings

_____ Basic first aid items like bandages and first aid cream

_____ Utility knife

_____ Emergency foil blanket

_____ Small noisemaker or air horn to deter uninvited wildlife

_____ Bear bells

- Sprouts

  _____ Mason jar

  _____ Cheesecloth and rubber band, or sprouting lid with screen

  _____ Sprouting seeds

  _____ Water

- Microgreens

  _____ Sprouting tray

  _____ Sprouting soil

  _____ Microgreen seeds in bulk

  _____ Grow light, if necessary

- Container gardening

  _____ Indoor light setup, if necessary

  _____ Containers with holes the appropriate size for your crop

  _____ Drip trays

  _____ Soil for container gardening

  _____ Fertilizer (for indoor or outdoor use as appropriate)

  _____ Watering can or hose with rain shower attachment

  _____ Mulch

- Raised beds

  _____ Board lumber

  _____ Bracing blocks

  _____ Three-inch outdoor/decking screws

  _____ Cordless drill

  _____ Soil for raised beds

  _____ Mulch

- Gardening supplies
  - _____ Shovels
  - _____ Shears/snips
  - _____ Hose or watering can with rain shower attachment
  - _____ Fertilizer
  - _____ Mulch
  - _____ Gardening gloves

- Composting
  - _____ Compost bin (outdoor or indoor, as appropriate)
  - _____ Green matter
  - _____ Brown matter
  - _____ Water
  - _____ Pitchfork
  - _____ Flat shovel
  - _____ Gardening gloves

CHAPTER 4

ORGANIZATION

The title of this chapter has either made your eyes sparkle, or bulge in fear. If you're the latter person, it's okay. We're in a judgment-free zone. Clutter has been linked to intelligence and creativity. After all, even Einstein's desk was notoriously messy! That said, we're pretty sure even Einstein would have to admit that it makes sense for disaster preparedness not to have to search high and low for what you need, or what you thought you had somewhere.

So, for our purposes, think of "organization" as freedom, space, less stress and frustration, and a more beautiful and functional place to live. And you don't have to be perfect—little tips and tricks add up to larger changes over time, and once you gain some good habits you'll never go back.

And for the anti-clutter crowd, according to a *New York Times* story, studies show that clutter can *induce a physiological response, including increased levels of cortisol, a stress hormone.* Nobody needs more stress hormones. So let's dive in.

THE RIGHT STUFF

If you're thinking that preparing for emergencies and creating a more sustainable way of living means you need more *stuff*, you're not entirely wrong. In a culture where we are finally seeing a trend of putting the brakes on acquiring a bunch of junk we don't really need, this may feel wrong. But stay with us.

It's not that you'll need *more* stuff overall, it's that you'll need the *right* stuff. You have to learn how to let some things go and make the most of the space you have.

Having the things you need for disaster preparedness and sustainability is important and should take priority. If it comes to choosing between the eighteen pairs of shoes you never use or having room to store an adequate amount of water, you know where we're going to land on that question. And you will too when you get the notice that your water isn't safe to drink. No amount of stylish purple sandals or bowling shoes will save you.

If you don't have room for the very things that can vastly improve (or even save) your life, then maybe it's time to take a deep breath, look at all those *other* things taking up your real estate, and prioritize. We're looking at *you*, box of deflated soccer balls, and the eighteen wooden spoons keeping you from opening the kitchen drawer.

We're not saying you need to become a Zen monk, but keeping it simple and making sure your stuff doesn't own *you* will be one of the best decisions you've ever made. Less clutter means more real storage space, less frustration, less waste, a smaller carbon footprint, and a more satisfying life knowing you have what you need when you need it—and where to find it. This is something that will bring you relief every day, not just during an emergency situation.

First, figure out your options. If you don't really need something, you can go one of several ways.

- **DONATING** items keeps them out of a landfill and allows someone else who really needs that item to reuse, repurpose, or recycle it. If you can donate, do it. It's good for you, the recipient, and the planet!
- **SELLING** items means you'll have a few extra bills in your wallet for that filtration system or water storage tank or vacuum sealer or hydroponic setup you've been eyeing. Online sales platforms or a good old-fashioned garage sale will get the job done.
- **USE IT!** If you've been saving fancy soaps, or beard oil, or anything else for a "special occasion" or because it seems too nice to use, use it! Life is short and you're special, so go ahead and indulge. This is your

official excuse to enjoy those things, which is what they're meant for, right? And before you go buy brake fluid or motor oil or antifreeze, ask yourself if there's already four or five half-empty bottles that you haven't used yet and use those first!

• **DISPOSE** of flat-out trash and junk. That's the quickest way to decrease the volume in your residence and increase the happiness!

THIRTY-FIVE ESSENTIAL DECLUTTERING AND STORAGE HACKS

To start you on your way, here are thirty-five tips and tricks to free up critical space in your prepper zones—closets, garage, car, kitchen, and bathroom. Follow these, and before you know it you'll be rid of the stuff weighing you down and have newfound room for the critical things that will ensure that you and your family are safe and well cared for if and when you need them.

1. BEYOND SPARKING JOY

The Queen of Tidiness, Marie Kondo, tells us to hold an item in our hands and ask ourselves if it "sparks joy," and if not, to thank it and let it go. That works if it's an elephant planter your aunt brought back as a present from her vacation. But if you're like most people, a two-year-old bag of dried beans or a camp stove you only used that one time may not spark joy when you hold it in your hands, but do *not* thank it and send it on its way. Under the right conditions it could be critical. So before you go crazy and load up the car to donate a bunch of "seldom-used" items, ask yourself, *Would this be important to have in an emergency? Could this be repurposed into something with a practical use?* If the answer is no to everything, then by all means, thank that ghastly elephant and send it to the thrift store.

2. ONE BITE AT A TIME

Speaking of elephants, there's a sage piece of advice that goes something like this: "How do you eat an elephant? One bite at a time." This is helpful both in decluttering and organizing your living space, *and* in obtaining your equipment and supplies. You won't be able to do it in one bite. Be thoughtful, consistent, and take things one step at a time. Start with small tasks, the ones you know you can finish quickly. By the time you've conquered a few of those, you'll notice a difference in your space, and you'll have a track record of success that is a great motivator to do more!

3. GET THE BIG PICTURE

If you get stuck, it may help to get everything in one category out at the same time. How many garlic presses do you really have in that giant drawer? And how many do you need? (Hint: One!) What to do with that garlic press in your hand becomes clearer when you realize that you have four. When you look at every pair of shoes you own in one place, it will be easier to gain perspective on what you need, what you use, and what's past its time. And make sure you save some good boots and work shoes for emergencies.

Papers and Records

4. GUARD THE GATE TO YOUR CASTLE!

Papers account for a lot of clutter. And clutter not only takes up space, it can just be plain demoralizing. When mail and papers that enter the house have an easy place to be recycled like *right where you enter*, they never make it to the kitchen counter, the table, or the desk. The clutter won't accumulate and you won't have to wade through it later when it looks and feels overwhelming. Piles of old papers? There's probably a lot you can ditch that seemed important earlier. Catalogs? You can find all that stuff online. Best of all, track down unwanted mail and get off that mailing list!

5. CREATE A DIGITAL FORTRESS

Digitize important documents. This is critical if you find yourself in a disaster situation, especially if you are asked to evacuate your home. Having this information at the ready will save untold amounts of stress. Make sure you have photos or scans of:

- Medical records: vaccine cards, immunization records, medical conditions, and special needs of everyone in your household
- Prescriptions: take photos of the labels.
- Insurance forms: health, dental, home, renters, cars, recreational vehicles

- ID: driver's license, state ID, school ID, passport, social security card, club membership cards, fishing/hunting licenses, military ID
- Bank information: account numbers
- Credit cards/debit cards: account numbers and customer service phone numbers
- Utilities: electric, heat, water, waste removal, cable, internet account numbers
- Monthly bills: rent, mortgage holder, vendors, dates due, contact phone numbers
- Photos: every family member and pet, in case you get separated
- Veterinary records: vaccine records including rabies, chip numbers, medications
- Emergency information: phone numbers and locations of emergency services and shelters
- Address book: phone numbers, emails, and physical addresses of family and friends

Once you're finished compiling all of the information, file it in the cloud. If Google Drive or Dropbox sound like something you don't want to deal with, just email it to yourself in a zip file called *important papers* or something you can easily find. Create folders and label them just as you would in a desk-drawer filing system.

6. BACK UP THE BACKUP

Then save all that information that you gathered on a thumb drive or external portable hard drive and keep it in a safe location like a fire/waterproof safe, or in your emergency evacuation bag, somewhere where no one but you can find it, but you always know where it is. This will keep your information safe and accessible even if the internet goes down or the cloud goes poof!

7. RECEIPTS

The humble paper receipt multiplied by everything you buy can become a super annoying clutter swarm. Snap a picture if you need a receipt for tax purposes, if it's a large or important purchase, if it's under warranty, or if you think you may need to return the item.

You do *not* need to keep a remembrance of every latté or pack of gum you ever bought. And if you have to keep a lot of receipts, consider getting a scanning app and uploading them onto Google Drive or another cloud platform where they are safe from fire, flood, and mishaps.

Car

If you've got a car, it is part of your living space and needs the same attention you pay to your non-mobile living quarters. And in a natural disaster or evacuation scenario, you don't need to be climbing over piles of dry cleaning or fast food bags or who knows what else in there. Even if your car is clean for the most part, you can still maximize space for the things you need.

8. SEPARATE AND STORE

A good trunk organizer is worth its weight in gold. AARP even gives out a free one for signing up, but it's not just a good lure for seniors—everyone can use one. Use one bin for outgoing things: donations, store returns, outgoing packages, and reusable shopping bags. Have another for items to go into the house: incoming mail and stuff you just bought. And finally, designate a space for a first aid kit and emergency supplies for your car (which we'll talk about later).

9. TRASH BAGS

Keep a few small-sized trash bags in the glove box or console so it's easy to do a periodic clean-out of empty water bottles, scrap paper, wrappers, and other accumulated trash.

Bedroom
10. OUT OF THE CLOSET

Clothing is like a goldfish: it has a way of growing to fit its container, filling every closet and drawer. The best thing you can do is fit *one* more thing in your closet—a donation box! That way, when you try on that not-so-you-anymore sweater, the I'm never-fitting-into-these-again jeans, or spot something you just haven't worn in five years, you've got a spot for it. When the box is full, bring it to the car to donate next time you're running errands. And if you have something that's ripped or unable to be saved, don't save it!

11. THE GOOD OLD DAYS

If you're hanging on to that junior varsity football jacket, or your wedding dress, or an old army uniform, make sure it gets the proper treatment as a sentimental keepsake. Wash or dry-clean it and tuck it away in a bin instead of giving it valuable real estate in your day-to-day space.

12. SHORT TO TALL

Hang all your clothes with the longest things on one side and the shortest on the other, and *boom!* You'll find you've got room under the short side for a shoe rack or a few storage drawers.

13. GO FLAT AND BACKWARDS

Replace your chubby hangers with flat velvet hangers and hang all your clothes backwards. Then after you use something, hang it the right way and take a tally at the end of a year. All the clothes you didn't wear that year will still be hung backwards, and you can have a conversation with yourself about whether someone else could use it more than you can. You'll find that you wear 20 percent of your clothes 80 percent of the time, so there's definitely room to streamline.

14. BANISH THE ORPHANS

No one knows how it happens, but it happens to all of us. I once did a massive sock match up including my kids' socks and I ended up with *thirty-one* sock orphans. Toss the orphans in a shopping bag and let a few laundry cycles go by. While this is happening, check under beds, in corners of closets, and in the car (because you know some of them will show up) and when you're ready and there are no more joyous sock reunions to be made—toss that bag! Sock liberation is a beautiful thing.

15. GROWING LIKE WEEDS

If there's one thing that grows faster than clothes, it's kids. Pull out every single piece of clothing and footwear from all the closets and drawers and go through it at least once a year (or every six months, depending on how fast they're growing). You'll be amazed at how much stuff is clearly too small and ready to go into the donation box.

Kitchen and Bathroom

Maximizing space in your kitchen and bathrooms, especially if you don't have large storage areas like a big garage or basement, is critical. Purging clutter and space-wasters can be quick and oh-so-satisfying in these zones.

16. THAT'S NOT SOUR CREAM

Let's start with the most obvious. If your cabinets look like something from an episode of *Hoarders*, it's time to get rid of those plastic tubs that used to hold sour cream or cottage cheese. Invest in a good set of clear glass containers you can safely microwave, with plastic lids for storing leftovers. You'll also be able to see what's inside when they're in the fridge. No more bracing yourself for a new species of slime mold when you peel back the lid on whatever that used to be. Also, match up other lids and containers of all kinds and get rid of any stragglers. And jars. We see you jar hoarders, too!

17. POTS AND PANS AND GADGETS, OH MY!

Pull all the pots and pans and cookie sheets out of your cabinets and sort them all by size. If you're like most people, there are some really obvious things you don't use and don't need. Get rid of duplicates and multiples you won't use at the same time. Definitely toss chipped Teflon and think about investing in ceramic nonstick or cast iron that will last a lifetime and doesn't contain nasty carcinogens that flake off into your omelet. It's also time to take a hard look at the electric cherry de-pitter, and the set of twelve plastic thingies that keep your tacos from falling over, and ask yourself what the heck you were thinking.

18. THE JUNK DRAWER

You'll never completely get rid of it, nor should you. Batteries, twine, paper clips, scissors—all good. What you can get rid of is the actual *junk*. Instruction manuals for appliances you don't own anymore or that you can easily find online? Chuck 'em. Bits and pieces of plastic and metal thingamabobs that you don't even know what they are? Ancient dehydrated rubber bands? Eight thousand plastic bread bag clips? It's okay to let them go.

19. PARE DOWN ON CLEANING SUPPLIES

Instead of having a bunch of bulky cleaning products that do virtually the same thing, whittle your collection down to the essentials. And let us stand on our soapbox (see what we did there?) and ask if you know that all those giant single-use plastic bottles of cleaners and detergents under your sink are mostly water? It's true. And many are also full of toxic chemicals that can be harsh on children and pets. You shouldn't have to toxify your environment and your family to keep clean or pay to have the weight of water transported to your store, right?

Modern refillable, nontoxic cleaning products that allow you to stock a lot of cleaning power in a small space really exist! And you won't be paying to ship water across the country or be adding plastic to landfills and oceans. The tiny concentrated refills also allow you to keep a big stock of reserve in a small area, which means you're less likely to run out. And guess what? All you really need to keep the kitchen and bathroom(s) clean and sanitary—on a budget—is good old-fashioned vinegar. Get a big bottle of white vinegar, dilute it in a spray bottle with water, and you're good to go.

A 1:1 ratio of white vinegar and water will clean and disinfect your countertop, sink, floor, microwave, plastic cutting boards, cloudy glassware, refrigerator and freezer, garbage cans, bathtubs and showers, and toilets. Vinegar is simply acetic acid, and it's a powerhouse for vanquishing grease, grime, dirt, and bacteria.

20. TRASH IT!

The other big space hog under your sink (or wherever you keep it) is that big ol' box of trash bags. And the box of bags stays the same giant size right to the end when you use your last bag. Next time, try taking the whole roll and storing it at the bottom of the trash can! This way, you always have a new trash bag in close proximity when you empty the trash, and you save a bunch of space.

21. OUT WITH THE OLD

Do a quick tour through your refrigerator, pantry, and bathroom and look at the expiration dates. We're not huge advocates of ditching food the second the date hits, because there's usually a built-in cushion of time. But if you've got a can of soup from 2003, or cottage cheese with green hair, or milk that no longer pours, you should probably deep-six that.

Same for the bathroom. Are you really keeping that conditioner you hate just because you spent good money on it and you don't want to admit failure and throw it away? We see you. We are you. But you now have permission, in the name of emergency preparedness space, to let that go. Same with old rancid beard oil, or oil-based lotions that smell "off." Oil doesn't stay good forever, and your nose knows. Condense multiples if you can, and just be honest with yourself about what you will never use and send it on its way.

22. PLAY THE ZONE

If you're lucky enough to have any larger storage spaces like a garage or a basement available to you, the key to organizing them is to create zones. What are your family's zones—sports, camping, gardening, seasonal decorating, fishing, crafts, hobbies? Zoning makes it simple to see what duplicates you have, how much you have, and makes it easy to find everything. And yes, everyone needs a zone for staging your emergency supplies because if you can't actually find what you need, you're not really prepared!

23. TOY OVERLOAD

Fun fact: the United States has 3.1 percent of the world's children but consumes 40 percent of the world's toys. So if you find yourself running out of toy space, and if your living room looks like a daycare center, it's probably time to donate the ones that were a hit for a few weeks, but no longer get attention, or the ones that are no longer age-appropriate, or the giant-sized play centers you couldn't resist and are now just taking up space.

Anticipating an epic meltdown? Ask your kids which of their toys they'd like to donate to a child who doesn't have toys and see what they say! Even if the toy isn't in good enough shape to donate, you'll know which toys your kids are willing to part with, and you'll empower them to help in decision-making and to do something nice for someone else.

24. AUTOMOTIVE

Treat your automotive materials just like you did the stuff in your kitchen and bathroom. Do you have eight bottles of motor oil, all half full? Do you have old tires for a car you no longer own or tires you're never going to use? How many lug wrenches does one person really need? And what about that wooden bead acupressure seat cover you got at the office holiday party? Time for some soul-searching.

25. KEEP, SELL, DONATE, THROW AWAY

Those four piles are the key to every zone you'll work on, from closets to kitchen to garage. If you're inside, use boxes. If you're outside (like on a garage project) you can use piles in the driveway or on the lawn. If you're going to be outside for *The Big Sort* make sure you plan for a day with nice weather.

26. EMPTY AND PURGE

Whatever zone you are working on, try to pull every single item out before you sort them. The more you can stick to this, the more effective your decluttering will be. If you can, pair like items together as you go (tools, sporting equipment, gardening supplies, hardware, automotive, emergency preparedness) so you can give another pass through your *keep* pile and see which items you really need and what duplicates you have.

27. HAVE A PLAN

Don't put those piles back in the garage unless you've got your zones figured out and a way to store everything where you can see it.

Maximize Your Space

Now that you've decluttered your closet, kitchen, bathroom(s), storage room, garage, basement, or all of the above, you can focus on maximizing the space you have, and utilizing space you never thought about.

28. SHELVES AND PEG BOARD

Garage walls, storage-shed walls, basement walls—anywhere you see a sad empty wall not fulfilling its potential, come to its rescue! Adjustable shelving and pegboard can help you get things out of boxes and visible. This helps you locate what you need and keeps you from buying something you already have.

29. UNDERUTILIZED STORAGE SPACES

Under-bed storage can be an organizational lifesaver in apartments or small spaces. You can utilize organizers made to fit in the space, or soft laundry or storage bags. What makes sense for this space? Seasonal clothing and outerwear, seldom worn shoes, sentimental cards, papers, and photos you want to save, even shelf-stable emergency food! You can put canned goods, dried pasta, dried beans, or other foods in airtight under-bed storage containers and voilà! They don't take up space in your kitchen.

30. UNEXPECTED PLACES

Look for storage opportunities in unexpected places. Take some time to look at your walls, behind doors, under furniture, and in out-of-the-way corners where you might be able to fit some small but effective storage solutions.

31. THINK VERTICAL IN THE KITCHEN

If you've ever said bad words after you've booby-trapped your own kitchen drawers with sharp things or stuff that makes them impossible to open, this is for you:

- Add a hanging bar on your backsplash or an island for dish towels.
- Put a utensil crock on the counter by the stove to keep often-used cooking utensils.
- Store sharp knives safely on a metal knife holder mounted on the wall.
- Hang potholders and measuring spoons on the fridge with a magnetic hook.
- Get a grocery bag organizer/dispenser for plastic bags if you use them. (Better still, use reusable shopping bags!)
- Use a set of hanging baskets to hold dish towels or produce. Just make sure, if you're using it for fruit or veggies, that you keep it out of the sun and away from the heat of your stove. I may or may not have learned this lesson with red potatoes after a game of *find that smell.*

32. HOOK HACKS

Use stick-on hooks (we recommend Command hooks) on available wall spaces or on the back of doors rather than using precious drawer space or cluttering surfaces or shelves. Use hooks for baseball caps, scarves, keys, and purses. And you can remove them with no damage to walls. There's a huge range of hooky goodness, from small ones that hold a pound to larger sturdy hooks that can hold up to eight pounds. That's like a gallon of milk! (Do not actually hang milk on a Command hook!)

33. POCKETS

Over-door pocket organizers work wonders to save space. They come in a variety of shapes and sizes to store shoes, toiletries, office supplies, papers, and are great for kids' toys like stuffed animals, action figures, and dolls.

34. SNEAKY STORAGE

When you buy or replace furniture, look for pieces that have additional storage like ottomans, benches, couches, loungers, or coffee tables that do double duty. Consider getting a behind-the-couch or foot-of-the bed chest, and an entertainment center with plenty of shelves and cabinets.

35. TOTES ARE THE GOAT

The stackable plastic tote, or action packer, is your new best friend. You can color-code for each zone or use clear acrylic ones so you can see what's inside. But either way, use big labels on the outward-facing side so you can read it without unstacking. Five-by-seven-inch index cards labeled in wide marker and affixed with clear packing tape work really well and are easy to read, even in areas that aren't well-lit. You can also use plastic binder sleeves with your inventory listed on a sheet of paper, ready to change easily when you need to.

Start with your emergency supplies, and you may like it so much you expand to seasonal decorations and clothing, sentimental items, tax documents, and more.

You can even get small containers or stackable drawers that will fit under the kitchen and bathroom sinks, and on the floor or top shelf of closets.

THE EMERGENCY BINDER

Sure, it's great to have all your important stuff digitized and saved on the cloud, but what if the internet goes down because of a natural disaster, power outage, cyberattack, or EMP? What's an EMP? That stands for ElectroMagnetic Pulse, a phenomenon that wreaks havoc with electronic devices of all kinds. It can be naturally occurring, like from a lightning strike, solar flare, or even a meteorite entering the atmosphere. Or it can be man-made and nefarious, like the result of a nuclear explosion or even a nonnuclear EMP weapon designed to cause chaos.

Even if you've been really good at backing up everything, how can you protect your information from a high-tech disaster? The answer is with a super low-tech backup.

Remember . . . paper? Yes, it used to be a thing, and there's nothing quite like it. So while you're sitting there, and everything is great, and your printer is working and has ink, or you have a few minutes to take that thumb drive with all your stuff to Kinko's or the library for printing, pretend you're back in school again and *get your binder organized*!

Your emergency binder should have a permanent home in your evacuation bag, and a good one will contain all the following information.

- Satellite views of your area on Google Maps showing terrain and water sources
- Several street maps of your area that cover evacuation routes and shelters
- Mailing and physical addresses and phone numbers of family and friends, and which ones still have landlines that will still work with no electricity or internet
- Stamps, envelopes, and postcards
- Prescriptions: photos of labels on all your family's meds—humans and pets!
- Copies of vaccination records/cards for COVID-19 and other vaccinations for every family member
- Living will: nobody likes to think of worst-case scenarios, and we're rooting for you, but have this, just in case.
- Copies of driver's licenses, state issued IDs, school IDs, military IDs, other photo IDs you need, passports
- Blank paper, pens, pencils
- Emergency contact numbers for fire, police, hospital—and don't forget 911. We know you know but write it down anyway to remind yourself it's an option if you're panicking.
- Locations of emergency shelters and directions on how to get to them
- Your evac list (we'll get to that)
- Printed photos of family members and pets in case of separation
- Phone numbers for:
    - Utilities—gas, electric, water, waste disposal, internet, cable
    - Home, vehicle, renters' insurance
    - Doctor—pediatrician, general practitioner, specialists
    - Local hospitals
    - Veterinarian and emergency pet clinic
    - Pharmacy
    - Landlord

- Banks
- School
- Local emergency helplines

Keep your emergency binder in your evacuation bag so everything is all together if you need to make a quick move.

STORAGE SOLUTION IDEAS

AMMO CANS. These are what they sound like—metal storage units designed to store ammunition. The good news is that you don't need to be an ammo hoarder or even know the first thing about ammunition to make great use of the handiest storage device you never thought of. Ammo cans are generally rectangular metal boxes that come in different sizes and have a hinged metal lid. They are painted to resist rusting, they float, and they are the cheapest, sturdiest, and most versatile waterproof storage out there. Important documents, photos, spare keys, thumb drives, electronics, you name it. If you can fit it in an ammo can, it's pretty darn safe.

FIREPROOF SAFE. Here's a purchase you hope will all be for nothing. But if you ever do need it, you'll be thanking yourself. For as little as sixty to seventy dollars you can find a Sentry fire/water safe that will keep your precious items secure and undamaged in case of fire. Passports, legal documents, jewelry, heirlooms, a spare checkbook, and emergency cash can all withstand an inferno. Remember, you may not be at home to grab all that stuff when a fire starts, so consider an extra layer of safety.

INDUSTRIAL STORAGE BOXES. The king of industrial storage boxes that are meant to last a lifetime are the Rubbermaid ActionPackers. They come in sizes from eight to forty-eight gallons and will hold pretty much anything you need to store—tools, auto supplies, clothing, outdoor gear, camping supplies, electronics, documents, photos, and more. They are engineered to be easily tied down with bungee cords for vehicle transport, are virtually indestructible, and come with a lifetime guarantee.

CANNING JARS. They're not just for jelly and pickled asparagus! Ball brand wide-mouth canning jars are available in sizes from eight ounces to one gallon and can be great for storing all kinds of things. Not only can you see what's in them (like nails, screws, drill bits, rubber bands, string, etc.), but if you keep some unused extras around you can use them for canning food.

LABEL MAKER. If you don't feel like making your own labels for boxes and totes, nothing beats the handy dandy label maker. It's quick, easy, and oh-so organized! Kids will love helping out too!

SHELVING. If you've got the room, do yourself a favor and invest in some NSF (National Sanitary Foundation) certified shelving. That's the restaurant-type steel shelving approved for food use that doesn't rust or sag, and lasts forever. It can work in the basement, garage, pantry, or any place you've got room. It will also keep your stored items off the floor and away from moisture, mice, or potential flooding.

If shelving isn't in your budget, you can use 2x4s or scrap lumber to stack boxes or bins on. Even a couple inches off the floor can save boxes and your precious things from getting mildewed or soaked in a flood.

ARE YOU READY?

_____ Do you have a system of storage that works for you: labeled boxes, totes, ActionPackers?

_____ If you are on the ground floor or are storing things in the basement, do you have items off the floor?

_____ Have you maximized storage space in each of the zones in your home: bedroom, bathroom, kitchen, living spaces, basement/attic/storage?

_____ Have you digitized your important documents to the cloud and a portable hard drive/thumb drive, and are they in a safe place like a fireproof safe?

_____ Have you assembled your emergency binder?

_____ Do you have enough room to keep emergency supplies accessible and safe? You may need to go through the rest of the book to determine the answer to this question.

CHAPTER 5

SHELTER

T he truth is that our relationship with home sweet home is complicated. During the worst of the COVID-19 pandemic, we were masking and vaxxing and distancing and boosting and putting on a parka to eat in an outdoor café at 35°F just to get some semblance of *normal life* back, and get *out* of the house. But during a hurricane or tornado, our priorities flip and we want to be barricaded *in*, safe, and out of harm's way.

This chapter will walk you through all the scenarios for staying safe from *all the things*, whether you're at home for months on end, at work overnight, or stuck on the highway. That means understanding your shelter, whatever and wherever it happens to be at the time.

YOU DON'T EVEN *KNOW* ME!

You may think you know everything you need to know about your home. I mean, you *live* there, right? But like any intimate relationship, there are still mysteries and things to discover. Now is the time to discover them, *not* during the hurricane, flood, or gas leak.

As enticing as it is to believe that "just call the repair guy" is an effective emergency plan, sadly it is not. If there's been a natural disaster, you can be sure all the repair people are going to have their hands full and can't drop everything to get to you first. This chapter shows how you become the master of your domain, because the goal is to stay in your shelter long-term if you can. Most of the time home is the safest and least stressful place to be.

Do not, we repeat, do *not* throw stuff in a backpack and head into the woods to survive on mice and pondwater. Take a breath and make the decision now, ahead of time, under what circumstances you would reach your *leave point*. How long could you stay with no power? No water? How long would you last with the supplies you have right now? What if something went wrong with the structural integrity of your house? Then decide how you can make your home stronger, safer, and more resilient as a long-term shelter so you can become a master hunker-downer.

HOME ASSESSMENT MASTER LIST

Give your home a good once-over to determine how resilient it would be in a disaster. Remember the *Three Little Pigs*? You want to be the one with the house made of bricks—metaphorically speaking. We're assuming *that* little pig didn't live in an earthquake zone.

After you do your own assessment, contact a professional to catch what you missed. Your self-assessment will help the auditor get a good start and more effectively analyze your home. Many utilities offer professional energy assessments *at no or reduced cost*. Take advantage of that to improve your comfort, your health, and also for potential ways you can save energy and money.

Here are the things to assess and fix if they need fixing. Keep a running checklist even if you're not going to do everything right away.

All right, grab your clipboard and let's go!

Roof

Check the roof for damage by using a pair of binoculars. Look for missing shingles that will need to be replaced. Check any chimneys to be sure that they aren't leaning and have no weird bulges, irregularities, or missing bricks. If you know the age of your roof and that it needs replacing, get a quote from a good roofing company so you know how much it will cost. Your top-of-the-line choice for roofing is a standing seam metal roofing system. They last up to fifty years, are tough as nails, and will withstand the elements. It's an expensive option, but you'll never have to think about roofing again.

Gutters

If leaves and other debris clog your gutters, rainwater can't flow properly and may spill over, causing water damage to your roof and the exterior and interior of your house. Fun fact: your gutters play a huge part in keeping your foundation safe. Pooling water can cause cracks and leaks, so don't blow off cleaning your gutters once or twice a year, and check the downspouts to make sure there are no clogs. The best option is installing a good metal gutter cover and you won't have to worry about cleaning out your gutters!

If your gutters need cleaning and you can't do it, find a professional service to take care of it. Climbing on ladders can be very hazardous. Hiring a professional might cost you a couple hundred dollars, but it will also prevent major expenses down the road (including hospital bills), and it will extend the life of the gutters themselves.

Not-so-fun fact: every year, in the United States, there are more than 164,000 injuries that require emergency room treatments, and three hundred deaths caused by falling from ladders. And most of those injuries and deaths come from falls of less than ten feet. So, even though you *can* clean your own gutters, you really might want to leave it to the professionals.

Drainage

If you have a floor drain in the garage or the basement, make sure it's clear and doesn't have anything sitting on top of it. This may seem obvious, but one of the authors (who shall remain unidentified) had a very close call and luckily only lost the box of office supplies that was sitting on top of the drain and not the precious photos and documents that were close by. Bullet dodged.

Drainage is also critical outside. Make sure when it rains or when the creek nearby rises that the water isn't going to pool around your foundation or run into a basement window or crack. If necessary, hire someone to slope or grade the area around your house to make sure water flows away. Money well spent. Also, if you own a house, invest in a drain snake. They are relatively inexpensive and can hook up to your cordless drill!

Window and Door Seals

Check your windows and doors for any looseness or compromised seals. If your windows and doors leak, you'll have higher energy bills and increase the chance of frozen pipes. Make sure windows and doors align correctly in their fittings and that they open and close smoothly. Caulking, weather stripping, and energy-efficient windows and doors can save you big on heating and cooling costs, cut down on street noise, and improve the resale value of your home. If you're in a rental unit with drafty windows, consider getting insulating window film for the windows you don't open, or just for use in the wintertime. Insulating film can save about twenty dollars a year per window in heating costs and make you much toastier and more comfortable.

Walls and Ceilings

Inspect the lines where ceilings and walls meet for any crookedness, cracks, or gaps that can indicate poor building or repair work, or natural settling. Look at the slopes of the ceilings and floors. Put a marble on the floor and see if it rolls. A noticeable slant can indicate a failing foundation.

Also look carefully at walls and ceilings for staining that could have been caused by water damage. Touch the discolored areas to see if they are soft, which may indicate rot or mold.

Check railings, stairs, and banisters to make sure they're sturdy and secure with no signs of rot.

Plumbing

Look at your pipes and valves for signs of corrosion or dripping water. Check all the fixtures to make sure they are operating properly by turning them on and off. If you can't turn a valve with your hand, don't use a tool or bang on the fixture. Get a plumber to do it. Make sure the water pressure is consistent throughout your home. If one fixture has noticeably weaker water pressure, it could indicate a problem that requires repair.

Electrical

Make sure all switches work properly and check for any visible damage or discoloration near outlets that could indicate electrical problems. Check the breaker box for any obvious damage such as scorching. *Scorching is bad.* Call an electrician if you have concerns about any of the wiring, plugs, or switches in your home.

Not-so-fun fact: 51,000 home electrical fires happen every year resulting in more than 500 deaths and 1,400 injuries. You don't want to be a part of that statistic, so make sure your electrical systems are safe and operating like they should.

Check all the light bulbs and make sure you are using efficient LEDs or energy-saving incandescent bulbs. Energy for lighting your home makes up about 10 percent of your electric bill, so also explore ways to use sensors, dimmers, and timers to reduce your lighting use.

Heating and Cooling

Get your furnace inspected before you start using it every fall and replace it when it gets old. Always go for energy-efficient models which will save you money in the long run. Most furnaces will last twenty or even thirty years, but after fifteen years do an assessment to see if you need to replace it. You may want to get a jump on it, especially if you've needed to have repairs. If a repair is going to cost more than half of what it takes to get a new furnace, it makes sense to get a new one. Replacing that furnace is something you definitely want to schedule for a nice warm day in the summer. We have no actual statistics on this but we're pretty sure furnaces really like to die on the coldest night of the year.

Siding

Check your siding for signs of rot, cracks or gaps, and bulging or damaged areas. To keep your house healthy and structurally sound, make sure to keep siding in good shape. Lazy? Just want to live your life without having to think about your siding? Scraping, sanding, and painting not your thing? Consider upgrading to vinyl siding which lasts a long, long time and increases the value of your home!

Insulation

Check when your house was built. Chances are that the recommended minimum amount of insulation in that year was much less than it is today, and think about beefing it up. Also make sure venting and vapor barriers are in place to avoid moisture problems that could lead to structural damage. Make sure your attic hatch door is as heavily insulated as the rest of the attic and that any gaps around pipes, ducts, and chimneys are sealed with noncombustible expanding foam caulk.

A professional will need to tell you if the insulation in your walls is adequate or if it has settled over the years, which it tends to do. They can also assist with insulating your floors if they sit over a basement or crawl space that is open to the outside.

Moisture and Mold

Check the inside of your home for the dreaded three Ms—and we don't mean musketeers. We mean moisture, mildew, and mold. Unwanted microbial house guests can make you really sick if you breathe in the spores. Mold flourishes almost anywhere that provides sufficient moisture or humidity— usually basements, crawl spaces, attics, closets, or bathrooms. If you live in a place that regularly has 70–90 percent humidity, you, my friend, are in the mold zone! Get a dehumidifier and keep your windows closed when the humidity goes over 80 percent or if it's foggy or rainy. Air conditioning also helps.

Mold is just waiting for leaks, floods, poor ventilation, humidity, and other sources of moisture to get the party started. A major key to mold prevention is to dry out your home thoroughly twenty-four to forty-eight hours after a water event like a leak or flood. If you have mold and can't figure out where it's coming from, it could mean your siding is compromised.

If you have mold, don't clean it up yourself if you have any allergies or respiratory challenges. Small areas of mold can be knocked out with detergent or a mold and mildew cleaner, but wear goggles, a mask, and gloves, and throw away any sponges or rags you use to clean the mold. It's also a good idea to bleach the area just to be safe. But your best option is to call a professional mold remediator if your problem is more than you want to handle—and it usually is.

Smoke Detectors

Make sure you have enough of them, that they are all in good working order, and that they have fresh batteries every year. Smoke detectors really do save lives, so don't endanger yourself or your family because you don't feel like checking batteries. Not a good trade. It's smart to check your smoke detectors at least twice a year, and many people do this on the same day they set the clocks ahead or back for daylight saving time. But you can pick any day and set a reminder on your calendar.

Some newer smoke detectors come with long-life batteries, but it's still good to check that the detector is working because dust and age can affect performance. If your smoke detectors are overly sensitive, or go off every time you fry a burger, try moving them farther away from the stove. But don't pull the batteries out in frustration like we *know* you want to do. Have a professional come to assess the situation or replace the smoke detector if you can't deal with it.

Escape Ladders

If your home has more than one floor, definitely invest in at least two escape ladders in case of fire. Ideally you should have two safe ways out of every bedroom where someone sleeps—the door and a window. If bedrooms are on upper floors, that means a ladder. Also, be sure that you have at least one ladder on each side of the stairwell in the upper floors. In a fire, the opening of the stairwell can act like a chimney, with flame, heat, and smoke dividing the upper floors into two sections. If you're worried about teenagers trying to sneak out, remember that deploying a huge aluminum ladder makes *a lot* of noise. So unless you sleep like the dead, they won't get away with it.

Fire Extinguishers

Be sure you have a working, non-expired fire extinguisher on every floor of your home including the attic and the basement, in the kitchen, near (but not too near) heat sources, the garage, and bedrooms. Teach everyone in your home, even kids, when and how to safely use a fire extinguisher.

BE BOOK SMART

We can't cover every situation here, so get a good, basic book on home maintenance and repair that covers the essentials of plumbing, carpentry, electrical, and minor repairs. We recommend *How Your House Works: A Visual Guide to Understanding and Maintaining Your Home,* by Charlie Wing, but there are lots of great books on the market. Learning the basics of your home will empower you, make you feel less stressed when small things go wrong, and let you live more self-sufficiently.

HOME TOOLS

Make sure you have a basic set of decent hand and cordless power tools. It's easy to get overwhelmed if you're not a *tool person* so here are the essentials:

- Cordless drill and screws of a couple different lengths
- Multi-bit screwdriver
- Power tools*
- 25-foot tape measure
- Locking pliers
- Retractable utility knife/box cutter with extra blades
- Claw hammer and assortment of nails
- Adjustable non-sparking wrench
- Pipe tape
- Stepladder
- Work light
- Work gloves
- Knee pads
- Twenty-five or fifty-foot extension cord
- Duct tape
- Staple gun (if you have kids, don't keep it loaded!)
- A good multi-tool like a Leatherman
- A manual can opener

THE THREE UTILITIES YOU MUST KNOW HOW TO SHUT OFF

Even though you've been hearing us say "call a professional" a lot, there are going to be times when no one is available, and it's going to fall on you. Especially after a natural disaster, you may be the closest thing to a professional you're going to get, so here are some basic skills you'll need to know and teach to everyone under your roof.

#1: Turning Off the Water

Cracked water lines or flooding outside can pollute your water supply and make it unsafe to drink for people and pets. That's why the Federal Emergency Management Agency (better known as FEMA) recommends that in case of potential contamination after an emergency, you shut off the water supply to your home until you know that the water is safe to drink.

---

* Milwaukee™ and DeWalt™ are always good bets for power tools, but if they're not in your budget remember: *something* is always *way* better than nothing.

That will keep the contaminated water out, so it never gets to infiltrate your plumbing and make people sick. (Good thing you read chapter 1 and stocked up on emergency water!)

Also, if you're going to be away from home for an extended period of time, it's a good idea to shut the water off before you leave, just in case something happens while you're gone.

To find where the water main enters your home and the location of its shut-off valve, you need to be a little bit of a sleuth. Plan ahead and locate key pieces of your utility structure before you *have* to locate it. If you have trouble finding it, you'll have time to ask your water utility representative or your plumber for help.

1. **FIND THE MAIN WATER VALVE.** If you live in a house with a basement or crawl space, the main valve is probably on an inside wall on or near the front of the house, near the water meter. If your home has no basement, look for the valve in the garage or near your hot water heater.

Illustration by Liliana Faiella.

If you're still stumped, look outside at the end of your property line near the street. You'll probably see a metal plate that looks like a little trap door, which is a cover for a box buried in the ground near your front curb.

You may need a special tool called a "meter key" to open this box. Meter keys can be purchased at many hardware stores. Insert the meter key into the slot, turn it counterclockwise, and push the handle toward the edge of the box to pry open the lid. You're in!

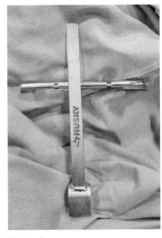

Meter key.

2. **SHUT OFF THE WATER AT THE MAIN VALVE.** Now shut the water off by turning the valve one-quarter turn to make it perpendicular (at a 90° angle) to the water pipe. Then your water will be shut off. If your valve has a handle that turns, turn it clockwise (to the right) to shut off the water.

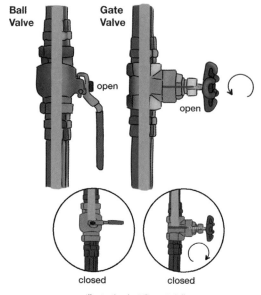

Illustration by Liliana Faiella.

If your valve is corroded or stuck shut and you can't turn it with your hand, *don't try to use a tool or force it.* Call a plumber who will get the valve in good working order without unintended consequences.

There also may be a pressure regulator near the main valve. You may be tempted to tweak it for a morning power shower, but don't touch it! Messing with water pressure is a task that should definitely be left to the professionals.

3. **RELEASE THE PRESSURE.** After you shut off your water, make sure to release the pressure in the pipes by turning on all the faucets (hot and cold) in your house and letting the water run out of the pipes.

4. **SHARE AND LABEL.** Make sure everyone in your household knows where the water main valve is located (and where the meter key is located if you needed one), and how to turn the water off. If the valve is inside, label it with a brightly colored tag or sticker so you can find it easily.

You can even draw a little diagram so you remember which way is on and which is off, or help someone else out if it isn't you shutting it off.

How to Prevent Frozen Pipes

Before the temperature gets below freezing, get your pipes ready! Consider these steps even if you think you live in an area where it won't get cold enough.

Most liquids contract and take up less space when they freeze, but when water freezes, it *expands*. That means frozen pipes aren't just a mild inconvenience. They can crack, burst, cause leaking, flooding, structural damage, and major costly repairs. Thanks, physics!

- **INSULATE:** Make sure that any exposed piping outside in your yard and in cold interior spaces (like attic, garage, basement areas) is properly insulated.
- **SEAL AIR LEAKS:** Cold air can be sneaky, and when it wafts in around drafty doors, broken window seals, vents, and anywhere it can get in from the outside, it can freeze pipes! So, seal those leaks with weather stripping, spray foam, or caulk. Weatherizing your home will also reduce your utility bills!
- **LET IT DRIP:** If you are worried about pipes freezing, turn the hot and cold water on just enough to allow for a constant drip. This method may mean an increase in your water bill, but if it keeps your pipes from exploding, it's totally worth it!
- **OPEN CABINETS:** Believe it or not, opening cabinet doors in the kitchen, bathroom, laundry, and utility rooms is an awesome hack to keep pipes from freezing. Open cabinets allow the warm air from the room to circulate around plumbing in the walls, keeping it closer to room temperature and preventing a freeze.
- **SPACE HEATERS:** Portable space heaters can be used during a cold snap in areas of your home where you are worried about freezing pipes.

Your Pipes Froze Anyway

It can happen, despite your valiant attempt to keep your pipes from freezing. Here's what to do after you yell bad words at Mother Nature.

- Locate the section of piping that is frozen. Find the frozen sections closest to your faucet and start from there.
- Turn the faucets on so when you successfully thaw the pipe, the water has somewhere to go.
- Soak some towels in hot water, wring them out well, and wrap them around the frozen section of pipe. Repeat after the towels cool off.
- You can also try using a hair dryer aimed at the frozen section of pipe. Be sure you are not standing in water and that the hair dryer is plugged into a GFCI breaker that will trip instead of electrocuting you!
- Don't do anything crazy like trying to blowtorch your pipes or expose them to extreme levels of heat. Stick with the blow dryer—it will get hot enough.

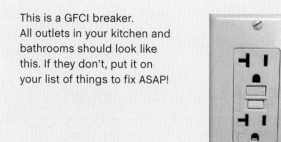

This is a GFCI breaker. All outlets in your kitchen and bathrooms should look like this. If they don't, put it on your list of things to fix ASAP!

#2: Turning Off the Gas

Natural gas leaks can be *extremely* dangerous, and if you have one it will require immediate attention and quick action. It's a good idea to contact your local gas company in advance of an emergency to help determine the exact steps for shutting off the gas and if you will need a special tool to do it. If you do need a tool, like a wrench, be sure it's the *non*-sparking kind that won't accidentally create a spark and ignite the gas. Talk about making a bad situation worse!

The first thing to do if you suspect problems is *call the gas company.* You will definitely want the gas shut off if you hear a hissing sound, if you smell gas, or if your gas meter is rising rapidly with no explanation, which could indicate a leak. If the leak was caused by a natural disaster, the gas company is going to be overwhelmed. The safest thing to do is get everyone out of the house if you suspect a leak, but in cases where this is not possible or if the gas company can't get to you, you may decide to turn off the gas yourself. Once you turn the gas off, *do not turn it back on again.* You will need to wait for a professional from the gas company to do it. In the aftermath of a major natural disaster, it could take days or even weeks for the local gas utility to make it to you, so be prepared.

- **FIND THE MAIN GAS VALVE:** The location of the main shutoff valve may vary from house to house. Find where the gas line first enters the house and follow it until you find a valve. It might be located right after the line enters the house, or possibly farther down, but it will always be found before a *T* in the pipe or the connection to an appliance.

- **TURN OFF THE MAIN VALVE:** Just like with your water valve, the valve lever will be parallel to the pipe when gas is flowing, so turn the valve perpendicular to the pipe to shut the gas off. See, this isn't so hard!

- **SHARE AND LABEL:** Make sure everyone in your household knows where the main gas valve

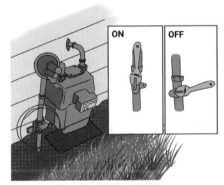

Illustration by Liliana Faiella.

is located, which tool to use if you need one, and how to turn the gas off. Label the valve with a brightly colored tag or sticker so you can find it easily and draw a little diagram so you remember which way is on and which is off. Think of it as a little gift to the future freaked-out you so you won't be trying to remember how to cut the gas while you're worried about the house blowing up.

#3: Turning Off the Electricity

This one is easy, but definitely crucial. Electricity doesn't mix with water, and it definitely doesn't mix with a gas leak. So, in those conditions you will want to shut off the electricity right away.

- **LOCATE YOUR CIRCUIT BREAKER BOX.** Most people know where it is, but if you don't, start by looking in the basement, garage, or utility closet. Look for the big metal panel, usually located at eye level.
- **TURN OFF ALL THE CIRCUITS INDIVIDUALLY, BEFORE FLIPPING THE MAIN CIRCUIT BREAKER SWITCH.** The main switch should be noticeably bigger than the others and is usually located at the top of the panel. No tools necessary!

- **POST INSTRUCTIONS ON THE INSIDE DOOR OF THE CIRCUIT BREAKER BOX** detailing how to shut off the electricity in an emergency. If you're feeling really motivated, now would also be a good time to label what area each circuit breaker goes to in your house.

Knowing how to locate and turn off the utilities in your home well in advance of an emergency is a good step toward disaster preparedness, so give yourself a high five. But now that you are sitting in your house in the dark with no light, heat, or water, you are going to need a plan. And plans start now, not then.

SECONDARY POWER SUPPLY

Generators

- *Never ever, ever, ever* run a generator inside. *Ever.* Generators must be outside of your house *and* outside your garage to avoid carbon monoxide poisoning, which can kill you. Keep portable generators twenty feet away from your house or garage and keep nearby windows closed.
- Disconnect your house from the power grid when using a generator. Staying connected to the grid while using a generator is extremely dangerous—not only for the people in your house, but for utility workers and your neighbors! So do *not* electrocute anyone! Disconnect and use a transfer switch. (See below for details.)

• Do not refill a hot generator. If you need to refuel your generator, make sure it has cooled down completely first.

When you store extra gasoline to fuel your generator, make sure to store it in proper containers certified for fuel storage and add a stabilizer, if necessary, for long-term storage.

When a natural disaster or weather event strikes, or when an overtaxed electrical grid goes down, you can bet there's going to be a rabid stampede to hardware stores, and guess what nobody will be able to find? Generators. Luckily this will not be you, because if you decide you want a generator, you're about to plan ahead and figure out which generator you want, how to install it (if needed), and how to operate it safely.

An emergency generator can keep your important appliances like your refrigerator running so you don't lose everything from that giant grocery haul. It will also keep the lights on and give you the ability to charge phones and other equipment. And if you have a sump pump, a generator can save your home from flooding. If you have kids—and we cannot stress this enough—it's in everyone's best interest to keep them happy and comfortable, with access to an electrical outlet for charging things.

Choosing a Generator

There are several types of generators, each with pluses and minuses. You'll need to do some research and figure out how many watts you will need to power and what budget you are working with.

1. HOME STANDBY GENERATORS

A whole-house standby generator is large and powerful and can automatically kick in when your power goes out. It should be permanently installed next to your house and will give you a seamless transfer of power when the grid goes down. It should be able to power all the things you have that need power. This is the gold standard and requires the least amount of effort, but of course it's also the most expensive. The generator itself will likely cost at least $4,000, and the installation may cost almost as much as the generator! It will also use a lot of fuel which you will have to store properly.

You will need to have a licensed electrician do the installation, including a transfer switch installed in your circuit breaker box, and a grid-tie disconnect so you don't overload your circuits or back-feed electrical current out into the grid, which can start fires or injure utility workers trying to fix the lines. It also keeps utility-supplied power from running into the house while the generator is running, so you won't set your fancy new generator or your whole house on fire.

If you live in a location where there are frequent outages and potentially life-threatening temperature extremes, this setup may be worth the investment. But if you live in a low-lying area where flooding is common, this is not an option. Generators don't like being under water.

2. PORTABLE GENERATORS

Portable generators range in size, and large ones can weigh up to several hundred pounds and generate a lot of power, also requiring expensive installation including the grid-tie disconnect and a tie-in port (a socket) on the outside of your house so you can plug the generator in from the outside where it should always be located. Smaller ones work well but are not designed to replace *all* of your regular energy usage. If you are on a budget, you'll need to figure out what things are critically important and buy the smallest generator that is adequate to fill that need. Don't ever max out your capacity because small surges in power (like when you start an appliance) can put you over the top.

Calculate the wattage of the things you want to run at one time and use that number to decide what you need and what will fit your budget. Here's an estimate of what it takes to run certain appliances and devices, but do calculate your own usage because it could vary.

Refrigerator (700W), laptop (200W), six or seven lights (250W), phone charger (20W), home security system (100W), 10K BTU air conditioner (1,000W), well pump (1,250W), sump pump (900W), gas or propane furnace (800W), one eight-inch burner on an electric range (2,000W).

Remember, you can close off lesser-used spaces of your home and just maintain power in a smaller area.

3. INVERTER GENERATORS

Inverter generators have several advantages. They are small, easy to move and transport, they don't need special installation, and they create a consistent current of electricity that is much friendlier to delicate electronics because they don't have all the spikes and surges that come with a regular generator. If you plan to be working on your laptop or charging cell phones or tablets, the inverter will reduce the likelihood of operating errors or device damage. They're also cleaner, quieter, and more fuel efficient.

So what's the downside? They're not capable of producing vast amounts of energy. An inverter may only provide you with about 7,000 watts rather than the almost 20,000 watts provided by large generators. This is why they are often used for recreational activities like camping or tailgating rather than as a whole-house solution. But if all you need is a small amount of power during serious emergencies or if you want a supplemental means to charge sensitive devices, the inverter may be just the ticket.

Powering Your Generator and Storing Fuel

Having a generator means you will need to make sure you have fuel available to run it, which usually means gasoline. Decide how much fuel you want to store and how long you'll be storing it. Typically you'll only need to use your generator for hours or maybe days. Storing enough fuel for weeks can be a daunting task, so choose the right amount for your situation and storage ability.

Gas cannot be stored indefinitely because it will degrade, so you'll need to use a stabilizer to keep that from happening. Choose a liquid fuel stabilizer designed for storage rather than performance. Follow the directions and your gas should be shelf-stable for two years! There are also diesel generators, and diesel will last longer than gasoline but also requires a stabilizer for long-term storage.

Make sure you store your gas in containers that are certified to store gas. No milk jugs, no Tupperware containers, no five-gallon buckets, and for the love of all that is holy, *do not fill plastic bags with gasoline.*

Yes, the US Consumer Product Safety Commission really had to tweet this during the pandemic when people were trying to hoard gas. Don't be those people. Certified plastic containers will work, or look for army surplus or metal gas cans.

Also, never store fuel in your home or car. Keep it in a dark, cool, dry location, filled only to the marked "fill line" and tightly sealed. And obviously no smoking or open flames near gas or any combustible fuel.

Clean Energy

What if you live in an apartment or a condo and you can't just store gallons of fuel off-site somewhere, or you don't physically have space outside your dwelling for a generator? Or if your brain is swimming from all this talk about engines, and licensed electricians, and carbon monoxide, and storing combustible fuels with chemical additives, this next part is for you.

1. **WIND GENERATORS**

Like gas-powered generators, home energy generated from wind spans the gamut of budgets. A full-sized wind generator that has the potential to provide all or most of your energy needs can run thirty thousand to sixty thousand dollars—or even more, depending on the size of your house. If you've got it in your budget, wind power from your own turbine can be a clean, reliable, and cost-saving way to power your home.

But if you're just looking for a small power source to light a bulb or charge a phone, or if you live in an urban or suburban area, new technology may have you covered.

Micro-sized omnidirectional wind turbines can be used to capture the unpredictable and complicated wind directions found in urban spaces. They won't allow you to turn on all the lights and run the vacuum and the microwave, but if you need a lightbulb and a cell phone charged, there's your answer. The developments in this technology are coming fast and will allow city dwellers to reduce their carbon footprint and their energy bills.

2. **SOLAR GENERATORS**

These are really not generators so much as they are storage devices that hold energy—like a battery. You can buy small portable solar panels that hang in or stand next to a window and can charge all kinds of electronic devices like cell phones, flashlights, your video doorbell system, or your laptop. Perfect for small spaces.

Light

If you don't have a generator, there are still plenty of ways to light a room.

Hurricane Lamps/Oil Lamps

Hurricane lamps are lanterns with a glass chimney that surrounds the flame and are designed to stay lit in windy conditions. They are fueled with kerosene (which can be a little stinky) or lamp oil (which is more expensive) and can be purchased in many hardware stores. You can also find oil lamps with handles for easier portability. It's important to keep the wick trimmed to cut down on soot. Also, don't turn the wick up too high or excessive heat could cause the lamp to explode. Never leave a burning lamp unattended.

Flashlights

Yes, your smartphone does have a flashlight, but you'll want to conserve the battery for communication, so it makes sense to have a good battery-powered flashlight (or several) on hand. If you don't want to worry about having fresh batteries, and you're diligent about keeping it charged, a rechargeable flashlight is also an option. There are also clever and low-tech flashlights that have a crank for charging or will charge simply by shaking them!

BATTERY PRO TIP: When you're buying flashlights or other battery-operated devices, make sure they take the same one or two kinds of batteries, instead of a bunch of different battery sizes. You'll save space and money, and be much more efficient. Also get rechargeable batteries so you can extend their use or charge them with a small solar panel.

LED Tap Lights

These little round lights are affixed to any surface with strong adhesive, operate on battery power, and turn on with a push of the finger. Be sure to keep an extra stock of batteries on hand and make sure that you're using LED lights to extend the battery life.

Solar-Charged LED Lanterns

These handy devices will charge using the sun or a USB. A full charge will provide bright light for hours with no danger of fire or injury. They come in many shapes and sizes, and some are even collapsible so they don't take up a lot of space. They are designed for camping but are great sources of light in an emergency, especially when you're looking for a portable light source.

Candles

When you think of emergency candles, don't think of those long, tapered dinner candles. You'll want a shorter, wider pillar-style candle with a solid base that can stand on its own without falling over and preferably one that comes in a metal tin. And although your pumpkin-caramel-apple-pie jar candle *will* create light in a pinch, it's smart to invest in a few good emergency candles designed specifically for that purpose.

- Liquid paraffin candles come in a small plastic container with a wick on top, and are sturdy and great for emergencies. No worries about melted wax or uneven burning!
- Multi-wick candles allow you to adjust light and heat output.
- Beeswax burns very cleanly and has a pleasant natural smell and a higher melting point than other natural waxes, so beeswax candles are less likely to melt in warm weather and will be easier on those with respiratory conditions.
- Tealight candles are very small, but last three to five hours and are easy to pack in an emergency bag.
- Always keep your wick trimmed to a maximum length of one-fourth inch to cut down on smoke and to prevent the flame from getting too tall, which will cause tunneling down the center of your candle and shorten its life.
- Keep lit candles away from drafts and at least two feet away from anything flammable like books, curtains, or clothing, and at least three inches away from another burning candle.
- Don't leave burning candles unattended, and don't let the candle burn all the way to the bottom. Discontinue burning when there's about one-half inch of wax left.

- And always make sure your candle is on a stable surface and sitting on a plate or other appropriate container to catch any melted wax.

Don't forget to keep a supply of matches and a lighter in a waterproof container!

Heat

Staying warm isn't just a problem in traditionally cold climates. Hypothermia, a condition where core body temperature drops to unsafe levels, is life-threatening. You know that Hollywood scenario where someone falls through the ice and is rescued and wrapped in blankets by the fire, shivering? That's not the way it usually plays out. The reality is that hypothermia can happen at 50 degrees indoors when you're bone dry! The elderly, babies, and children are particularly susceptible. Other risk factors include medical conditions, some prescription medications, working outside, dehydration, or alcohol use.

Establish a secondary heat source: Taking your climate into consideration, think of what conditions would be like if your heating system completely failed. Just, poof. Most heating systems and thermostats require electricity in some capacity to function, so if the lights are out, you may have no heat either.

And remember, you do not need to heat your whole living space. It's a lot easier and more efficient to choose one area of your home and make sure it's comfortable for everyone than to try to keep the whole house or apartment at your usual 74 degrees.

Wood-Burning Fireplace

If you've already got one you use for occasional snuggling with hot chocolate or on winter holidays when the house is full of guests, this is the most obvious secondary heat source to use. If you have a wood-burning fireplace, remember it will not function without . . . wood! Always make sure to have enough on hand. How much is enough? It all depends on how many rooms you want to heat and how long you'll want to heat them. But a good place to start for a comfortable emergency supply is half a cord—a cord is the unit of measurement by which people buy chopped wood, and one cord is 128 cubic feet. If you don't have room for half a cord, go smaller. A half-cord is essentially a four-foot cube.

Here are some safety tips and ways to maximize the heat output of your wood-burning fireplace:

- Install a fireback! A fireback is inserted at the back of the fireplace and reflects the heat from the fire out into your room. It will also radiate heat into the room after the fire goes out.
- Only use well-seasoned or kiln-dried wood to get the most heat and least smoke from your firewood. If your fire is smoky, wet wood could be the culprit.
- Hardwoods will generate the most heat over the life of the fire, but softwoods will give you hotter flames—they just won't last as long. Softwood also has more pitch and creosote which increases the risk of chimney fires, so you'll have to be sure you clean your chimney regularly if you burn a lot of softwood.
- If your fireplace has a damper, be sure it is all the way open to allow the maximum draw of air up the chimney and increase the output of heat from the fire. If you want the fire to last longer, don't open the damper all the way. There will be less heat, but your wood will burn longer. Shut the damper when the fire is out.
- Start a fire with smaller pieces of wood or kindling on the bottom, and once the fire has started, add larger logs on the top. Pack your logs close together to create more heat.
- Always make sure there is sufficient ventilation to improve heat output and keep smoke going up the chimney. You may need to crack a window open to allow air to flow up the chimney if your house is sealed well.
- Don't let the fire smolder into embers. Keep a visible flame at all times.
- Leave an inch or two of ash in the fireplace at all times to insulate the coals when you build a new fire, which will create more heat.
- Have your chimney cleaned at least once a year , and more often if you usually have softwood fires. This will make your fire burn hotter and reduce the chance of house fires.
- Have your chimney inspected every five years.
- Think about getting a fireplace insert that will convert your fireplace into a much more fuel- and energy-efficient woodstove.

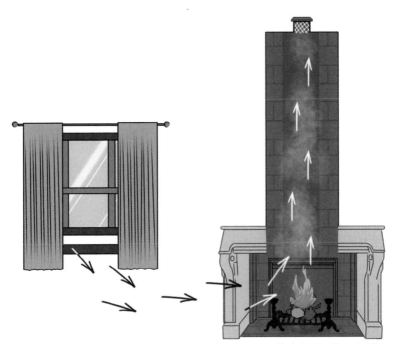

Illustration by Liliana Faiella.

- Always have a fireplace screen between open flames and the rest of your room so flaming embers or pieces of wood don't pop out into the room.
- Keep a supply of fatwood or other fire starters, matches, and a lighter on hand.

Gas Fireplace

These aren't usually designed for heating purposes, but there are some modifications you can make that will help get the most heat from your gas fireplace.

TO MAXIMIZE HEAT:

- Install a fireplace blower, a fireback, or a heat exchanger to maximize the heat.
- Keep the damper slightly open. If it's fully open you may lose more heat than you retain.
- Turn up the thermostat. This will increase your fuel consumption, but it will also keep you warmer.

- If you have a *decorative gas fireplace,* start looking for a different heat source because it may look nice, but it's not going to keep you warm.

Woodstove

While burning trees seems like a cringey way to get heat in the twenty-first century, the price of fossil fuels seems to always be on the rise, and the environmental impact of today's woodstoves is going way down. Woodstoves use radiant heat which means that the fire warms the stove itself that stays warm and, in turn, warms your room with an even, cozy heat, long after the fire goes out. And burning wood can be surprisingly more carbon-neutral than you think. If you make certain you are getting your firewood from a properly managed forest area and wood lot, the carbon you release when you burn it is the same amount of carbon the dead wood would release as it rots on the forest floor. If you just start chainsawing your trees down, this does not apply.

Most woodstoves are made of iron or steel, but if you've got some extra woodstove money burning a hole in your pocket, think about a high-end soapstone stove. They are highly efficient, and they store and radiate more heat than any other natural material. In fact, soapstone can absorb twice the heat of iron or steel, and that heat radiates for hours.

Here's what you need to know:

- Always buy EPA-certified woodstoves, which are quite energy efficient and up to eight times more cost efficient than using fossil fuels. EPA-certified models produce one-third to one-half the smoke of their ancient uncertified ancestors! Think about upgrading if you have an older stove.
- Always have a woodstove installed by a qualified professional who will know where and how to install it to ensure it can be operated safely and with a proper hearth.
- Get a model with a cooktop so it will be easy to cook a meal if the power goes out.
- Investigate the newest models that can connect to water heaters or radiators for even more energy efficiency!

Pellet Stove

Pellet stoves are similar to wood-burning stoves but have a few significant differences. The wood used in a pellet stove comes in the form of—you guessed it—recycled wood pellets. These are smaller and easier to store than wood but are also more expensive, and a pellet stove requires electricity to function properly. Pellet stoves are also quieter than wood stoves, so if you dig the snap, crackle, pop of a woodfire, that critical cozy-making component is missing from a pellet stove. But what you'll lack in sound effects you'll make up for with less ash and emissions, and a more consistent heat that's easier to cook on. And some even come with a programmable thermostat.

Woodstoves have the capacity for more heat output overall (up to 100,000 BTU) while pellet stoves top out at 50,000 BTU. Both are available as freestanding units or as fireplace inserts.

Space Heater

There are lots of small- to medium-sized electric space heaters on the market, but they can use a lot of energy from your generator if you're running one. Best to keep those for under your desk to keep your feet warm.

You can also consider propane or kerosene heaters. They both work, but for a variety of reasons, we think kerosene is the way to go.

Here's what you need to know:

- Make sure that whatever heater you get is rated for indoor use! Using a heater that isn't can cause death from carbon monoxide poisoning or make you very ill from fumes. There's no point in being warm if you're not around to enjoy it!
- Kerosene is a safe fuel and will not ignite unless you use a wick. You could drop a lit match into a can of kerosene and nothing would happen other than the flame would go out. Think of kerosene as a cleaner diesel fuel. They are interchangeable fuels, and you can use diesel in kerosene devices and kerosene in diesel devices if you ever need to.
- Kerosene is a stable fuel to store. No additives or rotating fuel here. You can store a can of kerosene for years or even decades and it's still good to go!

- Two gallons of kerosene will last approximately twelve hours on high and will heat a whole floor of most dwellings. Plan accordingly, but if you can store ten or twenty gallons of kerosene, do it.
- Run your new kerosene heater through a few gallons of fuel outside to get rid of the *new heater* fumes so you don't stink up your house when you need to use it inside.
- Make sure your heater has a carbon monoxide detector with an auto shutoff.
- You can purchase cans of kerosene from hardware or home stores, and if you're lucky there may even be a gas station near you with a kerosene pump.

Candles

Turns out candles can do more than provide light; they also provide heat. This should not be your go-to method for heating your home though, because it takes about twenty candles to heat a room. *But,* if you don't have power, and you're stuck without a better option, even minimal heat can be a lifesaver during times of extreme cold and a power outage. It's a good idea to keep a few tea lights or travel candles (little ones that come in a tin) in your car in case you ever get stuck. One little flame in a small cold space can keep fingers warm and heat the air just enough to keep you from freezing. You'll be very glad to have them if you need them.

Hand/Toe Warmers

Again, these are great to keep in the car. Once they are activated by shaking or clicking a metal disc, they begin to heat up and keep fingers operational and toes from getting frostbite. They come in disposable, reusable, and flameless catalytic varieties that (safely) use butane, are refillable, and can last twelve hours or more.

Wool Blankets

Low tech still works and should always be on your list of things to have on hand. Wool has been keeping people warm since at least 3000 BC. Its water-resistance and wicking ability means that although wool can absorb moisture, it keeps it away from your skin so you stay comfortable and dry, which is great because sweating and moisture can make hypothermia more likely. It's also eco-friendly, antibacterial, anti-odor, flame resistant, biodegradable, renewable, rarely needs to be washed, regulates your temperature, and is available in various grades of fineness. If you've found wool itchy or uncomfortable in the past, experiment with some finer non-itchy wools. Blankets, coats, mittens, socks, hat—wool is versatile and will keep you toasty warm. The sheep have you covered—literally.

Pendleton blankets are top-of-the-line, but you can find wool blankets for emergencies at thrift or army surplus stores too.

WATER AND WASTE

If you've made all the arrangements you should after reading chapter 1, you should be all set for water supply. But there's one thing you still may be used to having water to handle.

If your water is turned off, and you don't want to waste precious stored water to flush, you can easily create an emergency toilet. All you need is a five-gallon bucket, some small plastic trash bags, and absorbent clumping-style kitty litter.

If you want to get all fancy and comfy, you can get a seat for the top. After each use, dump a cup or so of 1:10 bleach water in there and sprinkle a little more kitty litter on top. Seal the bucket after use. When the bucket is full, take out the bags and tie them closed tightly. This is one instance when you definitely want to double bag! Keep the filled bags in a place where rodents or other animals can't get at them. Ideally, you should put them in a sealable outdoor recycling or trash container.

During emergencies you should be able to dispose of human waste with the rest of your trash.

And speaking of trash, the less of that you have the better—and that's not just during an emergency. This is another great example of how living a sustainable lifestyle is also the best way to be resilient, prepared, and also an all-around awesome human.

Living sustainably is a journey, so just be aware and take one step at a time.

Here are twelve ways to reduce the amount of waste you generate regularly, which you'll really appreciate during times when generating massive amounts of garbage is going to make things very difficult.

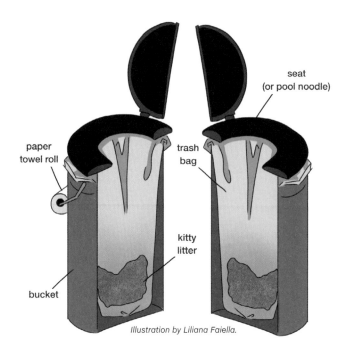

seat
(or pool noodle)

paper
towel roll

trash
bag

kitty
litter

bucket

Illustration by Liliana Faiella.

A Dozen Easy Ways to Reduce Waste

1. Use reusable shopping bags instead of plastic bags.
2. Use reusable wax wrap instead of plastic or foil wrap.
3. Get off mailing lists that send you junk you just throw away.
4. Use paperless bill paying when possible.
5. Buy food in bulk using your own containers when you can.
6. Buy food with minimal or biodegradable packaging.
7. Learn about recycling and composting programs in your area by searching online, and take advantage of all you can.
8. Get inspired by documentaries and follow bloggers and Instagrammers on sustainable living and a *zero waste* lifestyle.
9. Invest in a water filter and a glass or stainless steel water bottle instead of buying plastic one-use water bottles.
10. Use glass or stainless steel containers instead of putting every leftover in a plastic bag.
11. Prioritize buying packaged food in cardboard, glass, or cans—not plastic!
12. If you have a garden or have a friend or coworker with a garden, start composting all your organic matter.

SHELTER IN PLACE AT WORK

Nobody wants to think about the horror of being trapped at your workplace any longer than you have to be, but what if you end up having to shelter in place *at work* away from your TV, your end-of-the-world-as-we-know-it pantry, and your comfy bed? There's no reason to make it worse than it already is. Be prepared. What you'll be able to have depends on what kind of work environment you have. If you can, dedicate the back of a desk drawer or part of a locker for your emergency supplies so you have a couple days' worth of provisions that will last you until the emergency has passed, or until you can safely get back home.

If you don't have much room, think about what you can keep in your car or in a backpack or bag you take with you. Even if all you can manage is a little water, some power bars, and a foil emergency blanket, that's way better than nothing!

Office Food

Choose from the following list of high-protein, high-fat, high-energy nutrition in a small package.

- Nut bars/granola bars (try to stay away from high-sugar ones)
- Survival food like pemmican (or any hard-core survival food mentioned in chapter 2)
- Trail mix
- Canned tuna, sardines, or chicken with pull top can lids
- Peanut butter and crackers
- Pull-top cans of chili or thick soup like lentil or split pea
- Bottled water
- Instant coffee
- Powdered drink mixes with electrolytes like Gatorade or Powerade
- Multivitamins

Office Supplies

- Disposable utensils (preferably biodegradable ones)
- Napkins or paper towels
- Roll of toilet paper

- Flashlight
- A pair of fresh socks and underwear
- Jammies
- Comfortable shoes
- Phone charger
- Foil emergency blanket
- Crank radio
- Small inflatable pillow and air mattress, if you have room. (You can even use the pillow on a regular day if you lock the door. We won't tell.)
- Manual can opener

Know Your Office Space

Make sure you know how to get out of your place of work in an emergency.

- Look for evacuation maps on building doors and in public areas such as lobbies and stairwells.
- Know where the emergency exits are.
- Determine the best routes to take, and an alternate route if the shortest one is blocked.
- Do your windows open, and are you near the ground floor?
- Is there a fire escape handy?
- Know where all stairwells are, and don't take the elevator!
- Where are the fire alarms?
- Where are the fire extinguishers?
- Do you have any office mates with health or mobility issues who might need help evacuating?
- If you can't get out of the building, be prepared to call 911, report the nature of the emergency, and give them your exact location.

WHAT YOU SHOULD ALWAYS HAVE

Rather than having to doom scroll through your own brain, or a million weird Facebook groups, here are *all the lists*, because stress (in addition to being stressful) makes you forget stuff. Thanks, evolution.

Never Leave Home Without It: Wallet Edition

- Photo ID/driver's license
- Credit/debit card
- A blank check
- Photos of your family members and pets
- A multi-tool card or small keychain knife
- Cash
- Vaccine card(s)
- Important phone numbers
- Note with medical conditions, allergies, and emergency contacts
- Packet of salt

Never Leave Home Without It: Handbag Edition

All the above plus:

- Pack of tissues
- Pen/pencil and small pad of paper
- Tweezers
- Band-Aids, antibiotic ointment in a small ziplock bag
- Surgical and N95 masks
- A couple of healthy snack bars
- Refillable water bottle
- Tampons/pads—even if you yourself do not need them, do this anyway and be the hero on a disastrous day!
- Foil emergency blanket
- Multi-tool

Never Leave Home Without It: Kid Backpack Edition

- Laminated personal information card—name, address, two emergency contacts, health conditions, medications, allergies
- Small refillable water bottle
- A couple of healthy snack bars
- First Aid—a few Band-Aids and a couple of packets of antibiotic ointment in a small ziplock bag
- Hand sanitizer

- N95 mask in a ziplock bag for smoke, microbes, dust, etc.
- A foil emergency blanket

Never Leave Home Without It:
Special Items for Family Members and Pets

Depending on the age and health of family members, they may have critical needs that don't fall under the list headings above. Does your kid need an asthma inhaler? Does an elderly family member need special meds or extra hearing aid batteries? Should you tuck a couple of extra poop bags in your wallet or glove compartment for the dog? Have a good, deep think, and make sure those that depend on you are covered!

CAR SAFETY BAGS

Bags with an *S*? Plural? Yep, you'll need two of them—one to take care of your car and one to take care of you!

Mechanical Bag/Box
- Mechanic's tool kit or multipurpose tool
- Hose repair tape
- Bottle jack (to move heavy objects that might be blocking the road)
- Road flares—the type that burns with red phosphorus doesn't require batteries and lasts for about twenty minutes. They can also be seen from crazy-long distances and spotted easily by helicopters. They'll also start a campfire like nobody's business, even if the wood is wet. The battery-powered flashing flares last much longer, but require batteries and don't have the same visibility. It wouldn't hurt to have both.
- Powder-style radiator repair kit—this stuff is the closest thing to magic outside Hogwarts. Pour the powder in your radiator and wait for the dust to find and seal cooling-system leaks! It's not a permanent fix, but it will get you out of a jam.
- Work gloves
- Flashlight and extra batteries
- Twelve-volt air pump
- A can of Fix-a-Flat

- Red plastic sheet and/or reflective triangles to make your car more visible
- Duct tape
- Clear plastic sheeting to keep you off the ground and dry if you need to work on the car or change a tire. You can also use it (and the duct tape) to repair a broken window and keep heat in your car.
- Spark plug cleaner tool
- Jumper cables—good, heavy gauge ones
- Extra fuses
- Lug wrench to change a tire
- Car charger for your phone
- Properly inflated spare tire
- Tripod jack
- Multi-tool
- Fire extinguisher
- Seat belt cutter/emergency hammer combo tool

Survival Bag/Box

- First aid kit to include: gauze, tape, bandages, antibiotic ointment, QuikClot, Tylenol, a blanket, non-latex gloves, scissors, hydrocortisone, thermometer, tweezers, and instant cold compress. Adventure Medical and North American Rescue are great companies that have done the work for you and assembled a variety of first aid kits (including for dogs!) that you can choose from, based on your needs and budget.
- Sleeping bag, blanket, or emergency blanket.
- Maps and a compass
- Tea lights and lighter/waterproof matches (small candles that can help heat the air inside your car)
- Water—change it out every six months
- Water filtration device—like a LifeStraw
- Cliff bars/ready-to-eat meals/survival food
- CB radio—hand-held twelve-volt with adapter and battery pack adapter
- Rain poncho
- Foldable shovel

- Change of clothes or coveralls
- Jacket
- Toilet paper
- Toilet kit—coffee can, wastebasket liners, kitty litter, dryer sheets, toilet paper, personal wipes. You may never need this, but if you do, you're welcome!
- A bag of small candies (Jolly Ranchers, Werther's, Tootsie Rolls, etc.)
- Knife—we recommend the Ontario knife RAT-3.
- Parachute cord (550)—this versatile stuff can be used for scads of survival-y things. You can rig a shelter, hang clothes to dry, use it as bow string to make a fire, pull strands for fishing line, suspend food from a tree to keep it away from bears, make fishing lures and snares, tie up gear, create a sling or use with a splint, use it to haul firewood, or rescue someone who's fallen into a ravine or is stuck in the mud. There are probably a hundred more uses for paracord and if one of them comes up, you'll be happy you have it. They even sell woven paracord bracelets you can wear so it's on you at all times—if paracord is your fashion statement.
- Disposable lighters
- Waterproof matches
- Extra batteries
- Hand warmers
- Water
- Reflective vest in case you need to walk in search of help
- Tampons/pads
- Solar battery bank—we recommend the kit from Goal Zero. It is weatherproof, lightweight, portable, and contains solar panels, a solar-charged power bank, and a rechargeable lantern. It's ideal for charging your phone and providing light.

Cold-Weather Add-Ons

If you are in a cold-weather environment, supplement your car emergency supplies with a cold-weather bag too. Be especially mindful when you are taking a long trip or will be driving on rural roads without many people around, or if you live somewhere that has winter storms.

- Parka or warm coat with hood
- Knit or wool hat—Ibex has fantastic non-itchy sustainable merino wool beanies and outerwear!
- Mittens
- Functional cold-weather snow boots
- Snow brush/ice scraper
- Collapsible snow shovel
- Cat litter
- Wool blanket
- Backpack—if you need to leave your car to walk to safety or find help, you'll need to bring your survival gear with you. We recommend the Mystery Ranch thirty-five-liter backpack as a great solution. It's super well-made with glove-friendly buckles, expanding pocket, and is rugged and comfortable enough for an unanticipated hike to a gas station or to the nearest town. There are lots of backpacks on the market; just make sure you have one big enough to hold what you need.

ARE YOU READY?

Home shelter

_____ Complete home assessment and make a targeted to-do list.

_____ Get a good home repair manual.

_____ Have a professional inspect and assess your home.

Your utilities
Water

_____ Find and label your water main valve.

_____ Tell all household members where it is.

_____ Leave directions to shut off main water valve.

_____ Check individual fixture water valves.

Gas

_____ Find main gas valves.

_____ Label main gas valve with diagram.

_____ Find and check individual fixture gas valves.

_____ Tell all household members where the main gas valve is.

_____ Leave directions on how to shut off gas.

Electricity

_____ Locate circuit breaker box.

_____ Post directions on how to shut off electricity and label breakers.

Secondary utility requirements

_____ Assess needs and obtain backup energy sources for light and heat.

_____ Obtain gas cans, stabilizer, and gas to store if applicable.

_____ Have the components on hand to make an emergency toilet.

_____ Assemble your basic tool kit.

Office shelter

_____ Know evacuation routes and emergency procedures.

_____ Assemble emergency supplies.

Assemble preparedness kits

_____ Wallet

_____ Handbag

_____ Kids' backpacks

_____ Special items and pets

_____ Car mechanical

_____ Car survival

_____ Car cold-weather kit, if applicable

CHAPTER 6

SAFETY AND SECURITY

B uckle up, kiddos. Here's where it starts to get real.

Disasters bring out both the best and the worst in humanity. You've seen stories in the news about people who try to take advantage of the chaos during disasters and emergency situations. They know that emergency service providers have their hands full, and oftentimes homes and stores appear to be easy targets for thieves and vandals. Here's how you can increase the odds of staying safe and secure when everything around you seems to be falling apart.

PHYSICAL SAFETY

There's a fine line between being properly prepared, and being the crazy person who lives on top of a mountain encircled with *No Trespassing* signs and a barbed wire fence. Just as you can have your house inspected for structural soundness and energy efficiency, you can also take advantage of professionals who can perform a physical security assessment and then consult with you to sensibly create a more secure living space. For a nominal fee they will take a look at your house or apartment, produce a report of the vulnerabilities they see, and recommend solutions. This service also may provide what's called an *all threats*, or *total threats* assessment. These services will provide a localized and individualized assessment on security, natural disasters, political, and economic threats, and will identify ways you can mitigate those risks.

Commercial Security and Monitoring Systems

Don't worry about me, I have a security system! you may be saying. And during normal times, that's super. But in case you missed it, we're not talking about normal times. During disasters or wide-scale emergencies, typical security systems tend to give a *false* sense of security. Most of them only have one or two days' worth of battery backup, so during a power outage they will only operate for a short period of time.

One of the first things to collapse in a disaster is cellular networks. They go down hard because they simply don't have enough capacity to handle the surge of use during a crisis. If your security system works on the cellular network, it will be sending out an SOS into the void. And even if you get lucky and the call connects, police and other emergency services will also be overloaded, so the chances of their prioritizing your alarm call, or even responding at all, are slim to none.

So what can you do? Your goal, in a world of potential targets, is to be the most unappealing. You may never have thought you'd be trying to be the least attractive kid in town, but here we are.

Windows and Doors

One of the best ways to secure your entry doors is also the cheapest! Believe it or not, a six-inch doorstopper placed under the opening edge makes it two times harder to breach your door. And if it's nailed to the floor (which you can do when necessary unless you have in-floor heating), it's three times stronger!

Locks should be well-maintained and functional, and an interior or single-sided deadbolt should be installed on all entry doors. Ideally, you should have both a single-sided and double-sided deadbolt for maximum security, but the interior one will prevent anyone from tampering or trying to pick the lock from the outside when you are on the inside!

Barricade bars aren't just for gates either! You can install them on entry doors as well.

If raw lumber and ugly giant metal brackets don't match the aesthetic of your foyer, you can keep a pre-cut and fitted two-by-four with a ziplock bag containing the hardware taped to it in a hall closet, or labeled in your garage. It should only take a few minutes to install a barricade bar like the one shown here and you can wait until you need it to do so. Make sure you screw it into the studs on either side of the door.

Exterior doors should be in good repair with hinge hardware mounted on the interior.

Ideally, doors should be solid-core wood or metal with no windows. Peepholes with covers can help you see out without letting anyone else see in.

Interior entry door with bar installed.
Illustration by Liliana Faiella.

Sliding Glass Doors and Windows

Windows are problematic, and first-floor windows are a security specialist's personal nightmare. But there are things you can do to make those panes of glass a less obvious entry point. Windows and sliding doors should always be in good repair, fit snugly, and have locks that close, allowing no room to slip anything between the frame and the glass. For sliding windows and doors, insert a dowel/door bar that fits snugly between the door edge and the slider.

Ideally, you want steel shutters for all your ground-floor windows and glass doors. Yes, it's an eyesore, but the upside (especially in warm or sunny areas) is that lowering or closing the shutters when the sun comes up helps keep the heat outside and the cool air inside during times of intense heat when the power grid may fail.

Another option is hurricane film and or ballistic glass covers. These magical marvels will make your windows shatterproof, resistant to breakage, and literally bulletproof! These types of films also increase the *R-value* of your home which means they add insulation, so they are a security and environmental bonus all in one!

Garage Doors

Garage doors, just like entry doors, are commonly used as an entry point into homes. There are a couple of low-cost, quick fixes you can do to make them virtually impenetrable. First, make sure the garage door rests snugly against the ground with little-to-no space underneath. This prevents somebody from easily using a jack or a pry bar to wrench it open. Second, garage door slidelocks are cheap and incredibly effective. A padlock through the track of your garage door is almost as effective as a slide lock.

Padlock on garage door.

Plywood Covers

If you have room, you can store pre-cut plywood that you've cut to fit all your windows and glass doors. A pre-cut and pre-drilled cover can take just a few minutes to install. Store each piece with the screws attached in a ziplock bag with tape, and label each piece with what window it goes to, and an arrow pointing up so you know how to install it. This will help you when time is of the essence as well as in low-light conditions.

SAFETY MEASURES

Lighting

Did you know that lighting is the largest deterrent to crime? It's true! Bright, motion-detecting exterior security lights are worth their weight in gold. Using LED-based models not only means they will last ten times longer, but they will use a lot less power.

When looking at where to place exterior security lights, keep in mind that you want them to illuminate the full perimeter of your property with no dead spots. If you have a generator, make sure the lights are wired into it. There are also solar-powered models that eliminate the need for wiring as long as you have an appropriate place to mount them so they charge properly. Mount your lights as high as possible so they can't be accessed easily by folks who would prefer to work in the dark.

Security Cameras

Doorbell cameras are great, but they only cover a small area in front of your door and can't be accessed if the internet is down. Security cameras should be hardwired and cover the whole area around your house/property —or if you live in an apartment, the hallway and rear entrance. You want a system that records to its own hard drive vs. one that has a cloud drive and requires the internet or a cellular network to function.

Assaulting the Senses

Sirens and strobe lights are a great deterrent and can be easily wired to a light switch so you can manually operate them! Electricity down? There are even hand-crank sirens that don't require electricity and handheld air horns that will make any living thing run for the hills. The point is to make it as obnoxiously bright and loud as you possibly can so your neighbors know something is going on, and bad actors know *you* know they are there.

Building a Safe Room

We're not talking about a professional safe room that looks like Fort Knox or a nuclear bunker. But you should designate one room in your home as the *safe room* in case of a disaster. It's much easier to fully equip and secure one room where everyone can be, than to try to accomplish that in your whole house or apartment. If you have space in your designated safe room, you can even store some of your emergency food, water, and other preparations in it.

Make sure there is a solid-panel wooden door, put a deadbolt on it, and use hardware rated for exterior use. Don't forget to keep a wooden wedge in the room. If your safe room is on the second floor, that handy dandy escape ladder we talked about earlier will come into play, allowing you to safely evacuate.

Fake Dogs and Psychological Warfare

Dogs are great. Big dogs are also an amazing security asset in an emergency—from acting as an early-warning system to direct intervention, dogs are seriously our best friends. That being said, not everyone has the ability, the room, the budget, or the desire to own a dog. Dogs are treasured family members and require lots of care and time, so don't get a dog just for security, because now, for the dogless, technology has stepped in and provided a canine-esque deterrent. The motion-sensing dog bark alarm sounds real and will make any prospective bad guy think twice about messing with you. You can also post a *Beware of Dog* sign in the window or near the door just for added effect.

The Club.

Your Car

Yes, even your car gets a security makeover. You don't need a giant SUV with lightbars, bulletproof glass, and a twenty-four-inch lift. What you do need is to prevent your car from being stolen. *The Club.* Get one. It's been doing its thing keeping bad guys from driving off with cars since the 1980s. Even if someone wants your car more than you do, this will thwart their plans. Go with the safety-yellow one so people can see it easily and know right away that your car is going nowhere.

Be Prepared

My kids carry a laminated card with a map on one side and a list of information on the other. The map shows different points on the way home from school in numbered order; the other side of the card shows addresses of those points, phone numbers of friends and family, and vital information they can use. This is in a waterproof map bag with a watch and a Sharpie. My kids know to follow the map and then wait no longer than one hour for me at each location. If I'm not there, they are to write their initials, the time they left, and the number of the point they are heading to next with the Sharpie somewhere visible at each point. That way if I don't catch them at a certain place I know where and when they were there and where they are going. It also gives zero information out to anybody else that may stumble on their message. Make sure the watch is a mechanical watch with a second hand (less can go wrong). I like the simple Timex mechanical watches. They run for about five years on one battery and are built to withstand punishment.

Bill

Concealment

A great tactic to keep your stuff from being a target for thieves is concealment. You don't want to display to the world all that cool emergency preparedness equipment in the back of your car. If someone who isn't as well-prepared as you gets desperate, they can see all those tempting preps, smash your window, and steal all your hard work. Not cool, looter! Use a dark blanket or a drop cloth to cover your stuff. Some cars also come with a built-in rolling privacy shade you can pull over the contents of the trunk. Get into the habit of using it if you have it.

Have a Plan

The most effective thing you can do to ensure the safety and security of your family is to create your own personalized disaster plan, write it down, and distribute it to your family and loved ones. This plan should include who is responsible for what actions and at what time.

Just remember the KISS rule: Keep It Simple, Stupid. The more complex and detailed a plan is, the more prone that plan is to breaking down and becoming useless. And if a plan is useless, it's not really a plan. More on that in the Evacuation chapter.

The Rally Point

What happens if your home is somehow compromised and no longer safe, and what if you are at the office ten miles away and your kids are at school? The way to get everybody together is to have a *rally point*, or better yet, more than one. Choose a place that will be safe where you can meet up if you can't or shouldn't go home. Friends' houses work well or a local park or obvious landmark. Any place will work as long as everybody knows about it and it is relatively safe.

SITUATIONAL AWARENESS

Situational awareness is what 99.99 percent of personal or operational security is about. It is knowing where you are in relation to everything around you and having the ability to project and plan for the most likely outcomes of what may happen within your space. Unfortunately, most women in our society are already experts at situational awareness, even if they don't know it. Is that person walking down the sidewalk a threat? Is it dark or light out? Are there places someone could be hiding? Is there a place to get to quickly where there are people? Should I be taking a different route to my car? Being alert for immediate danger or possible danger is all part of situational awareness.

Try this exercise. The next time you're out in a public place, look around for a minute and then without looking up, jot down notes on your phone or a small pad of paper. What did you see? How many cars were there, what color were they, what about people and what they were wearing? What doors or businesses are nearby? Where were places to take shelter?

Once you're done writing it all down, look back up and see how much you noticed and how much you missed. You'll be amazed at how much you didn't see or how much you got wrong or immediately forgot. If you do this regularly, you'll see your notes getting better and better until eventually you won't even need the notepad; you can start doing it in your very own brain. You'll even start to expand what you see and begin assessing what or who may or may not be a threat. What situational awareness training really does is wake up that part of our brains that has kept human beings alive (and not dinner for some wild animal) for hundreds of thousands of years. You were made for this!

The next stage is threat assessment. You know that inner voice, the one that tells you something is off about a person—your intuition or gut feeling. Listen to that voice, have conversations with it, take it out for a drink, become friends. That voice is your subconscious mind collecting all the tens of thousands of points of information around you that your conscious mind isn't paying attention to because it's too busy doing other stuff like making dinner plans, or planning your next Netflix binge. The more you intentionally listen to the little voice, the louder it gets. When it pipes up, assess the threat and form plans on how to evade or overcome that threat. Now that you've started thinking about how to interpret the world around you, it's time to think about how that world interprets *you*!

When you did your exercise in situational awareness, you probably noticed the guy with the big loud laugh or the woman wearing the neon-green track suit. But you may not have noticed *the gray person*.

Go Gray

The *gray person* is somebody you don't notice, don't remember, can't recall any details about, because they didn't stand out in any way. If you need to be out and about in the aftermath of a disaster, when humanity is at its worst, that is who you want to be. The term *gray man* or *gray-manning* was coined by intelligence agencies to explain the trade craft of camouflaging yourself in plain sight. The less remarkable you are, the less attention you bring to yourself, the less of a target you become for criminals trying to capitalize on chaos. Here's how to become your sneakiest self and move through the world unnoticed. You can practice this and have fun being a stealth badass with the invisibility cloak.

Behavior

Don't walk too fast or too slowly, don't make eye contact, don't speak loudly or yell or cry. Don't give off a hyper-vigilant vibe with eyes scanning left to right. Be relaxed but not distracted; don't have your headphones in or your cellphone out. Be as regular and average as you can possibly be.

Appearance

For much of our lives we've been told to embrace our individuality, stand out from the crowd, be noticed. That is the exact opposite of what you should be doing in an emergency situation. If your hair is bright blue, tuck it under a cap. Have a beard that goes down to your belly button? Time to break out the scissors. Wear a lot of makeup? Go without or tone it down.

Your camouflage color palette: Autumn Ninja.

The color of your clothing, coat, shoes, and backpack or handbag should be earth tones. No bright reds, bright blues, neons, whites, or black. Pure black does not occur in nature and attracts the eye, which is why you'll never see soldiers wearing black uniforms in real life. Sorry, Hollywood, someone had to say it! So, a muted gray-black is fine, but no midnight jet-black Ninja suits allowed!

Clothing

Stay away from expensive designer brands. A well-worn pair of jeans with a pair of sensible walking shoes and a T-shirt is great *graywear*. That Rolex? Save it for another time. Timex or a G-Shock will work great. If your wedding ring could finance a small country, maybe wear a plain band, or leave your ring and all your other bling at home. On the flipside, don't dress down too far and stand out by looking disheveled. And never wear clothing with controversial or political messages. People are already riled up enough.

Under no circumstances should you try to look *tacti-cool*. No military surplus or tactical backpacks, no combat boots, no Punisher skull accessories, no head-to-toe military camo. Most important, never and we mean absolutely *never* carry a visible weapon in any emergency situation.

It's dangerous and automatically makes you a primary target. First, people may think *you* are the threat, or second, it makes people want to steal that weapon. Gray people do not walk around with visible armaments.

Camo Your Car

A candy apple red German sports car is not an effective doomsday survival car. Again, your best bet is a neutral-colored sensible vehicle without bumper stickers, signs, vanity plates, license plate frames, stuff hanging from the rearview mirror, or anything that telegraphs information about yourself.

Fight or Flight?

What happens if, after all the effort not to be noticed, you *do* get noticed and end up in a potential confrontation with someone? This is when our *fight or flight* instinct comes into play. And there's usually one right answer: *flight!* If you can get away, then *get away.* Don't try to be a hero, don't stand your ground, do not be a badass. Fighting is dangerous and risky and should be your *absolute last resort.*

THE LAST RESORT

Sometimes all else fails, and you find yourself in a situation where bad things are happening and you absolutely have to defend yourself. There are plenty of nonlethal, less lethal, and lethal options for self-defense. Use only what you feel comfortable with, but don't be afraid to learn. And please take note that many types of defensive weapons are regulated in most states, so *always check your local laws and regulations prior to purchasing, possessing, or using any weapon!*

Let There Be Light!

Believe it or not, one of the best passive defensive measures is a bright spotlight or strobing flashlight. Light can not only temporarily blind an opponent, but strobe lights can disorient them to the point where they are no longer a threat. There are even strobe and light combinations that cause nausea, known as *LED incapacitators.* The brighter the better when it comes to light, and there is only one company we recommend for flashlights:

SureFire. They have been making lights for the military and law enforcement for years because they are reliable and effective.

Tactical light gear.

Public domain photo courtesy of United States Navy.

Body Armor

While it may seem a little over-the-top, body armor is a legitimately effective passive defense measure if things are really bad. It ranges in price and effectiveness and is rated on the NIJ (National Institute of Justice) scale. The higher the NIJ number, the more it will protect you. Always buy new body armor that is fitted specifically for you. If your vest doesn't fit you correctly (and there are different vests designed for men and women) you could receive massive internal injuries that could result in death—even if a bullet doesn't make it through the armor! Crazy, right? You'll have a choice between hard armor with steel or ceramic plates, and soft armor made of flexible fabrics like Kevlar. Soft armor makes the most sense because it's lighter weight, easier to carry and conceal, easier to move around in, and costs a lot less. It's also great protection from handguns which are involved in 95 percent of shootings.

Ballistic sunglasses.

You can also purchase a ballistic blanket which is basically just a big sheet of soft armor and can be used to protect several people, a wall, or even your car. Sadly, there are even children's backpacks with soft body armor sewn in.

If you own a firearm, a good pair of ballistic glasses is a mandatory safety item. If you don't, they are still an excellent idea. Ballistic glasses will protect your eyes from most threats including flying debris or a direct shotgun blast with buckshot.

Smoke Bombs

No kidding! Smoke bombs are widely available due to airsoft and photography and can be mail-ordered just like anything else, and they are legal almost everywhere. Generated smoke is a great defensive tool because not only does it prevent folks from seeing you but it disorients them so they can't even see where they're going. Nobody expects a smoke bomb!

Smoke has some limitations though. Since it dissipates quickly, you may have only a few minutes so make the most of it and get the heck out of there. If it's windy, your well-placed smoke could be gone even faster. Always toss smoke bombs upwind of the area you want to cover. Even with its natural limitations, smoke is a great effective tool that most people aren't prepared to deal with, plus it comes in really neat colors. Most devices will deploy around forty thousand square feet of smoke within twenty seconds or so. That's a lot of smoke!

You can carry one in your car, in an emergency backpack, and keep some at home. The great thing about smoke is it doesn't hurt anybody, and it allows you to stop a potentially life-threatening situation in seconds.

ACTIVE DEFENSE

BRACE YOURSELF AND DON'T FREAK OUT: the following pages contain information about devices that can cause you and others great bodily harm, up to and including death. Never use any weapon without the proper training and adherence to manufacturers' limits and use recommendations.

"Active defense" means using measures to physically stop somebody from causing you or others harm. *Active defense measures should only be used in those circumstances where all other options have failed.* Once violence is brought into the equation, the possibility for life-altering and life-ending ramifications rises exponentially. Violence is a tool, and understanding it and its proper employment is important.

The Spice of Life: Mace and Pepper Spray

In the realm of less lethal self-defense options, mace and pepper spray are what most of us are familiar with. Mace contains CS or tear gas, and pepper spray is just what it sounds like—a big nasty spray of pepper. It's also known as OC. Some states have limits or outright bans on it, so check your local laws. OC/CS comes in many different shapes and sizes from small key chain canisters to giant blowers as big as fire extinguishers. Pepper spray isn't perfect; your assailant needs to be close to you, but normally not within touching distance. It's concealable in a pocket or purse, widely available, and has a track record of working.

Everybody was Kung Fu Fighting: Martial Arts

Don't do it—unless, of course, you have spent a lifetime training and practicing, and developing a deep understanding of hand-to-hand combat and all the dangers it entails. But that's not most of us—not by a long shot. The reality is that if the bad guy has a weapon of any type there is a good chance he is going to use it on you before you get a chance to land that sweet triple-flip head kick.

So, what can you do if you don't have a weapon and have to resort to using only your hands and wits? We all know about going for the groin, but don't forget about these other vulnerable areas.

KNEES: Try to get your opponent on the ground, which will give your body multiple points of support so you don't fall over. If you're having trouble doing this, try to raise your leg and bring your foot down hard on the top of their kneecap, pushing toward the ground. Fifteen pounds of pressure is all it takes to separate the kneecap. *Ouch!*

EYES: Use your thumbs to press on the eyes from the outside corner toward the bridge of the nose. Double ouch. And gross.

THROAT: It takes about ten pounds of pressure for eight to ten seconds on the carotid arteries to render someone unconscious. Thirty-three pounds of pressure will collapse the windpipe. And that's the end of that.

Knives (And Why They're a Bad Idea Most of the Time)

Knives are only effective at very close range, and as anyone who's ever been in a knife fight could tell you, nobody leaves a knife fight uninjured. Absolutely nobody, ever. A knife should only be used if and when an aggressor is physically touching you.

A knife is one of the most useful tools to have in a survival situation— but you really, really, don't want to be in a position to have to use it as a weapon.

And no, you are not a ninja, so if you think you can defeat a threat by throwing your knife and embedding it in your opponent's carotid artery, you are sadly mistaken and about to give that bad guy a weapon. Knives require you to be up close and personal, and if you are close enough to hurt somebody with a knife then they are close enough to hurt *you* with a knife, their hands, or anything else lying around, so the plan is to not get that close.

If all your plans have failed, and this is your Hail Mary, wait until the aggressor is so close that your bodies are pressing against each other in places they shouldn't be. This is the point where you take your knife out. No, you are not going to pull a *West Side Story* maneuver. There will be no taking your knife out and warning them, no circling around as you jab at each other. The more the aggressor doesn't know, the better. (This applies whenever you are planning on employing any weapon.) So pull your knife out only when you're ready to use it, and then use it.

Most states have rules and regulations regarding blades over three inches long, but, surprisingly, there are an amazing number of spots on the human body where three inches is more than enough to cause a bad guy to have a very bad day. Below is an illustration of fatal stab points that can be achieved with a three-inch blade.

If you are going to purchase a knife, there are two types to consider: folding knives and full-tang fixed blade knives. Full-tang fixed blade means the blade piece goes from the knife tip to the end of the handle as one solid piece of metal. Folding knives have a blade that folds over the handle. Folding knives are more concealable, more convenient to carry, and less threatening. Many states have laws prohibiting what's called *spring-assisted folders,* with a spring that helps the knife open faster. Almost all states have laws against automatic knives, where you just press a button and it pops open automatically.

9 Fatal Stab Points

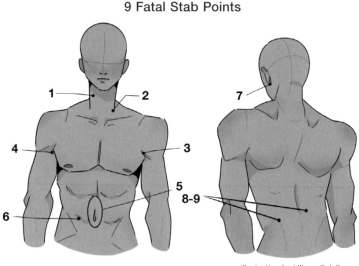

Illustration by Liliana Faiella.

Think *West Side Story* again, and the classic switchblade. If you're going to carry a folding knife, make sure it's legal where you are and any places you plan on taking it. Fixed blades don't have a weak spot in the middle like a folding knife, they won't collapse, and they can be deployed quicker, but you'll need a sheath. Whatever knife you choose to carry, remember it's a tool first, weapon last, so make sure your knife has some serration to make cutting rope and other objects easier.

Sticks and Stones (And Other Things That Will Break Your Bones)

Asps, batons, nunchucks, baseball bats, boards, spears, swords, cast-iron skillets, or any other weird stuff you plan on beating somebody with, all go right into the *dumb idea* category along with hand-to-hand combat and knife fighting. If you have nothing else, and all that's available is a bottle of wine, then by all means, swing for the fences. But batons, asps, and other weapons take training to use correctly and effectively and the bad guys need to be uncomfortably close for you to use them. Close will get you killed.

Zing Zing: Stun Guns

Let's talk stun guns. There are two types: ones that you have to make contact with the body of your assailant to use and ones that shoot out little barbs and stop the assailant at fifty feet away. Guess which one we advocate for? Yes, the one that lets you drop that bad guy fifty feet away from you. You can still have a handheld stun gun in your purse or bag just in case.

Stun guns, mace, and pepper spray are in a category of weapons classified as *less lethal*. Why *less lethal* instead of *non*lethal? Because, believe it or not, even pepper spray can kill somebody if they have underlying health conditions. Any time you use a weapon against another human being, there is a chance the encounter could be fatal. Understanding that will help you respect and use the weapon responsibly. Just because it's not as lethal as something else, by no means does that make it safe.

Firearms (That Escalated Quickly!)

Firearms are complicated operationally, emotionally, and politically; and the topic of firearm ownership is deadly serious. Don't ever buy a firearm on a whim. You need to be willing, prepared, and committed to properly train yourself, properly maintain the firearm, properly store the firearm, and only responsibly use the firearm. Make the decision thoughtfully and soberly.

A 2022 study found that living in a home in which there is a handgun doubles your risk of dying via handgun. That statistic alone should make it very clear to you why you must take your responsibility as a gun owner seriously if you decide you want to own one.

In a disaster/emergency situation or life in general, your biggest chance of ending up in a self-defense situation that you cannot flee from is one involving a firearm. As a self-protection measure, firearms are an equalizer. But a gun also immediately escalates any situation to life-and-death, so knowing when to employ your weapon and how to employ it is vital. A gun is not a warning device; it's not a threat to be waved around or used for intimidation. When you pull a gun on someone you must be prepared to shoot them—plain and simple. If it's not worth killing them for, it's not worth pulling a gun on them for.

Training

Before buying any gun, you should take at least twelve hours of instruction on basic gun safety and an additional twelve hours of training on a range, learning to handle a firearm safely and effectively. You should always spend some time using the model of gun you plan to purchase before you buy it. You should train on every gun you own a minimum of once every sixty days, including firing live ammunition. There are thousands of certified reputable weapons instructors out there who will make sure you know what you are doing. In addition, this training should be taken by anyone else in your home who will have access to the weapon. Make sure all children who live in or visit your home know that guns are not toys, and if they ever see one not to touch it and to tell an adult right away.

Storage

A good gun safe should be purchased and installed *before purchasing the gun itself*. Safes should be bolted to the wall or floor, optimally into concrete, but at a minimum into studs. Never bring a gun into your home that you do not have a safe for.

There are many sobering statistics about guns that were not properly stored. Almost all guns used in crimes in the United States are stolen, and almost all stolen guns are not in a safe. Suicides make up 60 percent of all gun deaths, and the vast majority of guns used for suicide that are not owned by the suicide victim are guns that were not locked up by a family member. Almost all accidental shootings committed by children are done with guns that were not properly stored. *It is absolutely imperative that you are prepared to store your gun properly prior to bringing it home.*

There are literally thousands of types and models of gun safes. Buy the largest safe you can afford. Why? First, it's harder to move, so if somebody breaks in when you're not at home they can't just throw the whole safe into the back of their car and open it elsewhere. Secondly, the bigger the safe the more room you have to lock up other vital things you want protected from theft or fire. Third, if you decide to buy an additional gun you won't have to buy an additional safe.

Make sure there is a way you can access the safe mechanically with either a mechanical combination lock or a bypass key. Biometric and electronic locks are okay, but if the battery dies or there's a lightning strike or an electromagnetic pulse, you'll still be able to get inside when the gizmos don't work. And don't write your combination down or store the key on or near the safe!

Never store a firearm with a magazine loaded or the firearm itself loaded. If possible, store ammunition in a completely separate safe, and always keep it away from the firearms. Firearms should be cleared of all ammunition, cleaned, and oiled, before placing them in the safe. When removing a firearm from the safe always check that it is empty or *clear.* Even if you *know* for sure there is no bullet in the chamber, check it anyway. It is a cardinal safety rule that anytime you pick up or are handed a firearm that hasn't been in your care and control, the first thing you do is point it in a safe direction and ensure it is unloaded. Always. Every time. No exceptions.

In addition to safes, there are pistol boxes that are used to keep a handgun readily accessible. They normally have a biometric feature with a key backup. A pistol box is basically a mini gun safe; it does not take the place of a larger safe which is bolted down. If you are going on vacation or leaving your house for an extended period of time, you should move anything in the pistol box to the main gun safe. Pistol boxes can be secured to the floor or walls just like a gun safe and should be. The same rule applies to pistol boxes. Don't ever store your gun loaded or with a magazine inserted in a pistol box.

Accessories

Before you purchase your firearm, you will need a pair of ballistic glasses, ear protection, an empty chamber indicator tool, and a general gun cleaning kit.

Buying a Firearm

Twelve hours of safety training? Check. Twelve hours of range training? Check. Safe storage purchased and installed? Check. Accessories purchased? Check. Ok, *now* you are ready to think about purchasing your firearm.

Always purchase your firearm new from a Federal Firearms License (FFL)-holder. Purchasing a new gun through an FFL-holder ensures that you are not purchasing a broken or damaged firearm, and also ensures that the gun isn't stolen. Even in states where it's legal to do a private sale, choosing an FFL-holder will ensure you're dealing with a reputable person, not just some rando online.

Handguns

There are a few factors to consider when purchasing a handgun—the biggest is fit. Make sure your FFL-holder shows you a variety of choices that fit you properly, feel comfortable in your hand, and aren't too heavy.

A good recommendation to consider is the 1911 model .45 ACP. The weapon is made by multiple manufacturers, has been around since, you guessed it, 1911, and has a proven track record in law enforcement and military use. It also has a unique two-safety system in which it can't be fired (even if the safety is off) when it's not held correctly. This helps prevent not only negligent discharges, but if somebody else gets your gun, they have to hold it correctly to use it on you. The 1911 has been around for so long that every gun store on the planet has parts and spare magazines in stock for it, and there is a vast array of ammunition available. The models range from micro compact to full-size and everything in between, so they will fit just about anybody's hand. It's popular and has stood the test of time for a reason.

Caliber refers to the size of ammunition; 9mm is the caliber of a handgun that shoots a bullet that is nine millimeters in size, and so on. Caliber is important because different calibers react differently in terms of penetration (how far it goes into a target), speed (how fast the round goes), and kinetic energy (how hard it hits). What you are looking for is a bullet that will knock down the target, but one that won't just keep going through your wall, and another wall, and into the street or another room and hit someone it wasn't intended for. That's called *overpenetration* and it's very dangerous. This is why having an assault rifle for home security is a bad idea. You can end up hitting all kinds of things on the other side of what you're aiming at.

For safety reasons, use either the .45 ACP or the 10mm. Both rounds are big and slow enough to not over-penetrate, while still knocking down your target. Forty-five and 10mm pistols also normally only carry seven rounds or so, and are well within most states' laws that have magazine size restrictions.

Shotguns

Pump shotguns are now, and have been since their inception, the best home defense weapon and the best general firearm ever made. A shotgun shoots both a slug (a very big piece of metal kind of like a bullet, but bigger and slower) and buckshot, which is a bunch of metal BBs. It can be used for hunting birds and game, as well as for home defense, so from a survival/emergency standpoint it really can't be beat.

The most common caliber for a shotgun, by far, is the twelve-gauge and for our purposes here, there is absolutely no reason you should go larger or smaller. One of the great things about a shotgun is that buckshot spreads out wide—think of a cloud of metal balls getting bigger the farther it moves away from the end of the barrel. What this means is you don't need to be a crack shot to use it effectively. Just aim for center mass and you will hit what you're shooting at. The other bonus with buckshot is it won't over-penetrate. Most buckshot will get stopped by drywall or particle board so there's less risk of hitting somebody in the room next to you or across the hall.

Pump shotguns also have a ton of barrel options that can be changed out in a minute or less. For home defense get an eighteen-inch barrel. This is the shortest legal barrel you can have without having to register the weapon with the Bureau of Alcohol, Tobacco, and Firearms. The shorter the weapon, the easier it is to maneuver in cramped indoor spaces like a hallway. Either the Remington 870 or the Mossberg 500 series in twelve-gauge are excellent choices. Both have extensive military and law enforcement usage and a ton of parts and accessories available.

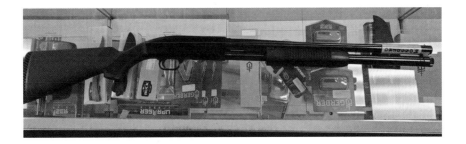

Ammunition

Your ammo is almost as important as what gun you fire it out of.

Ammunition should be stored in waterproof gasketed metal or plastic containers and stored in your gun safe or your ammunition safe if you have it. If you are storing ammunition in a removable magazine for more than a few days, never leave the magazine full. If the magazine holds ten rounds or less, take out one round; if it's eleven rounds or more, take out two. This prevents the spring from being compressed so long and far that it weakens over time and won't feed the ammunition into your gun properly.

A Final Word

Just remember, when a firearm is used safely and effectively by a properly trained person and stored in a safe way, it can be an asset, but that's the only time. We cannot stress this enough: If you do not feel comfortable with the idea of owning a firearm, don't own one. If there is already a firearm in your home and it isn't secured properly, secure it. If you decide to purchase a firearm, do it knowledgeably, confident in your commitment to safety at all times, and only when you and others with access are properly trained and properly equipped to secure it. Got it? Good.

ARE YOU READY?

_____ Are all locks on your property and in your home functional and well-maintained? Do you have dead bolts (preferably single-sided ones at entry doors as well)?

_____ Have you chosen and configured a safe room inside your home?

_____ Do you have wood wedges for all external doors and your internal safe room?

_____ Do all your windows have shatterproof glass, steel shutters, window film, or other reinforcements?

_____ Do sliding windows and doors have dowel bars?

_____ Do garage doors have slide locks or padlocks?

_____ Do you have adequate external lighting so you can see what's outside and who is coming or going?

_____ Do you have a security system with recording capability?

_____ Do you have a siren or strobe light to deter unwanted guests?

_____ Do you have a club safety device for your car?

_____ Do you have a dark blanket or privacy shade in your car?

_____ Have you practiced situational awareness exercises?

_____ Do you have at least a couple of sets of clothing that are *grey* and unremarkable so you can blend into a crowd?

_____ Is your car a neutral color and free from all bumper stickers or decoration?

_____ Have you read about and considered protective methods such as smoke bombs or body armor?

_____ Have you read about and considered carrying defensive sprays like mace or pepper spray?

_____ Do you know the weak points on the human body in case you are assaulted and must fight back?

IF YOU ARE GOING TO HAVE ACTIVE DEFENSIVE MEASURES LIKE OWNING A FIREARM, HAVE YOU:

_____ Considered thoughtfully what type of firearm and ammunition will serve your needs?

_____ Purchased and installed a gun safe prior to purchasing the weapon?

_____ Taken at least twelve hours of training in the weapon you will be using?

_____ Committed yourself to gun safety, educating all members of your household, locking the weapon at all times when it is not in use, and leaving it unloaded?

CHAPTER 7

DISASTERS

Before, During, and After

Not to be all doom and gloom, but it's not *if* you live in a disaster zone, it's *which* disaster zone(s) you live in. Climate change has ushered in an era of severe weather with unprecedented floods, storms, fires, mudslides, blizzards, and droughts. *#thankshumans*

Then there are the age-old events that work independently of climate, like earthquakes, volcanoes, and newer man-made catastrophes like nuclear accidents or chemical spills. We live our lives blissfully trying not to think about the consequences of these things because they're just not pleasant to think about. But here's where it's important to connect the dots; if you *do* think about these things and prepare for them, then you don't have to think about them as much. And when a disaster does happen, you'll be able to handle it better, and you'll thank yourself for taking care of you and your people ahead of time.

CUSTOMIZE YOUR PLAN

If you haven't already, it's critical that you take a good hard look at where you live and figure out which emergencies you are most likely to face so you can be prepared.

You probably don't need to be blizzard ready if you live in Honolulu, but try to think outside normal and make sure you are ready for "the big one," whatever that may be.

It's important to remember that these tips, tricks, and to-dos are all *in addition* to everything you've learned so far about basic preparedness—food, water, organization, shelter, security, and well-being.

FIND YOUR DISASTER ZONES

Earthquake Zone

Frequency of Damaging Earthquakes Shaking Around the U.S.

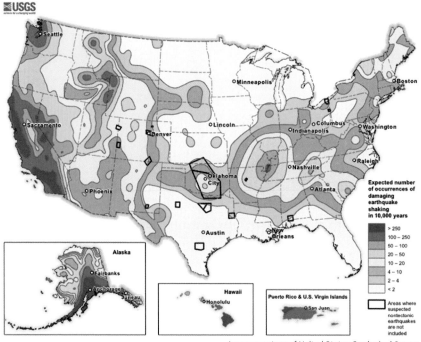

Image courtesy of United States Geological Survey.

Study this map. You may expect earthquakes in California, or Alaska, or Hawaii. But if you live in Missouri, Arkansas, Tennessee, Kentucky, Illinois, Washington, Utah, Oregon, or South Carolina, are you earthquake-ready? You should be.

Believe it or not, one of the largest earthquakes recorded in the continental United States happened in what is now Missouri. The year was 1811 and the magnitude was an unfathomable 8.2. Reports at the time told of the Mississippi River flowing backward and the shaking was so severe it rang church bells in Boston. Why haven't most people heard of it? Because there were few buildings and few people inhabiting the area at the time. Today with big cities, skyscrapers not retrofitted for earthquake resistance, and dense population zones, an earthquake like that would be absolutely devastating.

Because of the soft soils of the region, the effects would be far-reaching. Think Chicago, St. Louis, Memphis, Nashville, Indianapolis, Kansas City, and Cincinnati, just to name the big ones. Damage could even occur far beyond those boundaries if the quake were large enough.

But what are the odds? The US Geological Survey has calculated them, and they're going to make you want to start preparing now. For an earthquake with a magnitude of 7.5 to 8.0, the probability for occurrence is approximately 7–10 percent over the next fifty years. For a quake of 6.0 to 7.0, the probability is a whopping 28–46 percent over the next fifty years.

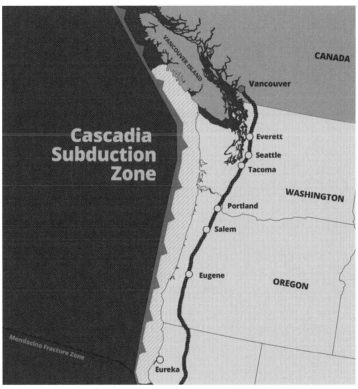

Image courtesy of National Weather Service.

On the West Coast, the San Andreas fault may get all the press, but the Cascadia fault which stretches for 680 miles off the coast of Oregon, Washington, and British Columbia could pose a much deadlier threat. A monster earthquake with astronomical magnitude happens there every few hundred years. The last one, in 1700, created a tsunami that made it all the way to Japan, causing coastal damage. And back in 1700, there was no Portland, no Seattle, no Vancouver. These modern and densely populated areas, just like the Midwest, haven't been built for earthquakes. We're already overdue for another big one, and some research puts the probability of a magnitude 8.0 or greater earthquake on the Cascadia fault as high as 75 percent in the next fifty years.

We're not trying to freak you out, but understanding dangers will help you be prepared for them, and there's nothing worse than the one you weren't expecting.

The bottom line is: you may live in an earthquake zone even if you don't think you live in an earthquake zone. So here's what you do, above and beyond what we've covered so far, to be ready.

Earthquake Preparedness List

- Make sure your furnace, hot water heater, and other utilities have earthquake straps that wrap around them and anchor them to the wall.
- Anchor bookcases and large or heavy furniture to a stud in the wall.
- Use museum putty to stick that heirloom vase to the shelf, and *don't hang a big, heavy anything over your bed*. Framed art or a chandelier in the face is not the wake-up call you want.
- Be very familiar with how to turn off your utilities, and make sure you have non-sparking tools to do it with.
- Some companies make earthquake sensors that will automatically turn off natural gas in a home if it detects significant shaking. Gas companies recommend that only trained professionals install those devices, but you may want to look into it if you are in the zone.
- Think about getting a bottle jack or high-lift jack to move heavy debris or trees.
- Add a battery-powered chain saw to your tool list if you are in a suburban or rural area.
- Don't ever store heavy things in high places.

- Have a portable hand-crank or battery-operated radio or TV to keep on top of emergency alerts.
- Keep an emergency whistle at work, in your car, and in your bedroom to signal rescue workers.
- Make sure all pets are microchipped and that the microchip is registered to your current address.
- Do an emergency earthquake hazard check and take note of heavy furniture, cabinets that could swing open, heavy things that could fall, the location of heavy masonry chimneys that could collapse, and other potential sources of injury. Most injuries and deaths caused by earthquakes come from falling objects—inside and outside.
- Know the location of emergency shelters near you.
- Download the Red Cross Emergency App by texting *GetEmergency* to 90999 or install it free from the App Store or Google Play. The Emergency app has an *I'm Safe* button you can click to update your social media accounts so family and friends know you're safe.
- Download the Red Cross First Aid App by texting *GetFirst* to 90999, or by downloading it free from the App Store or Google Play.

What to Do During an Earthquake

- If an earthquake strikes, FEMA says *Drop, Cover, and Hold On*. Get down on your hands and knees and cover your head and neck with your arms. The safest places to be are under a sturdy table or desk or against an inside wall, so crawl there if you can. Get to the closest safe spot and don't move around during an earthquake. Find those places at home and at work and discuss them with coworkers and family members.
- If you are outside, stay away from power lines, trees, buildings, bridges, and other structures that may collapse.
- If you are in your car, pull over to a safe open space on the side of the road as soon as possible and stay in your car.
- Only use your phone for emergencies.
- Be prepared for aftershocks that may cause additional damage. They almost always happen after a large quake and can be large themselves. So take advantage of the few minutes you may have after the first quake to find a safe spot if you weren't able to before.
- Review *ready.gov/earthquakes* to be fully informed.

You Haven't Thought of Everything

I was at work and about six miles from the epicenter of the huge 7.1 magnitude earthquake that hit Anchorage, Alaska, in November of 2018. I'd been through a lot of earthquakes, but this one felt like the world was ending! Almost immediately, cell service went down and I barely had time to post to social media that I was okay so family wouldn't worry. Aftershocks began minutes after the main event. The first one was a 5.7 and even closer to me than the first. Roads and overpasses by the airport and north of Anchorage buckled. Air and land traffic were disrupted. Parents were in a panic trying to pick kids up at schools. Luckily and miraculously no deaths were reported, and there were only minor injuries. I was lucky enough to have an artesian well that flowed even without the use of a pump so I hadn't been keeping a very large stockpile of water, because I was covered, or so I thought! The shaking of the ground disturbed the aquifer so much that my water ran orangey-brown for almost a week until all the particles in the natural reservoir had time to settle back down. Lesson learned. Even when you think you've thought of everything, you haven't thought of everything. And it is always better to have more water than you think you need!

Jeanne

My local grocery store with shattered windows and rubble from the storefront on the sidewalk, and well water full of sediment.

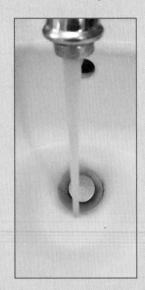

After an Earthquake

- Get out of a damaged building if you are in one, and don't enter damaged buildings.
- If you are trapped, bang on a pipe or a wall, send a text, or use your emergency whistle.
- If you are in a coastal area, listen for tsunami warnings and get to higher ground if needed.
- Treat yourself and others for injuries if you can. Seek advice from your healthcare provider, or call 911 in an emergency.
- If you fear your home or utilities have been compromised, shut them off. Call the gas company if you smell gas.
- Listen to the news media for information and instructions.
- Communicate via text with loved ones rather than voice-call.
- Be careful during cleanup. Wear protective clothes, wear a mask, don't touch floodwater or mold. Keep children, those with lung problems or other serious conditions, and elders out of the clean-up zone.
- Drink your stored water until you are sure your tap water is safe to drink.

Flood Zone

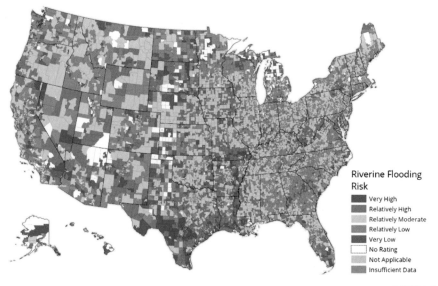

Riverine Flooding Risk

- Very High
- Relatively High
- Relatively Moderate
- Relatively Low
- Very Low
- No Rating
- Not Applicable
- Insufficient Data

Image courtesy of FEMA.

To find out how likely it is you may experience flooding and to determine your official flood zone, go to *floodsmart.gov* to find maps, flood zones, and contact information if you have questions.

Flood and Storm Surge Preparedness List

- Sign up for local alerts and monitor news reports.
- Learn evacuation routes, and the best way to get to high ground.
- Get flood insurance. Most homeowners' policies do not cover flooding, but even if you live in a low-to-moderate flood risk area, you are five times more likely to have a flood than a fire!
- Evaluate your property and make sure there is adequate drainage away from your house.
- If you've got about ten thousand dollars to spare, check out the AquaDam which is becoming more popular in flood-prone areas. It's a giant tube you pump full of water to encircle your house, creating a barrier for up to three feet of water, leaving your house and belongings dry. Spendy, yes, but if you're pretty sure you're a sitting duck for a flood, it might be worth it![*]
- Have a stack of empty sandbags stashed in the closet in case you need to fill them and stack them to hold back water.
- Make sure your boiler, air-conditioning unit, and other utilities are elevated off the floor.
- Think about installing a sewage backflow prevention valve (that sounds like a good investment already, doesn't it?).
- Use the heck out of flood-proofing sealants in your basement to keep the water out.
- Move your most valuable and sentimental items to the highest point in the house. In a hurricane, if you are worried about losing a roof, store them one floor down.
- Have irreplaceable photos and documents in waterproof bags and make digital copies to store in a water-resistant safe on the top floor, and in the cloud.
- Invest in a sump pump or other pumping system.

---

[*] https://www.wideopencountry.com/houston-man-uses-massive-inflatable-dam-save-house/

- Have some good strong fans and at least one big dehumidifier so you can dry everything out fast to avoid illness-causing mold and mildew.
- Have a good tall pair of rubber boots, hip waders, or chest waders.
- Make sure all pets are microchipped and that the microchip is registered to your current address.

What to Do During a Flood

- Evacuate immediately if officials call for evacuation and use designated evacuation routes.
- Don't wade or drive in floodwaters.
- Don't drink tap water until you know it's safe. Use your stored water.
- Do not use electrical equipment if it is wet or while you are standing in water.
- Stay out of floodwater as much as possible, and wash your hands well with soap and water or use hand sanitizer if you have come in contact with it.
- Dispose of any food that has come in contact with flood water.
- If water is entering your home, turn off the power while you can still do so from a dry location. *Never* turn power on or off yourself or use electric tools or appliances while standing in water.
- If you smell gas or suspect a leak, turn off the main gas valve, open all windows, and leave your house immediately if you can do so safely. Notify the gas company and the police or fire department. Do not turn on the lights or do anything that could cause a spark. If you leave, do not return until you are told it is safe to do so.

After a Flood

- As soon as possible ventilate your home. Open all windows and create as much air circulation as possible.
- Have an electrician check the house's electrical system before turning the power on again.
- If the house has been closed up for several days, enter briefly to open doors and windows to let the house air out for a while (at least thirty minutes) before you stay for any length of time. Wear an N95 or KN95 mask when in the house.

- If your home has been flooded and has been closed up for several days, assume your home has mold.
- Discard anything absorbent, like mattresses, pillows, and stuffed upholstered furniture that has come in contact with floodwater.
- Follow local guidance on whether your water is safe to drink, or what to do to treat it, and use your own stores of water or bottled water until you know tap water is safe.
- Get instructions from the utility company about using electrical equipment, including power generators. If a generator is online when electrical service is restored, it can become a major fire hazard and endanger line workers who are working to restore power.
- Have an electrician check appliances to make sure they are completely dry and can be safely operated before you use them.
- Once an electrician has told you it's safe to use electricity, turn on your sump pump, or use a wet/dry shop vac to remove water. Wear rubber boots when you do this.
- If you are using a generator or any other gasoline-powered tools, make sure they are outside your house and more than twenty feet away from the house and not near vents, garage, or any kind of air intake.
- Set up fans in windows to blow the air from the inside to the outside to get rid of moisture and mold.
- Use dehumidifiers where possible.
- Have your home heating, ventilating, and air-conditioning (HVAC) system checked and cleaned by a maintenance or service professional who is experienced in mold cleanup before you turn it on so you don't contaminate the whole house with mold.

Hurricane Zone

No matter what map you look at, remember that any information about hurricane frequency, severity, and reach, is already outdated. Climate change is increasing all of those things, and it's moving at a more accelerated pace than we first feared.

You know how they do the alphabetical list of hurricane names every year? In 2020, they started with Hurricane Arthur, then Bertha, then Cristobal, but after they went through the whole alphabet and got to tropical storm Zeta they actually ran out of names and had to start using Greek letters, giving the 2020 Atlantic hurricane season the largest number of named storms on record. Rising sea levels and heavier downpours mean higher flood risks during these storms and a wider reach into areas that normally haven't been affected. If you're on the map, whatever you think your risk is, bump it up a notch or two.

One thing on your side if you live in a hurricane zone is that you usually know when one is coming and have a little time to prepare. You'll be able to double-check your preparedness and food and water supplies for people and pets and make sure they are ready to go.

Hurricane Preparedness List
- Prepare as you would for a flood (above).
- Make sure your roof is rated for high winds.
- Be sure your property is landscaped and situated for maximum drainage so your basement doesn't flood.
- Keep trees pruned and healthy. Have a professional remove dead or diseased branches, and keep trees away from the house if you can.
- Sign up for local alerts and monitor news reports for storm development, warnings, and notifications.
- Locate the nearest shelter and different routes you can take to get there from your home.
- Fill your car's gas tank and put it in the garage, under a carport, or as sheltered as possible.
- Bring loose items inside like bicycles, patio furniture, garbage cans, and outdoor toys. Anchor items like barbecue grills, fuel tanks, swing sets, and other items that are unsafe or impossible to bring in.
- Put documents and valuables in waterproof bags.
- Get a NOAA weather radio or hand-crank emergency radio.
- Have pre-cut and labeled plywood to screw over windows, screws, and a cordless drill.
- Be ready to turn off your power. If you see flooding, downed power lines, or you have to leave your home, switch your power off.
- Get carbon monoxide detectors and make sure they are working.
- Consider constructing a *safe room* that meets FEMA criteria or a storm shelter that meets ICC 500 criteria.

- If you are in a suburban or rural area, think about getting a battery-powered chainsaw and a bottle jack to move heavy debris.
- Learn evacuation routes, and use them as soon as possible when instructed.
- Read the Flood Zone section above. If you are close to a water body, be prepared for a storm surge.

What to Do During a Hurricane

- Listen for official alerts which will tell you whether to shelter in place or evacuate. Always follow the instructions, and if you are told to evacuate, do it as soon as possible.
- Close and lock all windows, doors, and access to the outside.
- Bring all pets inside.
- Stay away from windows and doors, especially if they are not boarded up.
- Go to the safest spot in your house, as close to the center as you can, far from exterior walls and midway between roof and basement. This could be in a closet or interior bathroom.
- Have as much of what you need as possible in your safe room: other people, first aid kit, food, water, makeshift toilet, emergency radio, pets and pet supplies, blankets and pillows, flashlights, extra batteries, charged cell phones and battery pack, a deck of cards, medications, diapers, a change of clothes.
- Don't go outside even if things have calmed. You may be in the eye of the storm which means it's going to come back. Wait until there's an official announcement of safety.

After a Hurricane

- If your area is flooded, follow all of the flood instructions above.
- If your carbon monoxide detector is beeping, get everyone out of the house immediately and call 911.
- If you hear your structure making strange noises like groaning or shifting, get everyone out of the building. Noises may be a sign of impending collapse.
- Stay away from fallen power lines and report them to your local electrical utility.

- If you've had a power outage, dispose of food that has not had adequate refrigeration.
- Treat any wounds, even small ones, and make sure you prevent infection.
- Contact family and friends via text to let them know you are safe.

Volcano, Supervolcano, and Impact Zone

Meet the supervillains of natural disasters that can not only ruin your day, but potentially annihilate a big chunk of life on earth. Volcanic super-eruptions and space rock impacts may not be your first concern when preparing for natural disasters, but they do happen. And when they do, the aftereffects can be planet-wide.

The chances of a giant asteroid hitting Earth are pretty small. Nevertheless, NASA is hard at work studying the sky and figuring out ways to change the course of an asteroid if it looks like a large impact is likely. We won't candy coat this. If a giant asteroid lands on your house, there's no amount of canned beans and filtered water that will save you. But most people won't be at ground zero. Most will be dealing with the same problem as the aftereffect of a supervolcano—ash being thrown into the atmosphere keeping the sun from warming it and lowering global temperatures suddenly and drastically. Yes, global warming is real, but don't hope for a meteorite strike or a massive eruption to fix it. They just cause a whole other set of problems like crop failures, famine, and mass extinction.

Although both scenarios are rare, the supervolcano is far more likely. The most famous supervolcano site is probably the one in Yellowstone National Park in Wyoming. It has erupted three times in the past two million years, and the last time was 600,000 years ago. Unfortunately, there's no way to know for sure whether the next time will be in another one hundred thousand years, or next week, and throwing offerings or your mortal enemies into the cone won't appease it if it's ready to blow. Geologists tell us there's not enough magma built up to make Yellowstone an imminent threat right now, so fingers crossed they're right.

And don't forget, there are 161 potentially active *regular* volcanoes in the US that can wreak havoc despite their non-super status. Definitely be prepared if you live in Alaska, Hawaii, California, Washington, or Oregon. Other states and territories, and adjacent areas can also be affected depending on the amount of ash and direction of the wind. So, it makes sense to be prepared, even if you don't live on the slope of Vesuvius.

Ash Event Preparedness List

- Stockpiling food and water is critical because sheltering in place is the most likely action you'll be taking.
- Know safe places and evacuation routes in case you need them.
- Have enough HEPA filter units and replacement filters to keep the air in your home clean and breathable.
- Have a good supply of N95 or KN95 masks for all family members.
- Have good eye protection for all family members.
- Have a couple of pairs of large-sized nylon stockings. Cut one leg off and put it over your car's air filter if there is a lot of ash in the air. This will save your air filter from clogging and becoming ineffective. Change the stockings regularly.

What to Do During an Ash Event

- Close all doors, windows, and fireplace dampers; turn off fans, air conditioners, vents or anything bringing air into the house.
- Bring all people and pets inside.
- Prepare to hunker down.
- Do not go outside unless authorities have told you to evacuate because of a tsunami warning, lava flow, or other imminent threat to your physical health.
- If you *are* told to evacuate, do it as soon as possible and follow established evacuation routes.
- Follow evacuation plans if necessary and make sure everyone is wearing a properly fitted N95 or KN95 mask if you have to leave.
- Remove contact lenses that can trap irritants against your eye. Wear glasses instead.

After an Ash Event

- Go as long as possible without leaving your home, especially if road maintenance or traffic is continuing to kick up ash.
- Hold off from operating your car or other vehicle as long as possible to avoid internal damage.

- Do your best if going outside not to disrupt ash or kick up clouds.
- Do not let children or pets play in the ash.
- Always wear an N95 or KN95 mask until it is safe to breathe without one.
- Don't clean off your car or other important items with a sponge or rag. Ash is abrasive, so it's best to use a stream of water if you can.
- Check and replace air filters in vehicles and HEPA filtration systems often.
- Take extra care to prevent the elderly or those with respiratory conditions or illnesses from inhaling ash.
- You can continue to harvest and eat garden produce, just wash it thoroughly first, and preferably before bringing it into the house.
- Avoid areas downwind of the volcano or impact event where ash is likely to have accumulated heavily.
- Do not try to remove ash from your roof yourself unless you have been properly trained. Ash can be very slippery and is best removed by a professional.
- Do be aware that if it rains, ash can become very heavy and if there's a significant ash fall, there may be a danger of roof collapse if it isn't removed quickly.

Tornado Zone

We're not just talking Tornado Alley; if you live in it, you've heard of it. That's an area of the central United States where tornadoes happen *a lot*. It refers roughly to the areas of Nebraska, Iowa, South Dakota, Oklahoma, Kansas, Texas, and Louisiana. But looking at the map below gives *Tornado Alley* a much broader reach. Mississippi, Alabama, Arkansas, and Tennessee are solidly in the red zone, and many of the surrounding states are vulnerable too. If you live in an area where tornadoes are possible, but you've never really thought about how to prepare for one or what to do, here's your chance!

Before we get started, make sure you know the difference between a tornado watch and a tornado warning!

A TORNADO WATCH means, be prepared. Double check all your supplies and move them to your safe room. Move objects outside that could become flying projectiles. Shutter and close windows. Close and deadbolt all doors.

Contact loved ones and make sure they know to follow the emergency plan or locate a space where they can safely shelter. Get your ducks in a row.

A TORNADO WARNING means there is imminent danger to life and property because a tornado has been spotted in the immediate area. It means act now! Get to your safe room or shelter with family members right away and prepare for the worst. There's no time for any more preparations; just get to a safe space!

Tornado Preparedness List

- Know the name of the county or parish where you live. Tornado warnings are usually issued by those localities. Make sure everyone in the family knows this information.
- Be very familiar with how to turn off your utilities, including gas, electric, and water.
- Make sure you always have a battery-operated or hand-crank radio or other device so you can listen to the latest information.
- Choose a safe shelter in your home ahead of time. Tornado or storm shelters are ideal, followed by the center of the basement away from any windows, or a windowless room on the lower floor of your house. This could be a bathroom, a closet, or a hallway.
- Make sure your safe room is stocked with (or located near) water and food, your hand-crank radio, flashlight, medications, a first aid kit, sturdy shoes and clothing, and anything else you will need.
- You can purchase a professionally installed tornado shelter, but ensure the firm is reputable and that all materials are wind- and impact-resistant.
- Install a roof that is rated for high winds, and includes hurricane clips to help prevent it from being ripped off.
- Make sure all entry doors to your home have a two-inch dead bolt lock, three hinges, and that the framing is secure. That means drill into both the wall framing and the floor with screws that are longer than standard framing screws to keep the door from being pulled out of the framing.
- Brace your garage doors. You can do this when you know a threat is coming by installing a wooden brace cut to fit the framing of the wall

and the floor. But better still, have wood or metal bracing installed professionally before a tornado hits. A compromised garage door can lead to massive damage to your house.

- Reinforce your windows. You can install impact-resistant windows, storm shutters or roller blinds, or cut plywood to screw in over your windows. Again, preparing in advance is much better than trying to cover your windows during a tornado watch or warning.
- Have a heavy-duty document safe bolted to the basement floor where you store all your important papers and documents. Also have these documents on a thumb drive. Include a few hundred dollars in cash if you can, in case banks and ATMs are not available or functioning.
- Have an emergency plan for your family. If you live in a mobile home, make sure the plan includes a friend's or neighbor's home, or another secure location or shelter nearby. Do not stay in a mobile home, even if it is secured to the ground.
- Make sure that your child's school or elderly relatives' care facility has an emergency plan and know what that is.
- Take a basic first aid and CPR class.

What to Do During a Tornado

- Be diligent about monitoring conditions in your area. Watch TV, or the internet, or use your hand-crank or battery-operated radio.
- Sometimes tornados will happen without an official warning. Keep alert for weather conditions that could indicate a tornado in your area: large dark clouds, hail, a dark or greenish sky, and a roaring sound. Take cover right away if you notice them.
- Get to your shelter or safe room with family members and pets as soon as possible.
- If you are in your car, or outside unable to get to your shelter, find the nearest sturdy building and get inside to a safe location away from windows. Choose a small room in the center or basement of the building.
- If you can, shelter under a sturdy table or bench, or cover yourself with a mattress or blankets.

- If you can do so safely, alert others in your area if you have seen or heard a tornado, even if it isn't in the immediate area.
- If you are outside and aren't near buildings, find a low-lying area like a gully or a ditch, lie flat on the ground, and cover your head with your arms.

After a Tornado

- If you are able, assist anyone who may be injured or trapped.
- Give simple first aid to yourself and others, but do not try to move anyone who is seriously injured unless they are at risk of death or further injury.
- Do not enter damaged buildings. Get out of the building you are in if it is damaged or if you smell gas, fumes, or a chemical smell.
- Continue to monitor the latest emergency information. Weather conditions may create more than one tornado. Stay alert.
- Use the phone only for emergencies and use text and social media to tell loved ones you are safe.
- Once you know you are safe from any tornado threat, assess your shelter. Wear long sleeves, long pants, and sturdy footwear. Check to be sure utilities have not been compromised and clean up small spills of gasoline or flammable liquids.
- If you smell gas, hear a hissing noise, or have any reason to suspect a gas leak, turn the gas off at the main valve.
- If you see broken or frayed wires, or see sparks, shut off your main electrical breaker. Seek professional help if you can't do this without walking through water.
- If you smell or see sewage, flooding, or damaged water pipes, shut off the water and don't drink from the tap. Use your stored water or melt ice cubes.
- Avoid downed power lines and report any you see to the electric utility or 911.
- Help your neighbors with immediate needs if you can.
- Beware of insurance scammers who take advantage of catastrophes in damaged areas.
- Take photos of all damage as soon as possible for filing an insurance claim.

Heat Zone

U.S. Annual Temperature Compared to 20th-Century Average

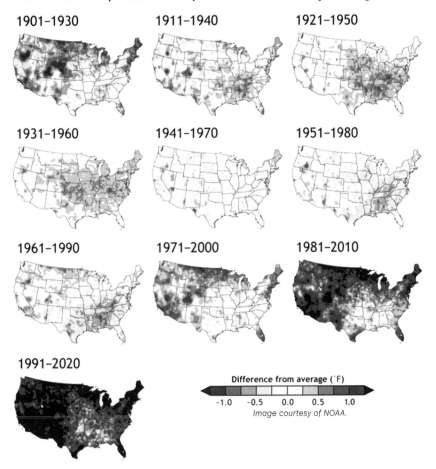

1901-1930   1911-1940   1921-1950

1931-1960   1941-1970   1951-1980

1961-1990   1971-2000   1981-2010

1991-2020

Difference from average (°F)

-1.0   -0.5   0.0   0.5   1.0

Image courtesy of NOAA.

If you haven't noticed the planet's warming trend in the last decade, we've got bad news for you. Extreme heat is going to become normal life for many of us and being prepared will be critical. Recent analyses show that the rate of warming of the planet is far exceeding previous predictive models, with large areas of the world destined to become uninhabitable in the coming decades. Even if we could snap our fingers and stop all CO_2 emissions right now, it would still take years before things stabilize. There's no getting out of it, there's only getting through it. Here's the down and dirty about what you need to be prepared for during a dangerous heat wave, and live to make it to the other side.

Heat Wave Preparedness List

- Be prepared for a power outage. Electrical grids get overtaxed when everyone is home and running an air conditioner.
- Have a secondary source of power in case the electrical grid goes down. Air-conditioning, water pumps, and refrigeration are all reliant on the power grid.
- Before the hot season, check that your refrigerator, freezer, fans, and air conditioners are all working well. Change filters as needed and vacuum the condenser coils on your fridge. Wipe down the gaskets too and make sure the seal is good.
- When you are thinking about purchasing a home, or renting one, take the architecture of the building into consideration. Stone or masonry buildings stay cooler. Stone or tile floors are cooler than carpet. Look for a place with natural shade, lots of cross-ventilation, high ceilings, and energy-efficient windows.
- Take a first aid class that covers the signs, symptoms, and treatment of heat exhaustion and heat stroke.
- Be sure you have several box fans.
- Have a bunch of cool packs in the refrigerator or freezer to help you and other members of your household cool down.
- Use LED light bulbs when possible. They produce 70 percent less heat than standard incandescent light bulbs.
- Make sure your house is properly insulated. Proper insulation will not only keep you warmer in winter, but cooler in summer!
- Invest in thick light-colored curtains, blackout shades, blinds, window shutters, or rolling shutters to block out the sun. Avoid metal venetian blinds which can absorb heat and transmit it into the room.
- Consider getting a window unit air conditioner or an energy-efficient mobile unit to keep one room or living area of your home cool. Remember you don't need to keep the whole house at 68 degrees. But it makes sense if you live in an area where temperatures can get dangerously high to have something that will cool you off.
- If you have a medical condition, talk to your doctor ahead of time and find out how the heat may affect your condition, and if any prescriptions you are taking will be affected.

- Have a buddy system and someone to check in with to make sure you are doing okay.

What to Do During a Heat Wave

- Try not to overtax the electrical grid which could cause outages. Keep your existing air-conditioning at 77 or 78 instead of 70 degrees or use a low-energy portable unit. You'll be fine if you follow these other hot-weather hacks.
- Look at the weather forecast. When the evening starts to bring cooler air, open all your windows and let the house cool off at night. Then when the sun comes up, pull curtains, close shutters and blinds, and keep out as much sun as you can. Your space will stay much cooler throughout the day. Then when it starts to cool off outside, repeat the cycle. This is how Europe, where the vast majority of buildings have no air-conditioning, survives during summer.
- You know how aluminum foil keeps food from burning even in an oven? It will do the same for you as an improvised window cover! Put the shiny side out to reflect the light and heat and wrap a layer of foil around a piece of cardboard cut to fit your window. This works especially well on older and single-pane windows. You can keep a room 20 degrees cooler than the outside this way.
- Hydrate regularly! Drink more than you think you need. Your body and internal organs will be stressed out and being properly hydrated will reduce strain on your heart and kidneys and keep you from getting dehydrated, or worse.
- Keep all pets indoors unless they have to go out. Once business is done, get them back in the house!
- Now is not the time for beef Wellington or a whole roasted turkey! Keep your oven off and go for lighter, high-water content foods like fruits and salads. Cold sandwiches and other fridge foods will do the trick, and they won't overtax your digestive system.
- If you do want warm food, try to run the oven at night when temperatures are cool and then reheat your meal in the microwave or on the stovetop the next day. Also, figure out what foods you normally cook in the oven or in boiling water, and see if you can figure out how

to use the microwave or outdoor grill instead. Microwaved baked potatoes and corn on the cob anyone?

• And speaking of heat, the other kind of hot food—spicy hot—may be worth trying. Foods that make you sweat will actually cool you off, if that's your thing! Think about hot sweltering places like Mexico, Thailand, and India. They know what they're doing!

• Rest! There's a reason siestas are a thing in warm climates. Keep your body still and at rest and it's less likely to show the physical signs of heat stress.

• Unplug! If you aren't using a device or appliance, unplug it; not your fridge of course, but laptops, microwaves, or other devices. Anything that stays plugged in is an energy vampire and is raising your electric bill and putting stress on the grid, even when it's switched off, and some of them are constantly putting out low-level heat. Connect several things to one power strip to make unplugging simple.

• Turn off unnecessary lights. Every light bulb you have is a little heating unit. Replace standard incandescent bulbs with compact fluorescents, and keep the halogen bulbs off altogether.

• Dress for warm weather. Wear breathable fabrics designed for warm-weather use. Sandals, loose shorts, and sleeveless tops are your friends. Baseball hats, socks and sneakers, and long sleeves and pants are not. And if you have long hair, it's ponytail time. Wear light colors that reflect heat, rather than dark colors that absorb heat.

• If you are outside, avoid sunburn that can mess with your body's ability to cool itself. Wear sunglasses, a straw hat with a brim or visor, and a good sunblock of at least 20 SPF that offers either broad spectrum or UVA/UVB protection.

• Take cool showers during the hottest part of the day. Even better, take them in your bathing suit or shorts and a T-shirt and keep those cool damp clothes on for a while.

• Put a big bowl of ice in front of your portable fan and blow air across the ice and onto you. It's low-tech but it works as it circulates cold air around the room. Mini-glacier!

• Put a bottle of water with a spray nozzle in the fridge and use it to mist your skin when you are feeling hot.

- Run major appliances like dishwashers, washing machines, and clothes driers at night when the windows are open. You can put up a clothesline indoors or outdoors and hang clothes to dry.
- Freeze your sheets! This is as amazing as it sounds. An hour before bedtime, take your sheets off the bed, fold them and put them in a gallon size ziplock bag or airtight container, then toss them in the freezer. Then when you're ready to crash, make the bed quickly and hop in. Ahhhh.
- Make a cold compress. Fill a sock with rice, tie the sock with a zip tie or string, and freeze it for two hours before bedtime. Then hold it, put it on your neck, or take it to bed with you! The rice will retain cold for a long time.
- Hang out in a cave! Humans have been doing that since there were humans because underground dwellings tend to retain a pretty constant temperature of (depending where the cave is located) between 50 and 70°F. But okay, we get it. You're not near a cave and you don't want to relocate to one. But use that principle and find places to hang out like basements or stone buildings or places that are naturally cool. Supermarkets and movie theaters work too!
- If the power is out or you have no other AC, try air-conditioning like ancient Egyptians, Greeks, and Romans. Create a cooling draft by hanging a damp sheet or other fabric in windows and doorways. Enjoy the nice cool breeze when the air comes in.
- Limit outdoor work or chores to early morning or evening. If you are outside performing physical activity, stay out of the sunlight and drink two to three cups of cool water every hour. Don't drink anything with sugar, caffeine, or alcohol that can all cause your body to lose fluid.
- If you are perspiring a lot, you'll need to replace the salts you lose in sweat. This can be done with sports beverages or electrolyte tablets. If you are on a low-salt diet, consult with your doctor before adding high-salt beverages or supplements.
- Create a *cool room* in your house or apartment. Make it a room where you can also sleep. Choose one with north- or east-facing windows. Keep it dark, put a portable AC unit in it, or a bowl of ice and a fan, or whatever alternate method you choose. Small spaces are easier to climate control than big ones.

- Keep any prescription meds you are using at the designated temperature and refrigerated if necessary. Many prescription meds can become toxic or less effective in extreme heat.
- Check in on elderly family members and neighbors, or people with disabilities or other medical conditions, and share tips to stay cool. We are all in this together.

Blizzard Zone

Climate change doesn't only make things hotter. Just to mix it up a little, areas that aren't used to ice storms, blizzards, and sub-zero temperatures can get walloped harder than they're used to, and people who live there may be ill-prepared to deal with the unique challenges of cold-weather survival.

Winter Storm/Cold-Weather Preparedness List

- Get a small camp stove to use for outdoor cooking or melting snow for water.
- Have one or two good snow shovels and a big bag of ice melt.
- Make sure you've got good warm winter clothes and outerwear.
- Prioritize having a good secondary heat source.
- Get a set of ice cleats for each person in the family.
- Have a stash of fire starters or fat wood and a portable outdoor fire pit. Do not use a fire pit or other stove meant for outdoor use indoors, or a blizzard will not be the worst of your problems.
- Make sure hand and foot warmers are part of your emergency supplies at home and in the car, and that they haven't expired.
- Insulate all water lines that run along exterior walls to help keep pipes from freezing.
- Caulk and install weather stripping on all doors and windows.
- Make sure you have adequate insulation in the walls and attic and that your insulation hasn't settled over time. If it has, beef it up!
- Install storm windows or thermal-pane windows. If that's not in your budget or you live in a rental unit, you can cover windows with plastic from the inside.
- Make sure your roof isn't leaking.
- Prune tree branches that could fall on your roof during a storm.

- Fireplaces or woodstove chimneys should be inspected at least once a year and cleaned accordingly, especially if it's your backup heat source. Also, keep a fire extinguisher nearby, and have operational smoke and carbon monoxide detectors on every floor. Also, be sure you have a supply of wood!
- Reread the section about alternate heat sources and heating safety, and make sure if you use a secondary heat source of any kind that you are doing so safely and in accordance with the manufacturer's instructions.
- Have your furnace checked once a year before it starts to get cold. If you rent, ask the property owner if this is being done.
- If you or anyone in your home is sixty-five or older, keep an easy-to-read thermometer inside. Our ability to feel the cold can decrease with age and hypothermia can set in with temperatures in the forties. Keep the indoor temperature over fifty degrees and make sure everyone stays dry and out of the wind.
- Get your car winterized before it's actually winter. Have the radiator serviced if needed, check antifreeze, use wintertime wiper fluid, make sure you have good wintertime tires with tread, fill tires to recommended pressure levels, check the heater, window defroster, brakes and fluid, exhaust, oil, battery, and emergency flashers.
- Keep your gas tank as full as possible to keep ice from getting in the tank or fuel lines.
- Make sure your car emergency kit is fully stocked and add hats, coats, and mittens or gloves. Make sure gloves and boots are not too tight. Restricted blood flow can make extremities cold. Also add tow straps/chains, jumper cables, a battery charger, a good sturdy ice scraper, a portable/collapsible snow shovel, and a can for melting snow into water. And don't forget a big jug of kitty litter to give your back end some weight and to use under your tires to help get unstuck from ice and snow.
- Invest in a sturdy ladder and safety harness in case you have to shovel off the roof.
- Invest in good all-weather snow tires and chains if your area permits them.
- Winter storms often come with power outages so make sure you're ready with flashlights and spare batteries in addition to other alternate sources of heat and light that we've already covered.

- Take a first aid course that includes how to treat hypothermia and frostbite injury.
- Take a CPR course. Sometimes a victim of hypothermia who appears to be dead can still be revived when CPR is performed for a period of time.

What to Do During a Winter Storm

If you are home:

- Listen for weather updates on TV, the internet, or by using a hand-crank or battery-operated radio.
- Don't let snow accumulate around the tailpipe of your car or around outside utility areas. If ventilation is blocked, lethal exhaust can fill your car or home.
- When keeping sidewalks and driveway clear, remember that shoveling a small amount of snow many times is better than shoveling a lot of snow all at once (just ask a cardiologist).
- Run a small stream of water from your faucets to help keep pipes from freezing, especially if they run up an outside wall.
- Close draperies, and cover windows with blankets at night.
- Keep all pets inside as much as possible. If they have to go out, keep them on a leash.
- Avoid unnecessarily opening windows and doors. But do make sure you allow some ventilation if you are using a fireplace.
- Keep tabs on the inside temperature, especially if you have elders in the house. Reach out to elderly neighbors and make sure they are keeping warm.
- Make sure you are getting enough calories. Your needs will go up if you are cold or doing a lot of shoveling.
- Avoid alcohol and caffeine. They actually cause your body to lose heat. Sorry.

If you are stranded in your vehicle:

- Use a flare, tie a brightly colored piece of fabric to your vehicle, turn on an emergency strobe, set up reflective triangles ten feet and one hundred feet behind your vehicle, or whatever else you can do to make sure nobody hits your car.

- Staying in your car is probably the safest choice.
- Don't try to drive if you can't see, or if road conditions are dangerous.
- Stay awake so you can spot the signs of hypothermia and frostbite.
- Don't eat snow, yellow or otherwise. It will lower your body temperature.
- Huddle with other people or animals (not wild ones) for warmth.
- Make sure snow isn't covering your tailpipe (a carbon monoxide risk) and run the car for ten to fifteen minutes per hour. Crack a window a little bit for ventilation.
- Wrap yourself up in blankets, a tarp, newspaper, extra clothing, whatever you have that will keep your body heat next to your body.
- Bring anything you'll need from the trunk into the vehicle so you don't have to repeatedly get in and out.
- Keep moving your extremities to keep your circulation going and to stay warm.

After a Winter Storm

- When going outside, follow some basic clothing rules for keeping warm.
  - Mittens keep you warmer than gloves.
  - Several lighter layers will keep you warmer than just one thicker layer. (The inner layer should ideally be wool, polypropylene, or silk; the second layer should insulate you—try wool, down, or fleece; the outer layer should be wind and moisture resistant.)
  - Make sure outerwear is not too tight. Pockets of air between layers will act as an insulator.
  - Wear a hat. Your mother was right.
  - A scarf, or balaclava will help keep cheeks and nose from getting frostbitten.
  - Boots should not be tight. Find a boot rated for cold weather and make sure there's plenty of room around your toes, even when you're wearing socks.
- Don't get wet. You will get chilled more easily and be more vulnerable to hypothermia. That means sweating too! If you get sweaty shoveling or doing other outdoor tasks, come in, unlayer, dry off, and warm up before you go out again.

- Know the signs of hypothermia. If body temperature drops to 95.5 degrees, seek medical attention right away.
- Use a broom or shake small ornamental trees that are covered in snow, especially if they still have leaves. Snow is heavy and you could save them from snapping under the load.
- Take utmost care if you are shoveling your roof. Wear the proper safety gear, including a harness, and make sure your boots have sturdy treads and won't slip. Only shovel your roof if there's a dangerous amount of snow on it. Find out what the building code is for your area and how many pounds per square foot your roof can hold.
- Knock off any icicles that are hanging over areas where people will be. People can be seriously injured or even killed by falling icicles!
- If you will be walking on ice or slippery surfaces, wear cleats over the soles of your boots. They are small and simple but can literally save your life.
- Avoid traveling if you can, but if you must—either by foot or in a vehicle—tell someone where you are going, when you expect to be back, and how you will check in if possible. Prepare for your car, snowmobile, or truck to break down.
- If everything else is taken care of, and everybody is safe and sound, you should definitely make a snowman!

Wildfire Zone

Where there is heat, there is dryness, and where there is dryness, there is risk of wildfire. The Proceedings of the National Academy of Sciences published an assessment that estimates nearly fifty million homes are currently in the *wildland-urban interface* in the United States, a number increasing by one million houses every three years. And when a lot of dry fuel in the wildland part is next to the houses in the populated part, you don't have to work for the National Academy of Sciences to get it.

And not only do you need to protect your family, your home, and your personal belongings if you are in the wildfire zone, you have to protect everyone from the sometimes-catastrophic health effects that come from smoke.

Better for the Next Time

Climate change isn't just making things warmer. In the Northeast US, my town was hit hard by a hellacious winter storm in 2022. The snow came, then rain, then the river flooded and caused a logjam that closed the bridge and the only road out of town. Fortunately, a bunch of people with tractors and big farm equipment were able to clear it. But the power went out too, and many of my neighbors were not prepared. My house has solar panels which cover most electric needs, and we use propane fuel and have a killer backup generator that automatically switches on. So in my house all we had was a little blip not even enough to reset the clocks. My food stayed cold, my family stayed warm, and my lights stayed on. But was it a perfect storm prep? Nope. Turns out the giant trampoline in my yard wasn't secured well enough and took off like a rogue UFO, ripping boards out of the deck and destroying part of the fence. Luckily that's where it got stuck until I detached it after the storm. Are you always going to have everything right? Nope. But each time you need to use any of this disaster information, you get better for the next time.

Bill

The name of the game for wildfires is preparedness. The best thing you can do ahead of time is prepare your home and your yard, and make sure your family and animals are safe. You don't want to wait until the last minute to try to deal with this stuff. Fires can advance quickly, change direction, and start without warning (stupid campers, anyone?) so be diligent and get prepared right away. It can make all the difference.

Wildfire Preparedness List
- Create a fire-resistant structure. When you are buying or renovating a home, go for flame-resistant building materials.
  - Avoid wooden or vinyl siding or anything that will burn or melt and go for concrete board or stone/brick veneer if you can.
  - Steel framing is great for exterior walls, and you should avoid wood decking/patio material in favor of concrete, stone, or brick.

- Avoid complex roofing with lots of ridges, and make sure you use fireproof roofing material.
- Use fire-retardant paints inside and out.
- Use Class A roofing material like slate, asphalt with underlayment, or tile if possible. If you are using shakes or shingles, make sure they are pressure-treated and fire resistant.
- Equip your home with double-pane windows or shatterproof safety glass which will be less likely to break from severe heat.
- Install fire doors. They can keep you and your home safe from flames and smoke for up to an hour, which will give you time to plan an escape or get help.
- Install fire sprinklers.
- Use fireproof shutters over windows and glass doors to protect them from heat.
- Make sure any wood used in construction is treated with fire-retarding chemicals.
- Embers are your enemy. Windblown embers can enter anywhere your home is open to the outside. Enclose eaves, soffits, and other openings in your structure, and use a fine-mesh barrier to cover crawl space openings, vents, and anywhere else where there's an opening to your house. Installing eighth-inch mesh screening is suggested if you're in a wildfire-prone area, but there are no guarantees, so make sure that attics and crawl spaces aren't full of combustible things that could ignite easily. Also, place mesh around areas under porches or decks where sneaky embers could wreak havoc.
- If you have central air-conditioning, use high-efficiency filters and change them regularly.

- Make sure your driveway is wide enough for emergency vehicles to be able to access your home.
- Have a high-intensity emergency light so rescuers can find where you are in the dark or smoke.
- Clearly mark your house number and full address in large type at the road so it can be easily found by first responders if there is smoke.
- Use fire-resistant landscaping plants. Avoid trees that burn easily like pine, spruce, cedar, and anything with needles. These trees tend to

have a large amount of sap, grow close together, and have branches close to the ground—all disastrous and fast-burning in wildfire situations. Find out what kind of fire-resistant trees are natural to your area and consider planting them instead. As a general rule, fruit trees don't burn easily, and orchards are often used by firefighting teams as a preexisting firebreak. Avoid tall grasses too, and bark or other flammable mulch.

- Keep your gutters clear of plant debris like leaves, twigs, and needles which can burn.
- Be aware of your community's emergency plan and know where to go if an evacuation is called.
- Make sure everyone in your household knows the evacuation plan, and where your designated shelters and meetup places are. Have a plan for home, school, office, and other areas you frequent.
- Clear your yard of all combustibles like brush, twigs and leaves, fuel, wood piles, and trees to a minimum of fifty feet from your home. As a bonus, this not only protects you from wildfires, it provides additional visibility for you to see what is happening outside your home. If you are going to have trees, keep them small. Fruit trees provide beauty and food, and don't interfere with visibility or create a huge fire hazard.
- Make sure you have adequate spigots on the outside of your home. One on each side is ideal.
- Have a good sturdy ladder for outside use. It should be fiberglass, which will not conduct heat, so you don't fry your hands and melt your shoes. For security purposes it's a good idea to store the ladder inside so you aren't providing bad guys an easy way to get in your house, but make sure it's accessible when you need it. Make sure all bedrooms on upper floors have an escape ladder.
- Make sure each floor of your home and the garage have fire extinguishers and that everyone knows where they are and how to use them.
- Mount a hose reel with a non-kink hose next to each spigot. The hoses should be long enough to be able to reach and soak all areas of your property. Most homes will be protected by a seventy-five-foot hose. Make sure the hoses have brass nozzles. The simple twist-style brass nozzle has fewer moving parts and will outlast plastic sprayers.

- Set up a smoke-free room that can be closed off from outside air. Make sure all the doors and windows are closed and set up a portable HEPA air cleaner to make sure indoor pollution levels are low. Stay in this room as much as you can.
- Get fire insurance if you don't have it and make sure it's sufficient to cover what you have in case of total loss.
- Keep important documents and small precious objects in a fire-proof safe.
- Sign up for text or email alerts from local authorities that will notify you of the latest emergency and safety information and evacuation alerts. For alerts available in your area, do an internet search for your location and enter the keyword *alerts*.
- Have a hand-crank or battery-operated radio (with extra batteries) in case the grid goes down. Consider getting a NOAA Weather Radio All Hazards receiver which will broadcast alerts directly from the National Weather Service. Some NOAA radios are designed to work with external notification devices and can provide visual or vibrating alerts for the hard of hearing.
- Have a supply of N95 or KN95 masks to save your lungs from smoke damage if you are in a smoky area or have to go outside. Put several masks in the glove compartment of your car.
- Know multiple evacuation routes from your location, and have a safe place for you, family, and pets to stay that is located out of your area in case you need to leave home.
- Go to *www.smokeybear.com* (yes, really!) to make sure you're not the problem or are starting fires without meaning to. Be responsible and share your knowledge with others.
- Take a first aid training course that teaches you basic first aid and CPR.
- If you have firearms in your home, never store them loaded. A fire can discharge a firearm the same as if you pulled the trigger, putting you, your family, and firefighters at risk. Store all ammunition in a fire-resistant ammo can inside a gun safe, and make sure all guns are unloaded.
- Review your homeowner's or renter's insurance at least once a year. Make sure you have a current inventory of things in your home

by taking photos, or doing a video walkthrough of your home, making sure to remember things in drawers and cabinets. If you need to file a claim or request assistance, this information will be critical.

What to Do During a Wildfire

- Implement your family's emergency plan.
- Monitor the situation diligently using your community's text or email alerts, news broadcasts, or NOAA radio. Follow all alerts and instructions. Evacuate immediately if told to do so!
- Check in with neighbors in the area to make sure they are able to connect to alerts and stay informed.
- Keep all pets inside.
- Stay in touch with family and friends who are not with you via text or social media. Cell service may not be the most reliable form of communication in any disaster.
- Move food, water, and supplies to your safe room/zone and run your HEPA air cleaner. Monitor alerts and stay safe in an area with as little smoke pollution as possible. Close all doors and windows but leave them unlocked. Charge all cell phones and a battery block.
- Remove flammable shades and curtains from windows and move all furniture and flammable materials to the center of the room.
- Close all windows and doors but leave them unlocked.
- If you have central air-conditioning with an outside intake, set your system to "recirculate," and close the intake damper to keep your inside air cleaner.
- Attach all hoses to outside spigots and turn the spigots on so the water is controlled by the twist nozzle on your hoses.
- Turn off the gas main and your air-conditioning but leave outside lights and water on.
- Back your car into the garage and close all the windows. Close the garage door. If you have an automatic garage door opener, disconnect it so you can raise and lower it without power. Leave the keys on the driver's seat. Don't leave them in the ignition because it could drain your battery.

- Fill all sinks and tubs with water. Fill outdoor and indoor plastic garbage cans and buckets with water as extra reservoirs. You can also have a pile of soaked towels or rugs which can be useful in beating out embers or smothering a small fire.

If the fire has trapped you in your house:
- Call 911, provide your exact location and explain your current situation. If you are going to be in your safe room, explain where it is in the house and how to reach it. Follow their instructions.
- Turn on all lights, inside and out, and shine your emergency light out a window to make it easier for first responders to find you.
- Make sure all outside access points like doors and windows are closed but unlocked.
- Stay inside, away from outside walls and windows.

If you are trapped in a car or outside:
- Use your best judgment to decide if it's safer to remain in your car or to leave. How far are you from the fire? Is it coming your way? Are you surrounded by brush or trees? Are you somewhere you can be easily found and rescued?
- If you are deciding where to move your vehicle, stay away from fuel sources like wooded areas. Try to stay in an area with rocks or a gravel pad, on a roadway or parking lot, or near a water source.
- Wear an N95 or KN95 mask (that you have stored in your glove compartment).
- Set your air-conditioning to recirculate, and keep windows and doors closed.
- If the heat is intense, cover yourself with a wool blanket or coat. You can even cover yourself in dirt if there is no other option and you are outside in harm's way.
- Call 911 if you are in fear for your safety or if you become trapped. If possible, tell them your exact location. If you are not in an easily locatable place, try to geo locate your position on your phone. Follow their instructions.
- Drive slowly and with your lights on if visibility is poor.
- Be alert for other vehicles, fleeing people, and animals.

After a Wildfire

- Do not return home until authorities say it is safe to do so!
- Debris may be hot. Avoid hot ash, charred or smoldering trees and debris, and live embers. The ground may contain pockets of heat that could not only burn you but spark another fire. The less you move this material around, the better.
- During cleanup, wear protective clothing including a long-sleeved shirt, long pants, heat-resistant work gloves, and sturdy shoes with thick soles.
- Use an N-95 or KN95 mask or respirator to limit your exposure to smoke and ash. If you are going to be in an area with ash, you can wet it down to minimize flying dust particles. People with respiratory conditions should be very careful in areas with ash, dust, and smoke.
- Take photos of the damage to document it for insurance purposes. You can call your insurance company for instructions and assistance.
- Send text messages or use social media to reach out to family and friends. Only use voice calls for emergencies.
- Check in on neighbors and see if you can offer assistance or support.

Nuclear or Military Zone

It doesn't have to be an all-out nuclear war to cause a radiation disaster. Accidents, natural disasters, terrorist attacks on power plants, and dirty bombs are all situations that make us and our nuclear infrastructure vulnerable. More than 65 percent of Americans live within fifty miles of an active nuclear power plant. About 10 percent of Americans live within twenty miles. And many of those power plants are in areas that are considered a seismic hazard.

Three Mile Island, Chernobyl, Fukushima—all names that give us chills. But there have been more than a hundred nuclear accidents around the world since the 1950s, the majority of which occurred in the United States. All have happened despite efforts to support safe nuclear power. Some accidents were caused by human error, and others, like the tragedy at the Fukushima Daiichi plant, involved a massive earthquake and tsunami that ultimately led to the compromise of the reactor. In an age of climate change when weather events like typhoons and hurricanes become ever more severe, nuclear power plants—like every other piece of infrastructure out there—become more vulnerable.

Figure out how close you are to a nuclear power plant, military facility, or population center that could be the target for a nuclear strike, an accident, or sabotage.

Nuclear Disaster and Radiation Exposure Preparedness List

- Determine what the safest place in your home or workspace would be in case of nuclear fallout. You'll want to be as far away from outside walls and the roof of the building as possible with as much protection as possible. In-ground basements, if you have one, provide a lot of protection. If not, try a bathroom in the center of the house with no outside walls, or anywhere as far away from windows and outside doors as you can get.
- Have an emergency crank-radio that can provide you with information, which will be critical.
- Have a family plan. If you have kids in school, a spouse elsewhere, and a parent in a care facility, you will all need to stay where you are and seek shelter there. Going out looking for each other is dangerous and could result in radiation sickness or worse. Schools and healthcare facilities should have an emergency plan, but you can double-check to be sure.
- Have a stash of potassium iodide pills. If you are exposed to radiation, these can minimize internal damage to your thyroid.

What to Do During a Radiation Event

- Get to the safest place possible right away. If you're in your house or at work, go to your predetermined safe zone.
- If you're outside or in your car, put a mask on (or cover your face with cloth or a towel) and get inside a building as quickly as possible. Ideally, you'll want to choose a building with thick walls, made of stone, concrete, or brick, with a basement where you can shelter. But do the best you can with what's available immediately. Anything inside is better than anything outside.

- Think of radioactive particles like dust you can't see. They will be settling on everything so if you are outside, just before you enter a building *remove your outer layer of clothing and shoes* carefully and put them as far away from you as you can. This will remove about 90 percent of the contamination you are carrying. No one will care that you are in your underwear during a radiation event. They should be in their underwear too!

- Wash all parts of your body that were in contact with the air: face, hands, arms, hair. This will help limit your exposure and keep you from spreading radioactive contamination. Keep cuts and abrasions covered while washing so radioactive material doesn't enter the wound.

- Close and lock all windows, doors, vents, fireplace dampers, or anything that is open to the outside. Turn off forced-air heat. Seal your space as much as possible.

- If your pet is outside, get them inside if you can and wash them with shampoo or soap and water and rinse well. Wear gloves and a face mask while doing this, especially if you have a cat. Wash your own hands and face well when you're done.

- When sending a message to friends and family, use text rather than your phone. It's more likely that your message will get through.

- Plan to shelter in place for at least twenty-four hours or until authorities tell you it's safe to come out or when a rescue plan is implemented. That means pets too, so shred some newspapers or use pee pads for your dog.

After a Radiation Event

- If your radiation exposure is the result of a nuclear reactor accident, take potassium iodide. This will help protect your thyroid gland from absorbing deadly radioiodines that could be released in a nuclear accident. It works best when taken within three or four hours of exposure, so take it as soon as you can after exposure to radiation. It is available without a prescription but check with your doctor first.

- The FDA recommends the following:

RECOMMENDED DOSES OF KI FOR THRESHOLD THYROID RADIOACTIVE EXPOSURES

	Predicted Thyroid gland exposure (cGy)	KI dose (mg)	Number or fraction of 130 mg tablets	Number or fraction of 65 mg tablets	Milliliters (mL) of oral solution, 65 mg/mL
Adults over 40	> 500	130	1	2	2 mL
Adults 18–40	> 10	130	1	2	2 mL
Pregnant or lactating women	> 5	130	1	2	2 mL
Adolescents 12–18	> 5	65	1/2	1	1 mL
Children 3–12	> 5	65	1/2	1	1 mL
Children 1 month–3 years	> 5	32	Use KI oral solution*	1/2	0.5 mL
Infants, birth–1 month	> 5	16	Use KI oral solution*	Use KI oral solution*	0.25 mL

* Each milliliter contains 65 mg of potassium iodide. You should take this dosage once every twenty-four hours until the danger has passed or as advised by a medical professional.

- Monitor your emergency radio or other sources for information and do not go outside until authorities tell you it is safe.
- Eat food in sealed containers, unspoiled food from the fridge or freezer, or food from a pantry or other area that's away from outside walls. If you had a pie cooling on the windowsill, you'll just have to write it off.
- Wipe off everything you're about to use or come into contact with, with a damp cloth or towel: food, countertops, table, plates. Put the towels in a plastic bag away from people.
- Do not eat food from your garden.
- Do not use drinking water from your tap. Use your bottled supply instead.

- Seek medical help for symptoms of radiation exposure, sickness, or injury as soon as it is safe to do so.

Pandemic Zone

Pan literally means everywhere, so yes, we are *all* in the pandemic zone. And we've been living the consequences of that for years. But just because people are still getting COVID-19, and we have vaccinations that have cut the mortality rate, it doesn't mean we couldn't get another pandemic on top of it at any time, or mutations could develop that are resistant to current vaccines.

The disease that poses the greatest pandemic threat to human beings isn't COVID-19 or any coronavirus for that matter, but influenza, according to information from the National Center for Biotechnology. The deadliest pandemic in the last century was the outbreak of *Spanish flu* in 1918 that killed a reported fifty million (probably closer to 100 million) people around the world. The next Spanish flu will travel around the world at the speed of the twenty-first century with the ease, pace, and frequency of travel making us much more vulnerable to it, whatever it will be. And there's nothing to say that it won't be more lethal than the last.

And while the world waits for successful treatment or a new vaccine, we already know the only non-medical intervention that really works. Nobody wants to hear it because we've had it up to here with it, but it's *isolation*. In 1918, American Samoa managed to isolate itself and escaped without one single case of the deadly flu. Just miles away, Western Samoa saw 22 percent of its entire population die. Fairbanks, Alaska, successfully isolated itself from influenza, but a full third of the Alaska Native population living in exposed villages died. Sometimes whole villages were wiped out. These are brutal statistics, but they illustrate the point.

Here's something interesting. In an account of the flu pandemic written in 1919 in rural Kentucky, the Red Cross reported people starving to death "not from lack of food, but because the well were panic-stricken, and would not go near the sick . . . A fear and panic of the influenza, akin to the terror of the Middle Ages regarding the Black Plague has been prevalent in many parts of the country." So, the sick were left alone to die with nothing, and no way to care for themselves. We like to think we're better than that now, but let's be real—human nature doesn't change that much.

And if there's a COVID pandemic marching along, that doesn't mean we couldn't get influenza on top of it. Or some new mutations. Or Rift Valley fever, Hantavirus, Crimean-Congo hemorrhagic fever, Marburg, Lassa fever, or something yet unknown. And yes, all these nasties are being studied and monitored right now as potential pandemic hazards. So, it could be a complete Chex Mix of suck.

The point we're trying to make is that whether it's self-isolation or isolation imposed by others, those who have it the easiest during hard times will be people who are prepared, have the supplies they need, the knowledge they need, and the learned adaptive behaviors that will put them ahead of the survival curve. And you are one of those people!

Pandemic Preparedness List
- Have enough food and water to last your family for two months if you can, or two weeks at a bare minimum.
- Try to have an *emergency fund* that consists of enough money to hold you over for two to three months if you couldn't work.
- Keep your body and mind healthy and better prepared to handle illness.
- Follow reliable news sources that will keep you posted about impending threats.
- Make sure you have all available and recommended vaccinations to protect you from existing illnesses. Nobody needs to have two things at once!
- Keep a stockpile of N95 or KN95 masks, hand sanitizer, bleach wipes, and latex or nitrile gloves.
- Be prepared with a plan if schools, your workplace, or commonly visited spaces close down.
- Don't hoard supplies all at once at the last minute. Panic buying is something you want to avoid so just add a couple of extra items here and there (like toilet paper) until you have as much as you want.
- Don't let yourself run low on things you absolutely need like prescription medications. Try to front-load critical medicines and medical supplies and get refills as soon as you are allowed.
- Make it a habit to keep your gas tank mostly full.

What to Do During a Pandemic

- As soon as there is a safe vaccine and you are eligible to get one, get vaccinated! Vaccines are a miracle of modern life, have saved millions of lives, and will either prevent disease or reduce the severity and lethality of it. Make sure elders, those with preexisting conditions, and children who are eligible also get vaccinated.

- Monitor reliable news and information about the pandemic. There is lots of misleading information out there. Conspiracy theories will flourish. Don't fall for it. There are doctors, virologists, epidemiologists, and research scientists who have dedicated their entire lives to knowing about this stuff. They think about it and prepare for it every day. Public health is their calling in life. Trust them. They know more than snake oil salesmen who like attention, or your Uncle Bob.

- Pass on reliable, science-based information only. Don't post unverified information on social media. Use your voice for good. Help educate people, and don't whip them into a frenzy. We don't need *Lord of the Flies* during a pandemic. Be part of keeping everyone calm and properly informed.

- Remember to closely monitor your own physical and mental well-being. Get outside if it's safe. Do creative work indoors. Learn a language or a new skill. Listen to music. Cook delicious healthy food. Do projects with your kids that will empower them and make them feel that they are doing something to help (like having a hardtack-making party!). Remember that it's totally normal to feel sad, stressed out, anxious, or depressed. Don't keep it inside. Reach out and talk to people.

- Connect with loved ones. If you live with them, hug them every day. We're not just being sappy; hugging is actually good for you! Snuggling your furry family members works too. If you don't live with anyone, use video chats or phone calls on a regular basis. Set up a Monday night chat or a socially distanced outdoor get-together on the weekends. Nothing beats one-on-one connection.

- Prevent the spread of disease as much as you can. Follow the guidelines of the day. Depending on the nature of the pandemic, you may need to cover coughs and sneezes (you should do this anyway), wear masks, wear gloves, stay home if you are sick, isolate for a period of time, keep surfaces clean and disinfected, wash your hands often or use hand sanitizer, and stay at least six feet away from those who are not part of your household.

- If you or a member of your family has been exposed to the disease, contact your medical provider and follow instructions. Quarantine, and monitor your symptoms. If there is a medical emergency, call 911.
- Don't be a jerk. We're all in this together. Be thoughtful. Consider other people, their situation, their needs, their vulnerability. Try to help where you can. Be kind.

After a Pandemic

- Keep all your good habits like washing your hands, sanitizing surfaces, and monitoring your own and others' physical and mental health.
- Continue to follow reliable news in case of resurgence or new outbreaks.
- It can take a while to recover from prolonged stress. Recognize this in yourself and others.
- Think of how you handled this pandemic. Would you do anything different next time?
- Restock any emergency supplies you may have used, and make sure you're ready for the next one.

LOOK FOR THE HELPERS (AND BE ONE!)

In times of toil, stress, and disaster, who can we turn to to make us all feel a little bit better? If you said Mr. Rogers, you are correct. And in this case, also his mom!

When I was a boy and I would see scary things in the news, my mother would say to me, "Look for the helpers. You will always find people who are helping." To this day, especially in times of disaster, I remember my mother's words and I am always comforted by realizing that there are still so many helpers—so many caring people in this world.

First, we should all strive to be helpers in a disaster and make Mr. Rogers and his mom proud. Assess your skills and abilities and use them, even if they are as basic as being able to drop off a meal to an elderly neighbor or bring the mail up to the door for someone, ask who needs what before going to the store, check in on those affected, and pitch in to ease the suffering of your fellow beings. It will not only make them feel better; it will make *you* feel better too, and if you have little ones watching, it's great role modeling for the next generation of humans.

Second, we should all be aware of the *official* helpers whose job it is to assist in the event of a disaster situation and how to connect with them when disaster strikes.

The Red Cross: redcross.org

For over 140 years, the American Red Cross has been dedicated to helping those in need. They provide services to members of the armed forces and their families, and to those impacted by disasters. You can not only learn from them, you can volunteer to help, and you can know that they will always be there for you and your family when you need them most. Whether you want to be a helper, or need a helper, reach out to the Red Cross.

Take a class! The Red Cross offers all kinds of certifications and training for adults, children, and babies: first aid, CPR, and how to use a defibrillator, for example. They also offer childcare classes, aquatics, basic water safety classes, workplace safety training, and more. Many classes are even available online!

DONATE BLOOD! This is something that really can save a life, especially if you have an unusual or rare blood type. You can find out by asking your doctor to test your blood the next time you have blood drawn, or, even better, you can find out by donating! The Red Cross organizes blood drives regularly, and especially needs donors during times when a disaster has resulted in injuries. Depending on your blood type, the best type of donation will vary, so find out what your type is and set up a regular visit to donate. Then sit back and have some OJ, you amazing giver of life!

Type	% of US Pop.	Best Donation	You Can Donate To	You Can Receive Donations From
A+	34%	Platelets Plasma	A+, AB+	A+, A-, O+, O-
A-	6%	Double Red Cells Whole Blood	A-, A+, AB-, AB+	A-, O-
B+	9%	Platelets Plasma	B+, AB+	B+, B-, O+, O-
B-	2%	Double Red Cells Whole Blood	B-, B+, AB-, AB+	B-, O-
O+	38%	Double Red Cells Whole Blood	O+, A+, B+, AB+	O+, O-
O-	7%	Double Red Cells Whole Blood	All Types	O-
AB+	3%	Platelets Plasma	AB+	All Types
AB-	1%	Platelets Plasma	AB-, AB+	AB-, A-, B-, O-

VOLUNTEER! From individual house fires to immense natural disasters, the Red Cross goes where they are needed to provide relief for those in need of clean water, food, and safe shelter. These emergency angels often set up shelters where people can gather after a disaster. They distribute emergency and cleanup supplies, and they provide medical and mental health assistance. And 95 percent of their disaster relief workers are volunteers.

GET HELP! You can contact the Red Cross before, during, or after a disaster at *redcross.org*. There's also a handy search tool where you can find your local chapter by clicking on *Get Help*. Bookmark your local chapter before you need it! Enter the information, including phone number, in your cell phone so you have it ready.

CHECK IN! Download the American Red Cross app or go to the Safe and Well website (findhelp.org) to let people know you're safe. The website is quite secure and allows friends and family to search for messages from friends and family. You can also register by texting SAFE to 78876.

Contact the Red Cross at 1-800-RedCross if you are missing a friend or relative.

FEMA: ready.gov

The Federal Emergency Management Agency (FEMA) is part of the Department of Homeland Security and was initially created by President Jimmy Carter in 1978. That's right, the government is here to help! Don't diss FEMA. They've got crucial information you'll need in times of distress and will be able to answer questions and guide you through some tough stuff.

DOWNLOAD THE FEMA APP! We cannot stress this enough. This app will provide you with real-time emergency information and weather forecasts for up to five different locations in the United States. If you need to evacuate your home, the app will tell you where you can find nearby shelter. After the danger has passed, the app will provide recovery tools and let you know if you are eligible for assistance, where to find Disaster Recovery Center locations, and answer any questions you have. Did we say download the app? Download the app!

GET HELP! You can also go to FEMA.gov/locations and enter your zip code to find out information for your specific area and disaster, and how to get in touch with your local emergency management offices.

CDC: cdc.gov and emergency.cdc.gov

The Centers for Disease Control and Prevention (CDC) is part of the Department of Health and Human Services. Their mission is to protect Americans from threats to their health, safety, and security, whether they are home or in other countries. They track and monitor threats to public health and keep the public and the media informed. They do the science and provide the best recommendations for prevention and treatment of disease. If you need all the latest on emerging diseases and advice on what to do, check out their website regularly. They also provide fact sheets and information on what to do in certain health disasters like nuclear or chemical attack, bioterrorism, natural disasters, and more. They should be your go-to source for everything relating to public health. Download their app so you have all the information ready at a glance.

WON'T YOU BE MY NEIGHBOR?

And finally, as we beat the Mr. Rogers theme to death, he had another thing right! There's nothing like a having a good neighbor. Reach out to the people in your building or your neighborhood.

Make connections. Not everyone will be as prepared or capable of handling a disaster situation as you are. Almost half of all Americans would need to rely on neighbors both before and after a natural disaster, but many Americans don't even know who their neighbors are! According to a 2018 study from the Pew Research Center, only 22 percent of younger adults ages eighteen to twenty-nine know all or most of their neighbors. The older you are, the more people you tend to know but only 40 percent of seniors report knowing all or most of their neighbors. Don't be one of those people. Figure out which neighbors will need to be checked on first after a disaster, and help them be prepared before it happens, because you are now brimming with knowledge, and there's nothing better to do with knowledge than share it to help people.

Among American adults who *do* know their neighbors, two-thirds would feel comfortable leaving them with a set of keys in case of an emergency. After a major disaster, response time from first responders may not be quick enough, and there may not be enough responders to attend to the needs of everyone affected. Others around you may be turning to you, and you may be turning to others. Working together as a community will improve everyone's ability to survive and rebound from calamity.

If you are comfortable, reach out, meet your neighbors and talk about how you and other neighbors might work together until help arrives. The conversation will depend on your neighborhood but here are some ideas of where to start.

- Talk about which disasters are most likely in your neighborhood, and find out how to stay in touch with each other in case something happens.
- Find out if there are doctors, nurses, or EMTs near you, or if there's someone who has special skills like first aid and CPR.
- Determine who might be available for childcare or to be a safe house where kids could go if parents can't get home.

- Find out who has a gas grill for outdoor cooking in case gas is shut off.
- Who has special equipment that might be useful during a disaster?
- Which neighbors may have special needs or disabilities and will need extra help?
- Ask everyone to share their own contact information and emergency contact information in case you need to call a relative or close friend to assist.
- Discuss the importance of everyone knowing how to shut off utilities and emphasize the importance of having basic supplies, including a first aid kit.
- How does everyone get around? Do your neighbors have cars or are they relying on public transportation?
- Find out who has pets and make arrangements for their housing and safety.
- Find out where your neighbors work in case something happens during work hours.
- Talk about ways you can all be better neighbors and meet others in the community by volunteering with the Red Cross, community response teams, Meals on Wheels, and other local organizations.

Remember, humans did not survive by being lone wolves. You're not going to take off into the woods and eat mice and build a lean-to out of sticks and moss to survive a disaster. A social safety structure and a community of people who are ready to help one another could be the best survival prep you have!

ARE YOU READY?

Be prepared

_____ Analyze and determine which disaster zones you live in and which disasters are most likely in your area

_____ Prepare in advance by using the customized disaster lists for *all* your potential disasters

_____ Know what to do during and after your likely emergencies

_____ Download the Red Cross app

_____ Download the FEMA app
_____ Download the CDC app

Be a helper

_____ Take a class from the Red Cross
_____ Donate blood
_____ Volunteer with the Red Cross, Meals on Wheels, or other community organization
_____ Reach out and meet your neighbors
_____ Create a neighborhood emergency group

CHAPTER 8

EVACUATION AND HOW TO PACK YOUR E-BAG

ead for the hills! is a lousy survival strategy. It's not really a survival strategy at all; it's more of a break your leg and get eaten by a bear strategy. In the vast majority of situations, you are far better off staying in your own secure and provisioned shelter. However, if your structure is compromised and unsafe, or if you are told by authorities that you must evacuate, you need a plan and certain essential items ready to grab and go.

THE PLAN

Have a plan, and make it well ahead of time. You can involve all members of your household in the discussion to help them remember and think about what they will need to do in an emergency situation.

- Know your local community's evacuation plan, staging areas, and shelters. They should have a plan!

221

- Identify where your family will go in case of an evacuation. If possible, think of more than one place in case your first choice is also in an evacuation zone. You can choose a hotel in another town or the home of a friend or family member. Also, know where your local shelter and the next closest shelter are and include them in your plan.
- Remember to take pets into consideration when formulating your plan. Many hotels will take pets, but sometimes hotels and even shelters will not allow pets.
- Have a paper map and figure out more than one route to get to your safe location in case roads are flooded or blocked. Remember, Google Maps may not be an option if the internet is down.
- Ask an out-of-town relative or friend to serve as a common contact person for your family.
- If your family is separated, arrange a designated meetup place and be as specific as possible. Use a landmark like a sign or a clock or a bench, so everyone knows exactly where to meet.
- Write everything down in detail including location, evacuation route, and contact phone numbers; and make sure every member of the family has it with them. It can be put in a wallet or backpack.
- Listen carefully and follow specific evacuation instructions from local authorities on TV, radio, or NOAA weather radio. Contact neighbors and vulnerable people in your neighborhood and tell them it's time to evacuate if you think they don't know.
- If you plan to evacuate by car, make sure you keep your car in good working condition and always with enough gas to comfortably drive a long distance.
- Have all your emergency car kit supplies stocked and ready to go.
- If you will be sharing transportation, have ironclad plans ahead of time and a backup plan in case the person with the car can't get to you or you can't get to them.
- If you are using public transportation, contact your town or local government and ask how public transit will be operating, how an evacuation will work, and where you can find the most current information on evacuating.

- Regularly discuss *what if* scenarios with your family and make sure everyone knows what to do. What if someone is at work, or school? What if someone is out of town?
- Download the Red Cross Shelter Finder app at *redcross.org/mobile-apps/shelter-finder-app*. It will list all open shelters, including their capacity and the current occupancy of each shelter.

EVACUATION BAGS

Here's where you're going to learn how to assemble an evacuation bag (e-bag) that will cover all the essentials you need, and the specialized supplies for individual conditions and disasters. And we promise it will not weigh 500 pounds.

Hint: You do not need to bring tools to build a shelter, or grind wild grain into flour, or trap large animals for their fur and meat. You just need essentials that will last you seventy-two hours while you move from your home to a safe location. Let's start with the basics.

The Basic E-Bag

No matter where you are, there are basic items you'll need in every e-bag. Your e-bag should be packed and ready to go, even when there is no disaster; because disasters do not politely let you know they're coming, and the last thing you want to be doing when something bad happens is trying to round up extra batteries and find your charger. Assemble the basic kit, add what you need from the specific disaster add-ons, and keep it somewhere near the door or a location where you can easily find it, grab it, and leave.

It's up to you to assess everyone's needs. What are the particular and specific things each member of your household will need in the three days following a disaster?

The bag itself should be a sturdy, well-made backpack-type bag. The last thing you want is a flimsy bag that will rip or fall apart, so go for a bag with sturdy construction and longevity.

And make sure what's inside your bag stays dry and is packed in sturdy ziplock bags or Snugpak dry bags which are waterproof, but thinner, lighter, and more flexible than normal rubber-coated dry bags. Here are some things to include:

- Every person's e-bag should have a waterproof tag that includes their name, emergency contact phone number, and physical address.
- You should also make an information card and keep it inside a plastic bag. The card should include name, age, address, medical conditions and medications the person is taking, any information emergency personnel should know, emergency contact phone numbers, and the designated meetup place in your emergency plan.
- Tarp or plastic sheeting (use as ground cloth or cover to stay dry)—four-by-four feet
- Rain poncho—military issue type with poncho liner or Snugpak jungle blanket
- Duct tape
- Topographical map of your local area
- A lensatic metal military-type compass like NDUR or Cammenga and/or a handheld GPS
- Water for each person in a three-liter CamelBak bladder with an inline life straw water filter system.
- High energy/lightweight foods that won't spoil like backpacker meals, military ready-to-eat meals, energy/power bars, and pemmican.
- Multi-tool that includes a manual can opener like Leatherman Charge TTI, SOG military issue, or Gerber MP600
- High-powered LED flashlight like SureFire (too see and to signal)
- Foil survival blanket for each person. Make sure these are the military-style casualty blankets, not the cheaper ones that lose the silver coating if they get wet!
- Paracord
- LifeStraw
- Baby wipes
- Ziplock bags—quart and gallon size
- Extra charger cords for phones
- Battery-powered or hand-crank radio, and a NOAA Weather Radio with tone alert like Easton Dynamo
- Extra rechargeable batteries
- Small solar panel with battery charger like Goal Zero Nomad 5 or equivalent
- First aid kit (You may already have one in your car.)

- Emergency whistle (to signal for help)
- N95 or KN95 masks
- Garbage bags and plastic ties (for personal sanitation)
- Manual can opener
- Small sewing kit including needles, thread, safety pins, and sewing scissors
- Battery brick (Try to charge this up monthly so it's ready.)
- Soap, hand sanitizer, and bleach wipes
- Prescription medications (Have *at least a week's worth* of vital meds ready to go in case it's difficult to refill or find a pharmacy.)
- A ziplock with a few doses of non-prescription medications such as pain relievers, anti-diarrhea medication, antacids, or laxatives.
- Cash and credit cards
- One complete change of clothing, two extra pairs of underwear, four extra pairs of socks.
- A thumb drive with all your important information
- Important family documents such as copies of insurance policies, identification, and bank account records saved electronically or in a waterproof, portable container
- Eight clothes pins (Use with paracord to make a clothesline to dry your stuff.)
- Matches in a waterproof container and BIC lighter with fire-starting kit (You can stuff dryer lint into empty toilet paper tubes to make excellent fire starters, and pack them flattened in a ziplock bag.)
- Five or six unscented low-smoke tea light candles
- Feminine hygiene products
- A gallon-sized ziplock bag with small travel-sized soap, shampoo, conditioner, lotion, toothpaste, deodorant, razor, and small brush and comb
- Mess kits, paper cups, plates, paper towels, and plastic utensils. Or get fancy with a metal collapsible cup and a titanium spork.
- Paper and pencil, and a Riteintherain waterproof notebook
- A roll of toilet paper and a roll of paper towels
- A copy of this book in a ziplock bag
- A shemagh (pronounced shmog). These brilliant all-purpose cloths originated in the Middle East as a head and face covering to protect

from sun, blowing dust, and sand. You can also use it as a bandage, a sling, or like a bag, rope, washcloth, towel, or baby sling.

- You may already have first aid kits packed in your home and car (see the Well-being chapter for assembly instructions) but you can buy one premade from Adventure Medical for basic first aid and a trauma kit from North American Rescue.

- Sleeping bag and pillow that fit in a waterproof bag or stuff-sack. This may be too big to fit in the backpack, so carry it separately if you can, or make do with the clothes you leave with and other items in the bag.

Customize Your E-Bag with Add-Ons

FOR BABIES

- Infant formula or pouched food and spoon
- Sterilized bottles
- Cloth and disposable diapers
- Comfortable onesies, pajamas, or separates
- Bibs and burp cloths
- Blanket
- Small toys and books
- Baby wipes
- Sling or carrier
- Diaper cream, lotion
- If baby is nursing, bring nursing pads, breast pump and containers, and whatever else is needed to keep a stable routine with mom and baby.

FOR CHILDREN

- Three changes of clothing (extra underwear and socks)
- Stuffed animals, dolls, action figures—whatever brings comfort
- A couple of books
- Handheld games
- A blanket and small pillow
- Batteries, chargers, and power cords for phone and games
- Pencil and paper
- Snacks

FOR THE ELDERLY AND THOSE WITH DISABILITIES

- A week's worth of all medications
- A medication plan with exactly what to take, how much, and when
- A record of all types of medical devices used, with model numbers
- Medical alert bracelet
- Adult pull-ups/incontinence pads and supplies
- Denture care items
- Any specialized medical equipment or gear needed to monitor and treat conditions and administer medication
- Extra eyeglasses
- Extra batteries for medical devices like hearing aids or blood sugar monitors
- A small cooler and cold packs to keep medication cool
- There may be items that are too large or expensive to have doubles just for an e-bag. Make a separate list of items that are used day-to-day that you must pack before evacuation. Leave that list inside and right on top in the e-bag.
- If a wheelchair is used, think about having a small, more easily portable one for emergency use.

FOR PETS

- Food—try for five or six days' worth. Changing a pet's diet (if you can't find their usual food) can have very unwanted consequences!
- Water
- Bowls—preferably lightweight and collapsible
- Treats
- Make sure your pet always has a collar with tags that have your contact phone number but have a spare in your e-bag just in case.
- Dogs: leash and harness or a carrier
- Newspaper or pee pads for dogs in case they get stuck inside and have to go
- A can of *Go Here* or other spray to encourage your dog to use the pee pad if s/he isn't used to it
- Cats: a portable/collapsible litter box and a couple of ziplock bags of cat litter.

- Portable carrier for birds, guinea pigs, hamsters, rabbits, snakes, lizards, chinchillas, or whatever else is in your menagerie
- Small toys
- If you use a hard-sided carrier to transport your dogs or cats, line the bottom with absorbent pee pads in case you don't have time to stop.
- Small fleece or blanket
- Wash cloth
- Pet wipes
- Poop bags
- A week's worth of any medication your pet is taking

COLD-WEATHER BAG

- Fire starters
- Hand/toe warmers
- Thick cold-weather socks
- Collapsible snow or avalanche shovel
- Extra emergency blankets, cold-weather sleeping bag, and Snugpak
- Emergency whistle
- Bright flashlight/emergency light
- Extra batteries

EARTHQUAKE BAG

- N95 masks for dust
- Emergency whistle
- Work gloves
- Small fire extinguisher
- Utility shut-off wrench

STORM BAG FOR FLOODS, HURRICANES, TORNADOES

- LifeStraw water filter
- Extra socks in ziplock bags
- Waterproof boots like XTRATUF or MUCK boots
- Ziplock bags
- Flares

- Glass breaker
- Water purification tablets

HEAT ZONE BAG
- Salt tablets
- Electrolyte supplements
- Small battery-operated fan with extra batteries
- Hand fans
- LifeStraw
- Extra water
- Sunscreen
- Aloe gel and pain reliever
- Sunglasses
- Sunshade
- Hat with visor or brim
- Small cooler

WILDFIRE BAG
- Safety goggles for eye protection
- Respirator
- N95/KN95 masks
- Small fire extinguisher
- Extra water
- Emergency light/strobe
- Extra batteries

Make a List and Check it Twice

There are certain things you can't pack months in advance. You may have medication that needs refrigeration. Your kid may have a special stuffed animal or toy they just can't live without. Any item you use in your day-to-day life but you don't have a spare to pack away is a good candidate for your e-bag list. Write these items clearly and large on a piece of paper and put it right on top of your e-bag. You should be able to unzip it and right away see that you need to grab your emergency light, or Snuffles the aardvark, or your mom's insulin and a cold pack. Pack those things quickly at the first sign you think you may need to evacuate.

Do not rely on your memory, no matter how obvious you may think these items are.

CLOTHING

If you are in an evacuation situation, what you are wearing when you leave is going to be critically important. Your body will be carrying several vital survival items critical to your health, safety, and comfort as you depart your shelter. Functionality and protection from the elements are the name of the game. Take some time to put together a good clothing list that will work for the most likely weather and disaster scenarios you might face. Once you know what you should be wearing during an evacuation, add that to your evacuation list in your e-bag. You're going to be rushed, and you may forget really obvious things like mittens or a rain poncho. Extra clothing that doesn't fit on your person or in your e-bag can be placed in a roll on the exterior of your pack, and if you have a poncho (you should have a poncho) just roll the clothes up in it to give them some weather protection.

A good rule for clothing choice is to be prepared for temperatures twenty degrees warmer and twenty degrees colder than the current temperature. And since you're not sure which way it's going to go, the key is *layers*.

Layers

Once you have left a shelter which has provided you with a comfortable climate-controlled environment and you are outside in the elements, you now have a new job. Congrats, you are now a sweat manager! During times of warm temperatures, physical exertion, and stress, our body temperature increases. To prevent overheating, our bodies perspire and the evaporation of that sweat cools our skin and our body. If you are wearing wet clothing, you will start to feel cold as soon as you stop moving or your body temperature goes down because moisture is staying in contact with your skin. The job of layers is to keep you dry and comfortable and allow you to manage moisture and temperature. You can do this by choosing the right fabrics for each layer and adding or removing layers to stay comfortable based on conditions.

Here's a crash course in the materials available and what they do!

MATERIALS

- **COTTON** is a natural breathable fabric and works well in hot weather when its moisture-absorbing qualities will keep you cool. It is hypo-allergenic and doesn't irritate skin. But in cold weather, avoid cotton! When you cool off, that absorbency can cause you to get even colder!

- **HEMP** is a great natural fabric that has been used throughout history to make tough durable fabrics that can take a beating. Think sails and ropes! Yet it can be woven into a very soft, comfortable fabric that naturally filters ultraviolet light, breathes, and resists bacterial growth. And it's four times stronger than cotton so it will last a long time and won't fall apart in the wash. It takes very little water to grow and doesn't deplete the soil, so it's a smart, eco-friendly, natural choice.

- **WOOL** actually absorbs moisture, which is not a characteristic you generally want for cooler temperatures, but wool is an exception. It can absorb 30 percent of its weight, but it wicks that moisture away from your skin and unlike absorbent materials like cotton, it acts as a great insulator to keep you warm, even when it's wet! It's also natural, sustainable, and new smart wool materials are able to be worn even by those who previously had reactions to it. Wool also resists odors, which is nice if you'll be in close quarters with other people.

- **POLYESTER/WOOL OR POLYESTER/COTTON BLENDS** are good for combining the best qualities of synthetic and natural fibers for keeping you dry. But the man-made fabrics are petroleum-based and not sustainable.

- **DOWN** has tremendous insulating qualities and is very lightweight. It gives three times the warmth of synthetics by weight. Sleeping bags and jackets can be stuffed in a small sack for easy portability. But down has drawbacks too. It loses its insulating ability when it gets wet, and it takes a long time to dry.

- **LEATHER** is another natural material that's been used by humans for a very long time. It's very heavy, but it provides great resistance to abrasion and can be treated to be waterproof. It can be prone to damage, is expensive, and requires upkeep.

- **GORE-TEX** gained a lot of notoriety when it hit the market as a breathable and water-resistant material, but it's not a miracle. It's good for about six hours of wet conditions but will eventually soak through.

Its breathability will also degrade over time as pores get clogged, and it needs yearly treatment. It also has some questionable and controversial chemicals in the mix like per- and poly-fluorinated chemicals, so we can't call it earth friendly.

- **RUBBER** is great for boots and rain gear. It is sustainable if sourced correctly, and it's biodegradable which means it's environmentally friendly, but it also doesn't last forever.
- **BALLISTIC NYLON**, as the name implies, was originally created to be used by pilots in World War II as flak jacket material. Anything designed to resist flying shrapnel is strong and tough. It is used today mostly in luggage, backpacks, knife sheaths, watchbands, and motorcycle jackets, or for reinforcing areas of clothing subjected to heavy wear and abrasion.
- **NEOPRENE** is a synthetic rubber which is waterproof, durable, chemical-resistant, and thermally stable. It remains functional and pliable in temperatures from -40°F to 120°F. Sport fishers adore neoprene for good reason, and a pair of neoprene waders (hip or chest height) is a great asset in flood areas, and the gloves work well in the cold as well because they insulate. Neoprene is waterproof but doesn't breathe well, so be sure to remove your neoprene and let your body dry out as needed.

How to Layer

LAYER ONE is your base layer and should be something that wicks moisture away from your skin so you stay dry. That means cotton T-shirts or other absorbent, slow-drying materials are a bad idea. Go for fabrics like polyester or merino wool. Base layers should have a snug but not tight fit for colder weather and be looser for warmer weather.

LAYER TWO is your mid-layer, or insulating layer. It's there to trap heat against your body and keep you warm. Wicking is also a good idea for layer two. Also, you may need to remove this layer depending on the temperature, so it should be lightweight and easy to pack. Think of polyester fleece or something with down fill.

LAYER THREE is your shell and is designed for protection from outside forces like wind, rain, and snow. Depending on the circumstances and the climate, you can go for a hard shell, a soft shell, or an insulated shell. You definitely want something that will repel water and wind so think fabrics like nylon, Gore-Tex, or neoprene.

Illustration by Liliana Faiella.

Closures

Zippers have been making people's lives easier (usually) since 1913. But what's even better than zippers is zippers and buttons, so look for clothing that has both. If all you can find is zippered clothing, make sure the zippers are made by YKK (you can see "YKK" stamped on the zipper pull) and buy a quarter-zip or pullover type so if the zipper jams or breaks you still have a usable piece of clothing.

See Appendix B for some more in-depth suggestions, followed by the companies we would recommend.

Evacuating from home in an emergency is one of the most stressful situations many people will ever experience. There is loads of anxiety, uncertainty, and fear. The more you can do to prepare ahead of time, the easier it will be. Think of assembling your e-bag, making a simple list of things to pack, having a preexisting emergency plan, and preparing in general as a gift to your future self and your family. If you ever need it, you will be incredibly grateful to have done the work in advance so all you have to do is pull your e-bags out of the closet, double-check your list, and get to safety.

ARE YOU READY?

_____ Have an official household emergency evacuation plan.

_____ Everyone in your household knows the plan and has a physical copy of it in a wallet or backpack.

_____ Know more than one route to your evacuation site.

_____ Know your local community's emergency plan and shelter locations.

_____ Establish a family member or friend to be a common contact for your household members in case they can't communicate with each other.

_____ Establish a physical location where household members can meet up if they get separated or if they are not together when a disaster happens.

_____ If you are using a car to evacuate, make sure your emergency supplies are in your car and your car is in good working order.

_____ If you are relying on someone else, make sure your plans are clear and cast in stone, and also have a Plan B—follow up periodically to make sure the plan is up-to-date.

_____ If you are using public transport, know routes and availability, and contact your local authorities to find out how it will operate in an emergency.

_____ Download the Red Cross Shelter Finder app.

_____ Pack your own basic e-bag.

_____ Customize your e-bag as appropriate.

_____ Pack customized e-bags for household members.

_____ Create your list of last-minute items and place on top of contents in everyone's e-bag.

_____ Acquire necessary survival clothing and make a clothing plan that's included on your e-bag list.

CHAPTER 9

WELL-BEING

For some, the prolonged COVID-19 hunker-down provided an opportunity to up their Peloton game, learn how to bake sourdough bread, and become fluent in Italian. For others, it provided the opportunity to hate on those people. Putting on pants felt like an act of heroism, and the big survival plan involved a box of wine and Netflix. Everyone reacts differently to trying times, and that's okay. But some coping mechanisms work better than others, and everyone is better off armed with the ability and skills to meet their basic physical and emotional needs.

During a disaster situation, what is the one thing, the critical thing, the *only* thing, that is keeping it all together and allowing you the best opportunity to come through it successfully? No pressure, but . . . it's *you*. But who's going to be making sure *you* are okay, and functioning at your optimal ability? If you're lucky, you have a good support system: a network of family, a group of friends, a supportive partner. But whether you do or don't, you need to be the one who takes the primary responsibility to ensure your own well-being, both physical *and* mental. In a disaster situation, you are your own best friend, but you can also be your own worst enemy. So you need to take care of yourself like it's your job. Because it is.

Self-care does not mean a hot-stone massage, or a snail facial, or a crystal-infused bath. In real life, it just means keeping your mind and body in good shape so you can handle whatever an unpredictable situation throws at you. Relaxing during a crisis is easier said than done. And *telling someone to relax* is sure to make the opposite happen. (Do not try this at home!)

This chapter will cover the practicalities of keeping your body alive and healthy but will also detail how to keep your brain firing on all cylinders so you think clearly, stay optimistic, and ensure your loved ones aren't secretly plotting to kill you in your sleep.

YOUR BODY AND PHYSICAL CARE

Basic Hygiene

You may have thought you'd never need to think about hygiene basics after Mrs. Stumpf's Health class in middle school. Welcome back to sixth grade, because it's time to go over it again, but this time you'll have a lot more to think about! What if you don't have water? What if the sewage system is clogged? What if you can't get to the store? What if you have to evacuate your house? These are all things that Mrs. Stumpf did not take into account when teaching you and your fellow adolescents how to use deodorant and soap.

It's not just about staying attractive and smelling nice in an emergency or disaster situation; good hygiene means good health. Depending on what the water system and sewers are doing, you may not be able to just hop in a hot shower any time you want. And dirt and grime harbor bacteria, viruses, fungi, parasites—any kind of nasty pathogen you can imagine. Wounds and injuries can get infected, so you'll have to be diligent about keeping everyone clean and healthy from top to toe. As circumstances allow, try to keep a hygiene routine as close to your usual one as possible.

Here's a list of stuff that you don't want to run out of if you can't get to the store, and the things that everyone else may have snapped up before you could get there. Don't wait until you're down to the last little sliver of soap before you put soap on your shopping list. *Always stockpile enough for a couple of months.* Then buy accordingly so you'll always have some inventory for emergencies.

HYGIENE ITEMS TO STOCKPILE
- Soap
- Toothpaste/dental floss
- Deodorant

- Q-tips
- Hand sanitizer
- Tampons and pads
- Laundry detergent
- Razors/shaving cream
- Shampoo/conditioner
- Trash bags/wastebasket liners
- Toilet paper
- Baby wipes
- Sunscreen
- Insect repellant
- Condoms
- Ziplock bags—all sizes
- Anything else you buy regularly to keep you clean, comfortable, and happy like moisturizer or aftershave
- Any requirements for elders, family members with special needs, children, or pets. Think denture supplies, medicated powders, muscle rub, bibs, diapers, baby wash/shampoo, puppy training pads, kitty litter, dog poop bags, diaper cream, etc.

First Aid

Everyone should take a basic first aid class that includes how to administer CPR, how to use a defibrillator, how to dress a wound, use a splint, and the basics of medication and its use. Understanding basic anatomy and what to do when someone is hurt is one of the most important skills you can have—a literal lifesaver. Contact your local Red Cross and find out about when classes are available in your area and take one. Even better, find out if you can arrange for a class in your workplace. The more people out there who know what they're doing, the better.

Traumatic Injuries

During natural disasters or other crisis situations, you may encounter people who have been seriously injured. If you see someone with a life-threatening injury, call 911 immediately, answer their questions as calmly as you can, and communicate the following information about the nature of the injury and the person needing help:

- Are they conscious or unconscious?
- Are they breathing, and if so, is their breathing labored?
- Do they have a pulse? Apply gentle pressure to the carotid artery on the side of the neck with two fingers. Find the pulse on yourself so you know where to feel.
- Are they bleeding, and if so from where and how badly?
- Do they have any obvious fractures?
- Have they been burned, and what does the burn injury look like?
- Do they have a head injury or signs of concussion like temporary loss of consciousness; blurred vision; ringing in the ears; dizziness; confusion; nausea or vomiting; headache; drowsiness or fatigue; slurred speech; appearing dazed or confused; repeating the same questions or statements?
- Are they showing signs of shock like cool, clammy skin; pale or ashen skin; bluish or greyish lips or fingernails; nausea or vomiting; rapid pulse (over 100); rapid breathing; weakness or fatigue; fainting or dizziness; enlarged pupils?

If a person appears to be in shock from a traumatic injury, immediately (after calling 911 or while someone else calls) take these steps to help:

IF THE PERSON IS NOT BREATHING
- Begin CPR and continue until help arrives.
- If you cannot administer CPR, ask those around you if anyone can.

IF THE PERSON IS BLEEDING HEAVILY FROM A LIMB
- Apply pressure to the wound with gauze or cloth or whatever you have.
- You can ask the injured person to assist if they are able.
- Use a clotting agent on the wound if pressure is not enough.
- Use a tourniquet if bleeding is severe and cannot be controlled by direct pressure and a clotting agent.
- Use the tourniquet from a first aid kit if available or if there isn't a commercially made one available, you can create a makeshift tourniquet with a piece of cloth and a stick or stick-like object.
    - Wear protective gear.
    - Apply the tourniquet about two inches above the wound.

- Tighten the tourniquet until the bleeding stops.
- Note the time that the tourniquet was applied.
- Wait with the person and do not release the tourniquet until first responders arrive.

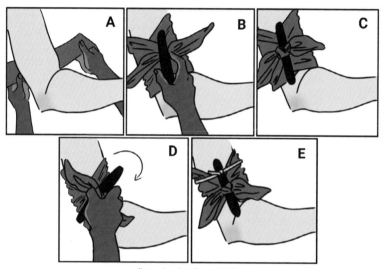

Illustration by Liliana Faiella.

- Proper application of a tourniquet can be quite painful. Always try direct pressure first before applying a tourniquet.
- Have the person lie down or lay them down and elevate their legs slightly. If possible, put something between them and the ground or a cold floor if that's where they are. A lot of body heat is lost through conduction.
- Keep the person still, and do not move them unless absolutely necessary.
- Loosen tight clothing and remove wet clothing unless you risk further injuring the person.
- Cover them with a blanket, jacket, warm and dry clothes, or emergency blanket if needed to prevent chilling.
- Don't give the person anything to eat or drink.
- If the person is conscious, tell them you will stay with them and that help is on the way. Be calm and reassuring. Injured people are afraid and need you to be the rock.

Basic First Aid Kit

You should have a well-stocked first aid kit in your home and another in your car. Make sure your workplace has one too, know where it is, and take a look at it to make sure it's fully stocked. The bag itself that contains your first aid kit should be waterproof, puncture resistant, and as compact as possible while still holding all the contents comfortably.

OVER-THE-COUNTER MEDICATIONS
(FOR ADULTS AND CHILDREN AS NEEDED)

- Painkillers and NSAIDs (Non-steroidal anti-inflammatories)—there are many over-the-counter remedies available. Tylenol (acetaminophen) is a common painkiller. Motrin (Ibuprofen) is a common NSAID. Be sure to read all labels and do not exceed recommended dosages unless advised by your physician.
- Antacid
- Antihistamine
- Anti-diarrheal
- Gentle laxative or anti-constipation tea bags
- Fever reducer
- Cough/cold medicines
- Antibiotic ointment
- Anti-itch cream
- Anti-fungal cream
- Antiseptic wipes/alcohol wipes
- Saline eye drops
- Anti-allergy medication
- Cortisone cream
- Burn ointment
- Blood clotting agent
- Potassium iodide (for radiation exposure)
- Syringes for giving liquid meds to babies and children, if necessary
- Honey sticks—great for low blood sugar/hypothermia

MINOR WOUND AND INJURY CARE

- Sterile gauze pads
- Roller bandages

- Medical tape and safety pins for keeping bandages secure
- Ace bandage
- Bendable foam-coated splint
- Adhesive bandages of various sizes and shapes
- Cotton balls and swabs
- 60 cc syringe with irrigation tip
- Medical scissors
- Skin glue for sealing cuts
- Moleskin for blister prevention and care
- Tweezers
- Nitrile gloves (These can be used on those with latex sensitivities.)
- Magnifying glass

DEVICES

- Forehead thermometer
- Blood oximeter—slips over your finger to read blood oxygen levels
- Small blood pressure cuff—especially if a member of your household has issues with high blood pressure or is at risk of a cardiac event
- EpiPen if needed by household members

TRAUMA RESPONSE

- Tourniquets. Have a few of these if you can in case you are in a multiple-injury situation.
- An assortment of regular bandages in various sizes, gauze, and tape
- Emergency pressure bandages (Israeli bandages)—a specialized sterile bandage designed to put pressure on bleeding wounds
- Hemostat dressing—these are wound-packing material meant to be packed inside the wound or over the top of lacerations, not to be wrapped around limbs like a pressure dressing or ace bandage. The dressing contains a blood clotting agent.
- Chest seals—to close open sucking chest wounds. These will not stop internal bleeding but can prevent a dangerous lung collapse by keeping air out of the chest cavity.
- Emergency blanket (military grade)—better than nothing but if a victim is in shock there will be less body heat to trap. External heat sources are better.

- At a minimum, think about getting a pocket trauma kit. These kits are made to slip in a thigh pocket and are sold vacuum-sealed so they are waterproof and sterile. North American Rescue makes a great pocket trauma kit!

Plan Ahead

According to the *Morbidity and Mortality Weekly Report* (yes, that's a thing) over 30 percent of emergency room visits after Hurricane Florence hit North Carolina were not for injuries but for refills of prescription meds! Think ahead, especially if those prescription meds are keeping you alive. Most states allow you to have an emergency refill on hand, so learn the rules and make a plan with your doctor.

Pro tip: Vacuum-seal your pills and they'll last up to *two years* past the expiration date! If your meds need refrigeration and the power goes out, put them in a ziplock bag and float them in the tank (not the bowl) of your toilet, which is usually 15–20 degrees cooler than the ambient temperature.

Contraception Refill Hell

If you live in one of those states that makes you refill birth control pills every single month, make sure you have a stash of condoms or an alternate method of birth control in case you can't get to the pharmacy. And always refill as soon as they let you, rather than waiting until the last pill. We're already facing a baby boom of *coronials*. Make sure you're covered! Literally.

Get Vaccinated

In a situation where disease is the emergency, and if you're lucky enough that a safe vaccine is available, get every member of the household vaccinated as soon as possible. Follow all safety guidelines. Make sure you are also getting vaccinations like your annual flu shot and tetanus boosters. Even if you end up getting ill, vaccines will tamp down symptoms and the severity of the infection.

Observe Good Health and Hygiene Practices

During times of disaster, especially during a pandemic or a situation involving flooding and flood waters, pathogens are everywhere. Flooding can breed bacterial and viral diseases, carry parasites and chemical hazards, make it more likely that existing wounds become infected, and make otherwise healthy people really sick.

Be sure to wash your hands like a germaphobe, use hand sanitizer, and wear gloves. Also, disinfect doorknobs, countertops, bathroom fixtures, banisters, and other commonly touched places with bleach wipes or other disinfectant.

Be Considerate of Others

Take care not only of your health, but the health and safety of others. Even if you are strong and healthy, many people are battling unseen and unknown (to others) health battles. People who are immunocompromised by disease, or who are taking medications that suppress their immune systems, or who have other serious underlying illnesses, or those who are members of vulnerable populations (the elderly, the young, etc.) need the help of the healthier members of society. Be sure to wear a mask, socially distance, and follow all protective health measures so you don't accidentally make others sick. Stay home from work if you feel ill, and keep sick kids home too.

Keep Your Regular Health Appointments

During the onset of the COVID-19 pandemic, many people delayed or canceled their regular health appointments or screenings. Every situation is different, but talk to your doctor and do the best you can to make sure you keep up on all your regular health-related prevention and maintenance. Don't skip mammograms, colonoscopies, cancer screenings, dental work, or any other appointments that could seriously affect your health. Due to lack of healthcare access for many Americans during the pandemic, telemedicine options have increased. If you are hesitant to go to see your doctor, find out if telemedicine is an option.

Be Wary of Substance Increase and Abuse

Stressful times bring out all kinds of coping mechanisms, and they aren't always good for us. Sometimes things that have short-term feel-good effects are bad for us in the long run. Be especially careful of alcohol, prescription drugs, and recreational drug use.

During the first year alone of COVID-19, there were 99,098 drug overdose deaths in the United States—a staggering increase of almost

30 percent from the year before. In June of 2020, 13 percent of Americans reported that they either started or increased use of substances as a way to cope with negative emotions and stress related to the pandemic.

If you've had substance abuse problems in the past, hang in there and actively seek out other ways of relieving stress, anxiety, and depression. Lean on those who helped you get a handle on it before, and contact a sponsor, professional counselor, or helpline. Be proud of your progress to date and stick with it. If you do slip, don't give up. Many people want to help you succeed.

Even if you have never had a substance abuse issue, these things can sneak up on you. Monitor carefully exactly how many glasses of wine you're having or if you're increasing your intake of recreational or prescription drugs. Try not to have more than one glass of beer or wine a day.

Move!

You hear all the time that exercise is key to good health. Well, we've got news for you—it is! Stress reduction, cardiac health, mental well-being, weight management, muscle tone, disease resistance—they all improve with regular exercise. If you could gain all the benefits of a half hour of exercise five days a week in a pill, people would be mall-brawling at Walgreens to get their hands on it. But it requires effort, which means that about half of all adults don't get enough exercise in the best of times, never mind the worst of times. But even if you get long-term stay-inside orders, you can still get exercise.

- **WALK.** Stuck inside? Walk laps around your house or apartment. Pace, even. Fitbits and other tracking devices are great for helping you set goals and letting you see over time what your patterns are so you can improve. And if you are stressed out or dealing with the aftermath of a disaster or emergency situation, a walk outside will make you feel better, guaranteed.
- **STANDING DESK.** Get a standing desk or improvise one. Get your laptop or paperwork pile off the table so you can stand while working. Using a standing desk, even if it's only for thirty minutes at a time during the day, can show improvement in your health: less back pain, lowered risk of heart disease, obesity, and high blood sugar that can

lead to diabetes. Plus, it can boost your productivity and make you feel better. Not bad!

- **STAIRS.** Does your house, apartment building, or office have stairs? Use them. It's a great habit to get into, and going up and down is a great improvised exercise when you can't get outside. Think of your stairs as a . . . Stairmaster! It will get your heart pumping and your leg muscles in shape.

- **YOGA.** People have been practicing yoga for over five thousand years, and there's a reason. Yoga reduces stress; keeps you limber and flexible; reduces injuries; improves sleep and muscle tone; improves balance, stability, and posture; lowers blood pressure; eases joint pain; elevates mood; and provides a deep awareness of the connection between your body and your mind. It's also gentle and it's simple to start easy and work your way up to more challenging poses as you improve. If you're a newbie, there are some great ways to start. Find yoga videos online that match your level and ability.

- **STRETCHING.** A simple stretching routine of five to ten minutes a day brings great benefit to your body and mind. It increases your flexibility, range of motion, your ability to perform physical tasks; calms the mind; reduces pain and stress; and decreases tension headaches. All this with very little time commitment! Here are three basic stretches for beginners so you can start right away. Search online for more in-depth stretching routines if you get hooked!

   - **FORWARD FOLD** (great for neck, back, hamstrings, calming the nervous system, reducing fatigue, and lowering blood pressure)

Illustration by Liliana Faiella.

- Stand up straight with your arms at your sides, and your feet hip-width apart.
- Inhale deeply, and as you exhale, slowly bend forward from your hips with your head and neck and spine relaxed.
- As you bend forward, try to bring your torso as close to your legs as you can without forcing it.
- Hold on to your elbows if it's comfortable, or you can also let your hands hang down.
- Relax your neck and allow your head to hang. Feel the gravity pull you down deeper into the stretch. Every time you exhale try to relax a little more and get closer to your legs and the ground. You can bend your knees if you feel too much tension in your back.
- Hold the stretch for 30 seconds to 1 minute if you can, taking slow, deep breaths, and feeling a nice stretch in the back of your legs and spine.
- Then slowly lift your torso back up to a full standing position.
- You can repeat the stretch 2-3 times, taking breaks in between if you need to. You'll see how much farther you can stretch by the end.

o **LEGS UP THE WALL** (great for stress relief, lower back pain, sleeping, relaxation, improved circulation, menstrual cramps, digestion, and constipation!)

Illustration by Liliana Faiella.

- Find an open wall space, and sit with your side against the wall.
- Lie down on your back, and swing your legs up the wall until they are straight up, keeping your hips as close to the wall as you can.
- Your legs should be straight up, with the bottom of your feet flexed towards the ceiling.
- Reach your arms out to your sides on the floor, palms up, and allow your shoulder blades to relax towards the floor.
- Close your eyes and focus on slow, deep breathing, and let your body completely relax into this stretch.
- Stay like this for at least 5 minutes, or up to 20 minutes if you want to.
- To end the stretch, slowly slide your legs down the wall, roll on to your side, and push up into a seated position.

- **CHILD'S POSE** (a classic yoga pose and a great back stretch that will also help you sleep better, improve digestion, and even lower blood pressure)

Illustration by Liliana Faiella.

- Start on your hands and knees, with your knees under your hips and your hands under your shoulders like a table.
- Lower your hips back towards your heels, keeping your arms straight, and if you can, rest your forehead on the floor. If you can't reach your forehead to the floor, no worries. Stack your fists on the floor and rest your forehead on top of them, or use a firm pillow.
- Relax your arms down alongside your body, palms facing up, or you can also stretch your arms straight out in front of you.
- Breathe deep and slow, and let your body relax into the stretch.

- Hold this position for at least 30 seconds, or up to a few minutes if you like.
- To finish, slowly lift back up to a kneeling position, bringing your hands to your thighs.

- **CALISTHENICS.** You remember gym class, right? Jumping jacks, running in place, imaginary jump rope, push-ups—that sort of thing. People reaped the benefits of movement before expensive gym memberships and fancy equipment! So, give yourself goals of time spent, or number of reps.

- **ISOMETRICS.** Wall sits and planking are great examples of isometric exercise, which involves working your muscles without lengthening and contracting them like you do when you are lifting weights. Isometrics can strengthen muscles and build endurance while going easy on joints. They also require no equipment!

- **DANCING.** Classes are great, but we're not talking ballroom dancing here. You don't need to tango to dance! Play your favorite danceable music and do it like nobody's watching! If you've got a partner or kids, get them in the act. Add some vacuuming, mopping, or countertop wiping to it and you're really accomplishing something!

- **WORK OUT ONLINE.** Search online and you'll find tons of great guided workouts and videos to exercise with. You are bound to find something that resonates with you. And if you get bored, find a new one!

And if you can get outside, all sorts of outdoor activities can provide healthy motion and exercise: run, walk, ski, go sledding, wrestle with the kids and the dog; play Frisbee, softball, basketball; ice skate, bike, hike, and do anything else that brings you joy and gets you moving! Remember, a soccer ball keeps most of the world happy and entertained.

Sleep

Sleep is absolutely essential for our physical and mental well-being. Whether we get good sleep or not affects our mood, our stamina, our ability to focus and think, our metabolism, our ability to fight disease and maintain immunity, and our long-term and chronic disease risk.

When we lose just one hour of sleep during daylight savings time, there is an uptick in motor vehicle accidents and even cardiac emergencies.

So don't treat sleep like a luxury, treat it like the necessity it is. Sleeping may be easier said than done in a disaster or crisis situation. The key is to recognize the importance of sleep and to do the best you can in your circumstances. Adolescents in particular need eight to ten hours of sleep a night to be functioning at peak performance. But even more than the number of hours people need, it's quality sleep we need the most. Here are some ways to get it!

SLEEP HACKS

- Have a consistent schedule! The more closely you can follow a set bedtime and a set wake-up time every day (with quality sleep time in between), the happier and healthier you will be.
- Eat a healthy diet, and don't eat for two hours before you sleep.
- No caffeine after 2:00 p.m. (if you have a normal daytime schedule).
- No alcohol within three hours of bedtime; it may make you fall asleep more quickly, but results in interrupted sleep patterns.
- No screen time an hour before bed. If you do have to look at your phone, make sure you have a blue-light blocker enabled, and wear blue light-blocking glasses so your brain isn't tricked into thinking it's daytime. And stick to light reading and things that don't make your heart race. No politics!
- Listen to a guided meditation before sleep; or there are plenty of other relaxing sounds and music you can try.
- Get a weighted blanket. They come in weights from two to twenty-four pounds, and advocates swear by them for getting to sleep faster and staying asleep.
- Supplements can help. Make sure you are getting enough vitamin D, magnesium, and fatty fish oil.
- Use blackout curtains and turn off all unnecessary lighted devices in your room.

THE MIND AND MENTAL HEALTH

Know Your Hormonal Frenemy

Meet your stress hormones: epinephrine, norepinephrine, and cortisol —the three amigos of a really crappy day. They used to be a human's best friend when they kicked in the fight-or-flight response that gave us that extra oomph to run from a brush fire, or punch a mammoth in the face, or whatever we had to do to get here today. But too much of a good thing is always bad, and modern humans are stressed out most of the time.

These hormones mess with digestion, spike blood sugar, and increase your risk of hypertension, heart attack, and stroke. They also make mental and physical ailments worse, and literally kill brain cells. Keeping these bad ombres in check isn't a luxury-it's critical, especially during times when you need to be thinking clearly, at your best, and ready to tackle challenges.

Think of your body as a machine, like a car. If you are too busy or stressed or too much in a hurry to get gas or an oil change, guess what's going to happen? Mechanics (and biology) don't care about extenuating circumstances. If you don't take care of the machinery (or the organism), it's going to fail.

How to Be a Happy Warrior and Win the Hormone Wars!

Dopamine is your happy hormone, the lethal foe of cortisol. So, what can you do during stressful times to stack the chemical deck in your favor? Science has answers.

- **EAT PROTEIN.** PB&J really is a wonder drug! Just ask any toddler. But no worries, poached salmon, macadamia nuts, or tofu work just as well.
- **AVOID SATURATED FAT,** which slows down dopamine signaling in the brain. Alas, there is no lasting happiness in that double bacon cheeseburger and fries.
- **CAFFEINE!** Coffee, tea, and dark chocolate wake up your dopamine receptors so they're ready to rumble when happiness presents itself. (You thought we were going to say no coffee, right? Gotcha!)
- **SUNLIGHT.** This one is just intuitive, but science backs it up. Exposure to sunlight increases both dopamine production and receptors! So, pull your comfy chair next to the window and hang out there. You and your houseplants know what's up.
- **MEDITATION.** This isn't woo-woo stuff, it's biochemistry. Meditating, even for just fifteen minutes a day, produces a 65 percent increase

in dopamine release. No wonder the Dalai Lama always looks so happy!

- **MUSIC.** Doesn't matter if you listen to it, or make it yourself, music wakes up your pleasure centers and reduces stress!
- **FOCUS.** If music isn't your thing, engage in another activity you enjoy like gardening, knitting, working out, sketching, tinkering with engines, or curating a collection of whatever you collect. The point is to focus on something you love that's detached from your day-to-day worries. It's healthy to get a break!
- **TOUCH.** Physical contact and touch increases dopamine production too: massage, dog/cat snuggles, hand holding, hugs, kisses, and . . . yes, that too!
- **EXERCISE.** If there's anything in life that's a free and effective health booster, it's exercise. Running, walking, skiing, and all sorts of outdoor activities are great, but even if you're stuck indoors there is plenty you can do. Walk indoor laps, run up and down the stairs, wrestle with the dog or the kids, do stretching exercises, use exercise bands, yoga, pilates, push-ups. All of these things will help you reduce anxiety and depression, improve your mood, and keep you physically in shape, even if the gym is closed.
- **KEEP A JOURNAL.** Writing down your thoughts and feelings can be a good release for otherwise pent-up emotions. Don't think about what to write, just let it happen. Write whatever comes to mind. No one else needs to read it, so don't strive for perfection in grammar or spelling. Just let your thoughts flow on paper—or the computer screen. Once you're finished, you can toss out what you wrote or save it to reflect on later.
- **TALK TO SOMEONE.** If none of the above are working and new and stressful situations are challenging your abilities to cope in a healthy way, or if you are feeling trapped or overwhelmed by circumstances, reach out to a professional. Their whole job is to help people cope and learn new and effective tools to live a happy and productive life.
- **KEEP INFORMED** about the current emergency or disaster situation, but also take intentional breaks from news stories, social media, and screen time. A constant barrage of information about stressful things can compound the stress.

PLAY!

Play is beneficial at any age. And this may come as a shock to anyone who has never lived pre-electronics, but people did stuff before video games! *Analog* games are still in existence and not restricted by electricity or batteries or cables or chargers. All it takes is paper, pencils, coins, cards, and dice! And all those things are super easy to pack in evacuation bags or keep in the car for when you might need them.

Here are a few games to get you started, but the internet is full of them. Find some favorites and then bust them out when your kids need a diversion from whatever's going on around them. Enjoying moments of closeness and laughter releases all kinds of endorphins, the feel-good hormones that give you a sense of contentment and well-being.

Dots and Boxes

For two or more players. You'll need paper and colored pencils. Make a square out of lines of dots on a piece of paper. You can start with a six-dot by six-dot box and work your way up to any size you want. Once your dot square is ready, players take turns connecting dots using different-color

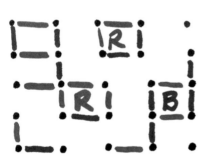

pencils. When a player completes a square with their own colored lines, they put their initial in that square and take another turn. The game continues until all the lines between all the dots have been filled in and whoever has the most completed boxes wins.

Salvo

For two players. You'll need a pencil and paper. Before there was Battleship for Xbox and PS4, there was the electronic Battleship board game, and before that there was just the regular Battleship board game, and before *that*, there was Salvo—also known as Broadsides.

In the game, players take turns trying to guess the locations of the other players' ships on a grid.

Each player draws two 10 x 10 grids and labels the vertical axis with letters and the horizontal axis with numbers. On the left-hand grid the player draws their fleet of ships of various sizes without letting the other player see it.

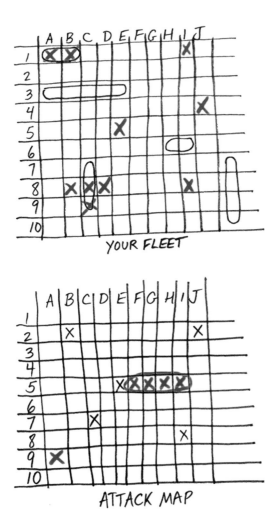

YOUR FLEET

ATTACK MAP

Each player's fleet consists of the following ships, and the ships occupy one or more consecutive boxes on the grid:

- 1 aircraft carrier—5 squares
- 1 battleship—4 squares
- 1 cruiser—3 squares

- 2 destroyers—2 squares each
- 2 submarines—1 square each

Players take turns firing a shot by calling out the coordinates of a square. The opponent responds with *hit* if the ship has been hit or *miss* if it has not. Once the player has hit the last remaining square of a ship, the opponent must announce the name of the ship and that it has been sunk. Each player records their opponent's shots on the left-hand grid, and their own shots on the right-hand grid, with X indicating a hit and O indicating a miss.

The first player to sink all their opponent's ships wins the game.

Knock Out!

For two or more players. You'll need two dice. Decide before the game starts what the winning score will be. Each player chooses a *knock out number* for themselves, which can be any number from six to nine. Then players take turns throwing the dice. The number of both dice added together becomes the player's score. If the player has thrown their *knock out* number they are knocked out until the next round and no score is added to their total.

Pitching Pennies

For two or more players. You'll need pennies or some other type of coin. Players line up an equal distance away from a wall. Each player takes a turn throwing a penny with the objective being to get as close as possible to the wall. After every player has pitched their penny, the player who made it closest to the wall takes all the pennies. Or you can just keep score with wins and reuse the pennies indefinitely!

Use your imagination and come up with games and activities the family can do together.

And you don't need to wait for a disaster to start a fun tradition of a weekly family game night or activity. Here are some ideas:

- **TREASURE HUNT:** Hide objects around the house. You can even leave clues to follow a trail from one to the next until the prize is found.
- **ARTS AND CRAFTS:** Always have craft supplies, drawing paper, watercolors and brushes, markers, charcoal, pastels, scissors, glue sticks,

tissue paper, construction paper, beads, pipe cleaners, felt, or whatever supplies you need for your favorite project.

- **MARBLES:** Another traditional game that's still fun to play.
- **DOMINOES:** Play the game or set up rows of dominoes to knock down!
- **TIDDLYWINKS:** Kids love these!
- **JACKS:** Simple, but harder than it looks!
- **JIGSAW PUZZLES:** Use a roll up mat if you don't have a lot of room so you can put the puzzle in progress away if you need to.
- **PLAYING CARDS AND BOARD GAMES:** There are dozens of card games and board games for every level of play. And do yourself a favor and invest a few dollars to get a *Hoyle's Rules of Games* book so you can learn how to play more than 250 card games and board games correctly and settle disputes!
- **OUTDOOR FUN FOR SOCIAL-DISTANCING SITUATIONS:** Isolation can get to everyone, especially kids. Sitting in front of screens can just make matters worse, so help your kids think of things they can do outside if weather permits. Dribble a basketball and learn some tricks; jump rope (single or double Dutch); have fun with sidewalk chalk; play Frisbee, corn hole, or horseshoes; press flowers and leaves; put up bird feeders and water and identify birds; play fetch with your dog; mess around in the garden; forage; hunt for and identify bugs, trees, flowers, and plants; try croquet; blow bubbles; paint rocks; make forts and trails for action figures. You get the idea—use your imagination and have fun!
- **BE SURE TO HAVE AT LEAST ONE BICYCLE FOR YOUR HOUSEHOLD.** It's not only a great way to get exercise and have fun; it can serve as a vital means of transportation if you don't have a car, as a supplement to a car, or if your car is not functional. They are also easier to use on streets that may be unpassable to cars, or if gas is hard to find. If you don't have a lot of space, look into getting a lightweight collapsible bike.

Electronic Backup

And for those times when you do need your kids (or yourself) to be able to plug in, even if the power and the internet are down, a solar charger for handheld devices, a battery backup, spare batteries, an old-school DVD player, and a binder full of DVDs might very well save your sanity!

CONNECT AND COMMUNICATE

The buddy system is not just for school field trips. Having a designated disaster buddy and a network of neighbors and friends to connect with during a crisis can make a huge difference in your ability to successfully navigate disasters and emergencies. Here's how to set up a communication network:

- Explain to trusted contacts that you are making a disaster plan and ask if they want to be part of your support network.
- Share addresses and phone numbers and be sure everyone has each other's information on their phone and on paper in case anyone loses power or connectivity. You can share emergency information, lend assistance when possible, and check in on each other in preparation, during, and in the aftermath of a crisis situation.
- Keep a stack of blank, stamped postcards to mail to seniors or people who are shut in, and tell them how to get in touch with you if they need something.
- Video call if you can, to keep in touch with family and friends. There's no substitute for seeing someone's face.
- If you have the ability and means, keep a landline for emergencies so you'll have a way to communicate if your cell tower or network is not operable. Find out which friends and relatives still have one and keep a record of it.
- While those paranoid bearded camo dudes are setting booby traps to keep people out, remember your humanity and reach out to help others when you can. Check in on neighbors, coworkers, and acquaintances, especially if they are elderly, disabled, have a medical condition, history of anxiety or depression, or don't have family close by. You can make a huge difference for someone who isn't as prepared or able to weather the storm as you are.
- Connect with your community or faith-based organization by volunteering to help. Use your skill set or learn a new one. Helping others is important not only for them but for you. Knowing you have purpose and acting on it provides fulfillment and is critical to mental health.

- Talk to others about how you are doing. If you are feeling anxious, depressed, sad, or angry, know that all these things are normal. But bottling them up inside is harmful. You can talk to friends, family members, community or faith leaders, a therapist or counselor, or call a helpline. That's what they are there for! Allow others to help you, just as you help others.

WATCH OUT FOR YOUR HOUSEHOLD

Sometimes when stress gets the best of us, we're the last to know! That's why everybody in your household should keep an eye out for each other. Pay attention to changes in behavior or worrisome symptoms of stress or depression. Reach out if you notice anyone exhibiting:

- Excessive sadness or lethargy
- Difficulties with attention and concentration
- Avoidance of activities they enjoyed in the past
- Increased use or starting the use of alcohol, tobacco, or drugs to cope
- Unexplainable headaches or body pains
- Excessive sleeping or insomnia
- Excessive paranoia, anxiety, or worry
- Drastic changes in eating patterns
- Social withdrawal
- Risk-taking or dangerous, out-of-control behaviors
- Detachment from reality
- Any talk of suicide or wishing to die from anyone of any age should be taken very seriously, even if you don't think the person is serious.

In children look for signs of stress like:

- Excessive crying or irritability in younger children
- A return to behaviors they have already outgrown (like bedwetting, not dressing themselves, tantrums, or fear of being separated from parents)
- Acting-out behaviors in teens
- Avoiding school and schoolwork, and sudden poor performance

- Increased arguing with siblings and parents
- Feelings of helplessness and lack of control, especially in children and adults with special needs, or the elderly who are dependent on others

Usually signs of distress will fade over time, but sometimes traumatic response can resurface even after the threat is over. Be there for your people. Listen to them, hug them, support them, and if they need help beyond what you can provide, get it for them.

WHEN TO CALL 911

Call 911 for immediate help in a medical or safety crisis. The 911 dispatcher will ask you a series of questions so they can understand the nature of your emergency. Answer all the questions as directly as you can and be prepared to explain details of the situation. Even if a cell phone is not registered with a plan, it will still be able to call 911. Be careful though because your location will not be trackable, and the 911 operator will not be able to call you back if you get disconnected. Be sure to give your precise location first thing if you are calling on one of those phones.

MEDICAL REASONS TO CALL 911:
- Any serious or life-threatening injury or situation
- Difficulty breathing
- Chest pain or pressure or other symptoms of a heart attack
- Large cut or burn or one that involves the head, chest, or abdomen.
- Head injury with loss of consciousness, confusion, vomiting, or poor skin color
- Skin or lips looking blue, purple, or grey
- Seizures
- Choking
- Inability to move all or part of the body, confusion, inability to speak, severe sudden headache, blurred vision, or other signs of a stroke
- Miscarriage
- Amputation of fingers, toes, or limbs
- Coughing or vomiting blood
- Asthma attack, severe allergic reaction

- Unconsciousness due to alcohol, medication or drug overdose, or ingestion of poison
- When someone is too ill to speak

OTHER REASONS TO CALL 911:

- Car accidents that are more than a fender bender
- Vehicle or building fire
- Home invasion
- A tree or power line has fallen on your home
- Drowning or someone clearly in distress in the water
- Any accident that has injured people or poses a threat to life, health, and safety
- An emergency situation you find yourself in that endangers you or others

If you accidentally call 911, don't just hang up or officials may think that you are in an emergency but couldn't talk, or that the emergency call was inadvertently cut off. So just stay on the line, explain the mistake, and make sure vital resources aren't wasted pursuing a mistaken call.

Don't make the mistake of thinking that emergency preparedness is all about hand tools and trauma response. Your body and your brain are the most powerful tools and trauma response mitigators you have, and their operating systems have nothing to do with nuts and bolts. Caring for your body, being gentle and kind to yourself and others, finding a way to make positive social connections, maintaining a sense of purpose, and allowing some time for actual fun, are all critical. So is maintaining a healthy balance of all the hormones and chemicals that allow you to function. What we're trying to say is that all the caretaking and warm fuzzy stuff is important in its own right and will help you handle all the other stuff better. So give yourself and somebody else a big hug. You've got this.

ARE YOU READY?

_____ Review basic hygiene items and build a two- to three-month supply.
_____ Take a basic first aid class that includes CPR, defibrillator training, and traumatic injury care.

_____ See if your workplace is interested in taking a group first aid training.

_____ Assemble home first aid kit.

_____ Assemble car first aid kit.

_____ Check on the first aid kit at work. Does it exist? Is it stocked?

_____ Make sure everyone in your household is current on all vaccines in consultation with your doctor.

_____ Talk to your doctor about having an extra supply of prescription medication for emergencies.

_____ Keep track of your sleeping patterns and try to improve them.

_____ Get into good exercise habits before a disaster so you are healthier and better able to cope.

_____ Learn some new games and ways to keep everyone entertained without screens.

_____ Ask neighbors and friends if they want to be included in your disaster network for check-ins and assistance.

_____ Have an electronic copy _and_ a hard copy of all names and contact numbers of your list of friends and neighbors in your home, on your phone, in your car, and in your evacuation bag.

_____ Get at least one bicycle for your household for exercise and transportation in an emergency situation.

_____ Think about a solar charger for devices, and always have spare batteries and an external battery storage device.

_____ Have a landline.

_____ Keep a copy of all emergency numbers in an obvious place: on the refrigerator, on the door, on a corkboard, next to a landline, etc. There's also a place to write them at the end of this book.

_____ Always look out for yourself and be good to your body and mind.

_____ Always look out for your people.

AFTERWORD

Well, that's it! You did it! Congratulations for being proactive about your own and your family's safety, security, and resilience in the face of an uncertain future. You've learned what you need to have, the skills that will help you, how to plan, and important steps to take in preparing for, surviving, and recovering from disaster situations. You've learned how to bolster yourself against natural and man-made threats, and you've got a checklist a mile long to help you on your way!

At this point, we hope you've picked up on a few important themes.

1. **YOU CAN'T DO THIS ALONE.** Your success at creating a sustainable and resilient lifestyle that prepares you for adversity requires group effort. The myth of the lone survivor matching wits with nature and living off the land is just that—a myth. Your community is the most important survival tool you have—those who will be an extra set of eyes, or hands, and who will have your back, just like you will have theirs. That's how humankind survived until now, and that's how we'll do it to get through what the future has in store.

2. **SUSTAINABILITY IS SURVIVAL.** Every tiny step you take to be more capable and self-reliant (from canning peaches to kneecapping a bad guy) will help you and those you love. The bottom line is that the less you need to rely on supermarkets, gas stations, utilities, repair people, and luck, the better off you will be. This book isn't designed

to be a quick fix; it's meant to get you on the path to sustainability for your sake and for the sake of the planet.

3. **SHARING KNOWLEDGE IS KEY.** As you learn and implement steps to surviving and thriving through adversity, share what you learn with your community! We all have many communities: our physical neighbors, our family (including our children), our friends, faith groups, community organizations, and work friends and associates. Tell them what you are doing and why; get them in on it. Give them a copy of this book! Shameless plug? Perhaps, but it's also good sense. The stronger and more resilient your community is, the more it benefits everyone in it, including you and your household! Plus, you could be the most popular person at the holiday gift exchange, or a good neighbor with a welcome or housewarming gift for anyone in your circle.

Thanks for taking this journey with us. We're really glad you've decided to survive and thrive!

Jeanne and Bill

RECIPES AND NUTRITION

BADASS SURVIVAL FOOD RECIPES FROM HISTORY

Remember that the best recipes are the ones handed down through generations. In today's world that means all those links you've saved, and digital files don't count. Be sure to keep actual recipe books or some of your own favorite recipes on paper in a binder or an old-fashioned recipe box so you have them in case the internet goes down or your hard drive is compromised. Your recipe file will be no good to you if you can't get at it!

As with many survival-related tips and tricks, there's a lot we can learn from our ancestors. Those people were figuring out how to eat and what to eat when the whole world was like a giant TV survival show. The fact that any of us are even here means our forebears were, in fact, badasses who learned, taught, and applied the lessons of food preservation successfully enough to create new generations without dying of food poisoning. So, give the old ones a pat on the back and learn how to make some fascinating food that can last sometimes for decades!

Hardtack

Hardtack is definitely not going to grace the cover of *Bon Apétit* any time soon, but if you ever really need it, you won't care. Relive some culinary history and whip up a batch of hardtack, used by our ancestors to carry on long journeys. Hardtack is as basic as it gets and about as yummy as it sounds. With only three ingredients—flour, water, and salt—it's got a long and storied history dating at least as far back as 6000 BC!

Hardtack has been known by many names (pilot bread, sea biscuit, molar breakers, sheet iron) and was used during long sea voyages, as a necessity of frontier life, and as standard ration for armies and navies from the seventeenth until the early twentieth century. Hardtack was often baked multiple times to remove as much moisture as possible so it would last longer.

Civil War soldiers (who started off using leftover hardtack from the Mexican-American War almost two decades earlier) soaked it in water or coffee to avoid that molar-breaking hazard, but it kept them alive and it stays edible for a *very* long time. If you could get your hands on some original Civil War hardtack, you could still eat it. At the very least, you could frame it and sell it at auction for five hundred dollars. Yep, that happened.

Sailor Boy brand pilot bread (a commercial brand which is softer than traditional hardtack) is still a staple in one US state. Alaskans consume more than 95 percent of all the pilot bread made, and for good reason. Outdoorspeople, campers, and the large numbers of Alaskans who live in the bush consume it regularly. A PB&J on pilot bread is as Alaskan as the midnight sun, and just as dependable.

Even if you're lucky enough to live in an area where you can find this arctic treat in the grocery store, hardtack is also a fun foolproof recipe to make with your kids, while explaining preparedness and giving a little history lesson at the same time.

Basic and Indestructible Hardtack Recipe

Don't use self-rising flour. White all-purpose flour will give you a product that lasts much longer than if you use other flours. Additionally, the salt is optional, but it will act as a preservative and your hardtack will stay good longer.

INGREDIENTS:

3 cups white all-purpose flour

1 cup water

2 tsp salt

DIRECTIONS (MAKES 12–16 CRACKERS):

Preheat oven to 375° F.

Combine the flour, salt, and water in a bowl and stir.

Your dough should be dry enough that it doesn't stick to your fingers. If your dough is too wet, sprinkle small amounts of flour into the dough until it reaches a drier consistency.

When your dough holds together, knead it into a ball. Work the dough with both hands until it has a uniform consistency that feels like Play-Doh.

Lightly flour a surface and roll out the dough to a uniform thickness of one-quarter to one-third inch. The thickness is important to make sure that your dough dries out thoroughly when you bake it.

Cut the dough into square pieces, roughly 2–3 inches each.

Poke 9–12 holes in rows in the hardtack with a chop stick, a nail, or a skewer. This will help keep the hardtack flat and dry. Make sure the hole goes all the way through the dough.

Place the pieces on a baking sheet and bake for thirty minutes.

Flip the pieces and bake for an additional thirty minutes.

When the hardtack has finished baking, remove the pieces with a spatula and let them cool on a rack. (Air circulation will keep the hardtack dry. Are you sensing a theme? Dry is what we want.)

After they have completely cooled, put the hardtack in an airtight container until you, or your children, or your children's children's children want to use it!

Remember to soak your hardtack before eating it so you don't destroy any dental work! This recipe is not meant to be a delightful crispy cracker or soft biscuit. These are hard-core last-forever calories. You can soak your creation in water, coffee, milk, or broths and soups (and some soldiers even smashed it up and soaked it in whiskey). Do what you need to do.

Pemmican

Pemmican traces its roots to Native Americans who used it as a staple. It's much better tasting than hardtack (which, granted, is not a high bar) *and* it actually contains enough nutrients that you could eat nothing but pemmican and survive for a very long time. Fur-trade journals and other records from the nineteenth century speak of pemmican as *the bread of the wilderness.*

It's easy to carry and store, doesn't require refrigeration, and there are only a few ingredients, although you can get creative and add nuts, honey, or experiment with different types of meats and berries. All these things make it a top-notch survival food that's also fun to make and eat.

Super basic pemmican requires only one ingredient: meat. But you can significantly add to the taste and nutritional value of pemmican by adding blueberries, currants or other berries; walnuts, pistachios, or almonds; and even honey.

Pemmican was originally made using wild game meat like buffalo, moose, caribou, or venison, which tend to be lean. You can also use a lean cut of beef which is what most people use now. Avoid pork which is too fatty. Also don't use bear and porcupine—you know . . . if you happen to have some lying around.

The idea is to completely dehydrate the meat and berries, crush them into a powder, and then bind them together with liquid fat. Then you can cut or shape the pemmican into little cakes and store it. Pemmican is basically like an Armageddon breakfast bar.

Ten pounds of pemmican is enough for one person to survive on for a month in a lockdown situation. To make ten pounds of pemmican you'll need to start with about fifty pounds of meat. Of course, if you don't want to go through all that, there are now companies that sell pemmican and you can go online and order it. But then you won't have bragging rights.

INGREDIENTS:
- 6 pounds beef
- 2 pounds tallow
- ½ cup berries

TOOLS:

Food dehydrator (optional, but nice)

Vacuum sealer (also optional, also nice)

Sharp knife

Food processor, blender, or mortar and pestle

DIRECTIONS:

Trim as much fat as possible off the meat and cut the meat into *very* thin strips.

Dry in a food dehydrator until the meat cracks and breaks. If it bends, there's still too much moisture. If you don't have a dehydrator, you can use your oven at the lowest setting possible (about 130 degrees) and put the meat strips directly on the rack. Be sure to put some foil at the bottom of the oven to catch drips.

Do the same thing with the berries. Put the berries on a sheet of aluminum foil with the sides turned up, and spread the berries out into a single layer. Then put the foil on the rack.

As you are dehydrating, leave the oven door open a crack so you don't trap moisture inside. This is especially crucial if you have a gas oven which tends to generate a moister heat than an electric oven.

Leave the meat and berries in the oven until the meat is completely crunchy and breakable. This will take about twelve to fifteen hours. Yes, *hours*. You're going to have to plan a Pemmican Day when you're barbecuing or getting takeout for dinner.

Render the tallow into a liquid form by cutting into small pieces, putting it in a pot on medium heat on the stovetop, stirring every few minutes, and waiting for it to liquefy. This takes patience, but you've already spent fifteen hours watching meat dry, so you're a champ. You'll end up with some *cracklins* that don't melt away and have turned a nice golden brown. You can spoon those out and eat them with salt or seasoning, or earn huge human points by saving them for your dog who has been patiently watching you this whole time and smelling meat all day.

Crush the fully dehydrated meat and berries (and nuts if you use them) into a fine powder using a food processor or a blender. If you don't have either, you can try rolling up your sleeves and do it the old-fashioned way with a mortar and pestle. You can even smash the meat with a hammer, a block of wood, a rock, or whatever you have. The objective is to get the meat as finely ground up as you can. If there is smashing involved, remember that the original pemmican makers laid down a buffalo hide first to catch all the bits of flying meat particles. If you don't have a buffalo hide, a tarp is acceptable.

When you've blended the dry ingredients, pour in *just enough* fat and work it in so that everything is totally coated and sticks together in a cohesive way. Don't add so much fat that there's residue in the bottom of the bowl.

If you have a vacuum sealer, seal the pemmican in bags, or put it in ziplock bags and press it flat, squeezing out all the air you can before sealing. The less air, the longer your pemmican will last.

Store in a cool, dry place.

Fruitcake

The Cake that Never Dies

When you think of delicious baked goods, what springs to mind? Brownies? Fresh blueberry muffins? Rarely does anyone think about the baked good that is the king of them all, a storied treat from the annals of history that will outlive and outlast generations of mere mortals. One that actually improves with age. A sweet so decadent that it was outlawed in Continental Europe in the 1800s for being *sinfully rich*, and yet so nutritious that it passed the stringent standards of NASA as an astronaut survival food and even went to the moon! A dessert so very regal it is the traditional wedding cake of the British royal family to this day. We refer, of course, to the noble fruitcake.

Deep dark, rich, brandy-soaked fruitcakes are so long-lasting they truly rate as a survival food. They take time and patience to make, but when prepared and stored correctly they will stay delicious and safe to eat for many years.

In ancient Rome, soldiers brought a fruitcake called *satura* to the battle-field. It was a mixture of barley mash, pine nuts, pomegranate seeds, raisins, and honeyed wine. That sure beats the heck out of hardtack for a wartime snack! Gold star for the Romans!

The ingredients have morphed over the course of history and geography depending on which fruits and nuts were available. The fruitcake we know today can trace its culinary origins to the Middle Ages in Europe. As sugar became more affordable and people discovered it could preserve fruit, they began soaking fruit in sugar, and then all of that nummy sugar-soaked and preserved fruit was added to fruitcake. Throw in a few nuts, and you've pretty much got the fruitcake of today.

The long-lasting nature of fruitcake made it a traditional wedding cake, a slice of which could be enjoyed at an anniversary way down the road. As a matter of fact, my grandmother saved a slice of her wedding fruitcake from 1915 for so long that I got to taste a bite as a little kid in 1978. Take *that*, devil's food cake!

In Manitou Springs, Colorado, there's an annual fruitcake toss in which unwanted fruitcakes are catapulted across a field for prizes. *Your* fruitcake will definitely not be among them. When you are enjoying your decadent fruitcake some dark and stormy night when the power goes out, or when the next pandemic keeps you home, you will get the last laugh.

Use the fruits, nuts, and the preservative alcohol of your choice to make your own one-of-a-kind fruitcake that can last for years. This is easily customizable, so make it your own!

INGREDIENTS:

$1/2$ cup (1.5 oz, 45g) almonds, coarsely ground

1 cup walnuts or pecans, chopped

2 cups dark raisins

1 $1/4$ cups light raisins

$1/3$ cup candied orange peel

$1/3$ cup candied cherries

1 cup currants

Grated zest and juice from 1 lemon

$2/3$ cup brandy, rum, or whiskey for recipe (and more during the aging process)

1 $1/2$ cups all-purpose flour

1 $1/2$ tsp baking powder

1 tsp cinnamon

$1/2$ tsp nutmeg

$1/2$ tsp dried ginger or 2 tbs. fresh grated ginger

$1/2$ tsp kosher salt

$3/4$ cup room temperature, unsalted butter

$3/4$ cup brown sugar

4 large eggs, room temperature

Powdered sugar (for long-term storage)

TOOLS:

9" cake pan

Mixing bowl

Cheesecloth or muslin cloth

Airtight container

DIRECTIONS:

In a bowl, combine the dried fruits with the lemon zest and juice. Add the nuts, the ginger (if you're using fresh), $1/3$ cup of the brandy (save the rest for later), and mix well. Cover the bowl and let it sit for 24–48 hours. Give it a toss now and then to make sure everything is well-soaked in the brandy.

Take the eggs and butter out of the refrigerator and let them get to room temperature.

Preheat the oven to 350°F. Line a 9-inch cake pan with a round piece of parchment paper.

Sift together the flour, baking powder, cinnamon, nutmeg, ginger (if you're using powdered), and salt.

In a large mixing bowl, cream the butter and sugar together until light and fluffy. Add the eggs one at a time. Mix until combined.

With the mixer running on low speed, add the dry ingredients a little at a time and mix until combined.

Fold in the soaked fruit and all the liquid by hand until mixed.

Pour the batter into the cake pan and spread it evenly.

Bake 50–55 minutes until it passes the toothpick test. (Insert a toothpick into the center of the cake. If it comes out clean it's done.)

Remove from the oven and drizzle the second $1/3$ cup of brandy, rum, or whiskey evenly over the top of the cake.

Cool the cake to room temperature and remove it from the pan.

Soak cheesecloth in whatever liquor you used and wrap it around the cake.

Then wrap the cake and cheesecloth in two layers of plastic wrap and set aside at room temperature.

Once a week for 4–6 weeks, unwrap the cake, brush it with liquor, and then re-soak the same cheesecloth in more liquor and re-wrap the cake.

After 4–6 weeks, continue the soaking process monthly for at least three months and up to a year. You can also brush the cake with liquor after unwrapping. The goal is to make sure that the alcohol has completely permeated the cake.

If you are going to be storing your fruitcake for a year, make sure your cake is well-soaked, and wrapped in a soaked flour sack or muslin towels. Then find an airtight container as close to the size of the cake as you can, put a layer of powdered sugar on the bottom, place the wrapped cake on top, and then cover with another thick layer of powdered sugar. Seal the container and leave it in a cool, dark place away from sunlight until you are ready to serve it.

The more you continue to brush the cake and wrap in soaked towels, and the more time that passes, the darker and boozier and more flavorful your masterpiece will become.

Despite your best efforts, it's possible that even a well-preserved fruitcake can go bad. If it wasn't soaked enough in alcohol, the cake may become hard and dry. If you notice mold, or if the cake tastes bad or sour, don't take any chances and discard it.

DIY Sourdough Starter Recipe

If you're like many people, the COVID-19 pandemic turned you into a home baker or amped up your existing skills. And you may have found that when you went to the store to get some baker's yeast for some bread baking, the shelves were bare. But the miracle of breadmaking does not rely on packets of yeast being in stock at Safeway. Humans have been making bread for thousands of years using sourdough starter, and newfangled baker's yeast has only been around for about 150 of those years. So how did they do it? Did they just make yeast out of thin air? The short answer is yes!

If you want to, you can go down a very deep yeast rabbit hole and learn about its chemistry, its history, and the 1,500 different strains that have been identified. We'll keep it simple. Yeast is a leavening agent (something that makes bread rise) that is made up of zillions of tiny living organisms perfectly adapted to the environment where they live. Yeast is everywhere around you: on crops, in the air, and even on your skin.

You can create a yeast colony of your very own with nothing more than flour and water, which is the preferred food and drink of your little yeasty beasties. Keep feeding them, and they will multiply. When you see bubbles, it means you're making them happy. And when the colony is super happy, it's time to bake! And forget that sourdough starter you've heard about that's been across the Oregon Trail and up the Yukon. Yeasts change over time and adapt to whomever is feeding them. Your yeast is all you, baby, and if you get it from someone else it will become yours and only yours over time.

You won't get instant gratification making yeast, but when the gratification comes in about a week, the triumph is sweet!

DAY 1: IT BEGINS!

In a quart Mason jar, combine 1/2 cup (60g) of all-purpose flour and 1/4 cup (60g) of filtered water. Chlorinated water can slow your process. Mix it up with a fork until the lumps are gone and the consistency is smooth, and thick.

Do yourself a favor and get a digital kitchen scale that measures in grams.

If you're doing any amount of baking (or cooking in general) it will always give you a superior product with proper ratios.

Place the jar in a small cereal bowl or saucer with the lid loosely on top and let it rest in a warm spot for twenty-four hours. You can put it on top of the refrigerator or turn on the oven light and give it a perfect warm fermentation cave. Just don't forget it's there and inadvertently incinerate your yeast!

DAY 2: BUBBLE WATCH

It's possible small bubbles may appear on the surface of your starter. This indicates that fermentation has begun! But if you don't see any, no worries. Just leave the yeast in its warm cozy home for another day.

DAY 3: FEEDING DAY!

Check again for bubbles. Don't freak out if you see a mysterious brown liquid on top of your starter. This liquid is called *hooch* and it indicates that your little colony is getting hungry. That means it's feeding day! Even if you don't see bubbles or brown liquid, it's time.

Discard about half of your starter from the jar and try not to feel like a mass murderer. This is just part of the process. Your colony will take over your refrigerator and your life if you don't discard the starter. When I first started

It's aliiiiiive!

making sourdough, I had seven—literally *seven*—jars of bubbling yeast all over the place. I was the mad scientist of bread and was going through copious amounts of flour to feed the masses until I finally stopped the insanity and started discarding starter. So use a spoon and just dump it right in the trash. No one will judge you.

Then, add $\frac{1}{2}$ cup (60g) of flour and $\frac{1}{4}$ cup (60g) of filtered water. At this stage your starter should have the consistency of a very thick pancake batter. Put the lid on the jar and put it back in its safe place for another day.

DAY 4: REPEAT

Repeat the process of discarding half the starter and feeding it with flour. Try to feed your starter around the same time every day and always use the same all-purpose flour. You like variety in your diet; your yeast does not. You'll notice that your colony is becoming more robust and you may realize why we had you put the Mason jar in a bowl. Sometimes your yeast parties so hardy it runs over the top! You'll notice your starter rising and falling as it consumes its food and water and then as it relaxes. Normally it will double in size after a feeding.

DAYS 5+: KEEP IT UP!

If your yeast is taking longer to get going, don't worry. It will happen eventually. It may be that you have it at a cooler temperature than it likes, or there is chlorine in your water, which slows down the fermentation process.

You'll be ready to bake when you take about a half a teaspoon of yeast, drop it in a glass of water at room temperature, and it floats! Congratulations, you did it! You are a *yeastmaster* and you may now name your yeast. Yes, this is a thing among sourdough aficionados. (One of Jeanne's favorites is William Butler Yeast. She also knows a Yeasty Boys and a Gerald. But you do you.)

If you aren't going to be baking for a while, you can put your starter in the refrigerator and feed it about once a week. If you forget, don't sweat it—you can bring it back. You should also freeze some yeast in an airtight container as insurance in case you have a disaster and lose your yeast. Short of super-high temperatures, or smashing it on the floor, or someone throwing it away, your yeast should be able to withstand all kinds of abuse and neglect. To revitalize a sleepy yeast, even one you haven't fed in months, just pour off any hooch, and repeat the process of feeding above. You can feed once or twice a day. If you feed twice, wait for the yeast to relax between feedings.

Super Simple Three-Ingredient No Fuss Sourdough Bread

There are all kinds of sourdough recipes out there, and a lot of them are complicated, time-consuming, and have sometimes discouraged people from baking sourdough at all, which is a real shame. But no worries if you're not into making sourdough a way of life. Here's a fantastic super-simple recipe for basic beginner sourdough that will knock your socks off. You'll have to plan ahead a little, but it shouldn't take any longer than fifteen minutes on day one, and even less (if you don't include baking time) on day two. No Sourdough Master Class required.

INGREDIENTS:

Sourdough starter
All-purpose or white bread flour
Non-iodized salt

TOOLS:

Kitchen scale
Dutch oven or loaf pan
Flour sack cloth (if using Dutch oven)
Scissors
Thermometer

DAY 1

In a large bowl, mix 4 oz (113g) sourdough starter at 100 percent hydration, which just means you have fed for a couple days with equal *weights* of flour and water. You don't need to feed your starter first before baking.

Add 12 oz (340g) filtered room-temperature water.

Dissolve the starter in the water.

Add 1 lb 4 oz (567g) bread flour or unbleached all-purpose flour.

Add 3/4 oz (20g) non-iodized salt.

Stir together until the dry flour is incorporated. You can sprinkle little bits of water on the dough if you can't incorporate all the dry flour. Then knead the dough for twenty seconds or so into a cohesive raggedy ball. Cover the bowl with a dish towel and let the dough rise for twelve to twenty-four hours on the countertop.

DAY 2

After the dough has roughly doubled in size, shape into a loaf. Depending on how recently you fed your starter it may double in anywhere from twelve (recently fed) to twenty-four hours or longer (not recently fed).

Turn the bowl upside down and let the dough release itself onto a slightly floured surface like your countertop. Shape it into a loaf by flouring your hands well and pulling the outside edge of one hand around the side and into the bottom of the dough ball, gently tucking the side of the ball underneath the main mass. Perform this action a few times, working around the perimeter of the ball until it is round and smooth.

If you are using a Dutch oven, let this dough ball rise in a bowl of about the same size as the Dutch oven. The bowl should be lined with a smooth cloth like a flour sack towel or linen napkin that has been heavily floured to prevent sticking. If you are using a loaf pan, let the dough rise right in the oiled loaf pan.

Let the dough rise again until it doubles in size. This should usually take about two to five hours.

BAKING

An hour before you're ready to put the loaf in the oven, make sure the oven rack is in the second-to-lowest position and preheat the oven to 500°F. If you are using a Dutch oven, preheat that in the oven as well and be very careful handling it!

After the Dutch oven is heated, put it on the stovetop with the lid off.

Score the dough. No need to be fancy here. Take a pair of scissors and snip the top of the dough with three parallel snips across the top of the loaf that go about half an inch deep. Drop or flip the loaf into the Dutch oven so it lands scored-side up and put the lid back on. If you are using a loaf pan, do the same thing with three diagonal snips across the top. Scoring allows your bread to expand and rise.

Turn the oven temperature down to 425 degrees.

In a Dutch oven, bake for thirty minutes covered, then remove the lid and continue baking for another ten to fifteen minutes until the bread is dark golden brown and the internal temperature is 205 degrees.

In a loaf pan, the bread should be ready in about thirty-five minutes.

As tempted as you may be to have some hot sourdough right out of the oven, let it rest until fully cooled to avoid gumminess. If you have no willpower, try to at least wait thirty minutes!

Boom! You made delicious sourdough from scratch with minimal time invested! Now, feed your starter and get ready to make another loaf because this one is not going to last. And the more you bake sourdough, the better and faster you get at it.

Puffy Cloud Sourdough Pancakes

If you'd rather not dump all that hard-earned starter in the trash every day, here's a phenomenal way to use your unwanted sourdough discard that yields the most cloud-like, scrumptious pancakes you can imagine! The lives of your yeast shall not have been in vain!

INGREDIENTS:

- 2 cups all-purpose flour
- 2 tsp baking powder
- 1 tsp baking soda
- 2 tbsp sugar
- 1 tsp salt
- 1 cup of your amazing homemade sourdough starter!
- 1 1/2 cups milk
- 1 egg
- 2 tbsp vegetable oil

DIRECTIONS:

In a large bowl, whisk together the flour, and other dry ingredients to combine.

Then add the wet ingredients. Mix, just until nicely combined.

Heat a pan or griddle to medium heat and spray with cooking spray or use butter. Pour 1/4 cup pancake batter on the hot griddle. Cook until bubbles burst on the top of the pancake, then flip.

Cook for an additional minute or so until the pancake is cooked through and golden brown on the bottom.

Serve!

Bone Broth

Bone broth and stock are not the same. Stock is usually made from simmering vegetables and meat for long periods of time. Bone broth is made from the collagen-rich bones of beef, chicken, pork, or turkey (usually). The key to making a good bone broth is to allow all the rich, nutritious connective tissue and collagen-filled marrow lurking inside the bones, *out*. And to do that you may need to elicit the help of your local butcher, especially if you are making beef bone broth. If you are making chicken or turkey bone broth you can simply break the bones yourself. But beef bones will require cutting to access the marrow within.

For beef bone broth ask your butcher for knuckles, oxtail, neck, and cut leg bones that will fit in your pot. For chicken you can use the carcass of a whole roasted bird and break the bones yourself.

INGREDIENTS:

Bones

2–3 carrots

1 large onion

2 stalks of celery

1 head of garlic cut in half crosswise

1 tsp peppercorns

2 bay leaves

1 tbs apple cider vinegar

12 cups of water

Kosher salt to taste

Water

TOOLS:

Stock pot, crock pot, or Instapot

Roasting pans

DIRECTIONS:

If you are using beef bones, blanch them first by dropping them into boiling water for ten to fifteen minutes to clean them. This will remove residual material and make your broth taste better.

If you are starting off with uncooked bones (including ones you blanched), place them on a roasting pan in a preheated 425°F oven for thirty to thirty-five minutes.

If you are starting with an already cooked chicken carcass, break the bones to expose marrow.

Bring the water to a boil.

Rough chop your vegetables and put them and the rest of the ingredients into the boiling water. There's no need to peel anything (including the garlic or onion) because you're going to be straining at the end.

Turn the heat down to the lowest setting, so the liquid is just barely simmering

Simmer for fourteen to eighteen hours, adding water when/if necessary to keep roughly the same amount you started with.

When you are finished, fill the sink with ice water and place the pot in the water to help cool it.

Then you can put your broth (which will be gelatinous when cold!) into Mason jars or other airtight containers in the refrigerator for a week, or you can freeze your broth in freezer bags or jars for later use.

Use bone broth for sipping, for soups and stews, for making rice or risotto, or any recipe that calls for chicken or beef stock.

I also like to save up vegetable scraps like the ends of onions or celery, or carrot peels, kale ribs, etc., and throw them in a freezer bag for use in making bone broth, or vegetable or meat stocks. It's a great way to squeeze all the nutrition and flavor you can from your produce, save money, and waste less food!

Simple Sautéed Dandelion Greens

This basic recipe works well on all sorts of forageable greens, and you can get creative with it. Add shallots or onion, experiment with different spices, use a dab of butter, a little bacon, whatever suits your taste. Use the very first young tender greens you see. If the leaves get too big, they can be bitter!

INGREDIENTS:

3–4 cups of freshly picked and washed dandelion greens

1–2 cloves of garlic, finely minced

$1/4$ tsp of red pepper flakes (optional or to taste)

1–2 tbsp olive oil

Salt and pepper to taste

DIRECTIONS:

Heat olive oil in a skillet on low-medium heat, then add garlic and sauté for thirty seconds to a minute until it becomes fragrant.

Toss in greens and red pepper flakes and move them around the pan until the greens wilt and become tender.

Serve immediately.

NUTRITION

Sample 2,000-Calorie-A-Day Menus

FINISHING OFF WHAT'S ALREADY IN YOUR HOUSE:

BREAKFAST: two scrambled eggs (156 cal.), 1 tbs olive oil (119 cal.), 2 slices Canadian bacon (89 cal.), coffee with milk (12 cal.), 8 oz. orange juice (103 cal.) *479 calories*

SNACK: ¼ cup nuts (160 cal.) *160 calories*

LUNCH: Two slices of whole wheat bread (138 cal.), with 3 oz. turkey (162 cal.), lettuce (10 cal.), tomato (10 cal.), swiss cheese (200 cal.), mustard (5 cal.), celery sticks (15 cal.) *540 calories*

SNACK: Six whole grain crackers (120 cal.) with 1 slice cheddar cheese or 2 oz. hummus (100 cal.) *220 calories*

DINNER: two baked chicken thighs (200 cal.), 1 cup cooked spinach (45 cal.), sweet potato (114 cal.), 2 pats butter (72 cal.), lettuce and tomato (40 cal.) with 1 tsp. olive oil (40 cal.) and apple cider vinegar (3 cal.) *514 calories*

DESSERT: one whole-grain granola bar or a container of strawberry yogurt (150 cal) *150 calories*

TOTAL: *2063 calories*

USING ONLY PANTRY STAPLES WHEN FRESH FOOD HAS RUN OUT:

BREAKFAST: 1.5 cups cooked oatmeal (237 cal.) with ¼ cup reconstituted powdered milk (150 cal.), 1 tbs. honey (64 cal.), cranberry juice (92 cal.), black coffee *543 calories*

SNACK: ¼ cup trail mix (175 cal.) *175 calories*

LUNCH: 2 cups of canned beef or lentil stew (400 cal.), 6 whole grain crackers (120 cal.) *520 calories*

SNACK: half a bag of microwave popcorn or a can of sardines (200 calories) *200 calories*

DINNER: 2 cups cooked whole wheat spaghetti (375 cal.), ¾ cup jarred sauce (110 cal.), 1 c. canned green beans (35 cal.) *520 calories*

DESSERT: one can fruit cocktail in water (80 cal.) *80 calories*

TOTAL: *2038 calories*

VEGAN MENU:

BREAKFAST: two biscuits shredded wheat cereal (155 cal.) with ½ cup almond milk (20 cal.), ¼ cup blueberries (20 cal.), drizzle of honey (20 cal.) black coffee. *195 calories*

SNACK: ¼ cup trail mix. *175 calories*

LUNCH: 3 tbs. peanut butter (240 cal.) 2 tbs. jelly (112 cal.), on homemade sourdough bread (250 cal.) *602 calories*

SNACK: six whole-grain crackers (120 cal.), 2 oz. hummus (94 cal.) *214 calories*

DINNER: 1 cup rice (206 cal.) with ½ cup canned tomatoes (35 cal.), ½ cup canned corn (70 cal.), ½ cup black beans (115 cal.), garlic, cumin, onion powder, vegetarian protein of choice (150 cal.) *576 calories*

DESSERT: 1 cup vanilla chia pudding (232 cal.) with ½ oz. dark chocolate chips (68 cal.) *300 calories*

TOTAL: *2062 calories*

PRODUCT RECOMMENDATIONS

WATER STORAGE

Water Bricks

Water bricks are made in the US and are the product of an effort (inspired by Jean-Michel Cousteau, son of legendary oceanographer Jacques Cousteau) to reduce plastic waste, provide ease of water delivery to remote and third-world areas, and provide a building material for transitional housing. So you can feel good about supporting this innovative and eco-aware company.

A ten-pack, which will store a total of thirty-five gallons of water, will cost about $130–$180.

Semi-Stackable Five-to-Seven-Gallon Jug

LCI makes all its products in the USA, and their sole mission is to create meaningful employment for the blind and visually impaired. They provide training and advancement opportunities for their employees and engage in philanthropic efforts for research into blindness and treatment for the visually impaired.

waterBOB Water Bladder

The waterBOB bathtub bladder is a thick 100-gallon plastic bag that fits in your tub and lets you store and pump out water—like a giant dooms-day Capri Sun.

It uses food-grade plastic, and only costs about $35, so it's a pretty good bang for your water-storage buck. There are also smaller collapsible water containers if you don't have a tub.

Budget-Friendly Water Storage

AQUA-TAINER rigid storage containers from Reliance Products will do the job best when stored upright and used gently. And they're a budget prepper's best friend at only about $15 for a seven-gallon jug. But don't let cost prevent you from having what you need when you need it! You can start with one container and add more over time. Something is always better than nothing.

RELIANCE PRODUCTS is a Canadian company which focuses on creating products that can be recycled to produce more packaging, minimizing plastic waste during the manufacturing process, and supporting responsible manufacturing. They've also been a national corporate partner with Habitat for Humanity since 2014, providing lots of volunteer hours and fundraising efforts supporting affordable housing for families in need.

UPCYCLE PRODUCTS sells fantastic eco-friendly fifty-five-gallon rain barrels that are actually repurposed Greek olive barrels! They measure 38"x 22" and are high-density food-grade plastic that can even be left outside during the winter months. Heavy-duty screening will keep mosquitoes and other unwanted visitors out. The spigot at the bottom of the barrel is designed to fit a garden hose. Think about adding a twelve-inch stand (about $40) for the barrel to set on to keep the spigot higher off the ground so you can fill a watering can or other container right from the barrel.

The Gold Standard for Rainwater Collection

If you want to really nerd out on rainwater collection, RainHarvest Systems LLC offers complete above-ground rainwater collection systems that will store from 350 gallons (about $500) to 500 gallons (about $1,700), cisterns that can run into the tens of thousands, up to a mammoth underground storage tank system that stores 50,000 gallons for a cool $170,000, and everything in between.

LifeStraw

If budget and space don't allow, there's even a compact water filtration device called LifeStraw that can fit in your pocket, lets you drink right from any water source, and only costs about $20.

LifeStraw sells a wide assortment of small-sized water filtration systems that are easy to carry with you, store in your house, or keep in your car or office. Their largest system runs almost $500 and holds thirteen gallons at a time with a whopping lifetime delivery of 26,000 gallons! Use all that rainwater you collected, run it through, and you've got a hard-core emergency backup water supply!

Grayl

Another company, Grayl, has a fabulous product that acts like a French press coffee maker and can provide twenty-four ounces of drinkable water from virtually any fresh water source in just eight seconds! Fill, press, drink—from anywhere. This design is super convenient, and great not only for emergency use, but for travel to areas where drinking water might be a little sketchy. They cost around $90, and are worth every penny.

Backpackers and hikers know what's up when it comes to portable water filtration, and outdoor stores and online retailers have a host of products to choose from that can render drinkable water from outdoor sources.

FOOD PRESERVATION

Prepackaged Freeze-Dried Foods

We love Mountain House, which offers good-tasting breakfasts, lunches, dinners, and desserts, either individually or in premade variety packs designed to last a couple of days up to a full year. They also have gluten-free and some vegetarian options.

In addition to their freeze-dried choices, they offer a large variety of foods in #10 cans that include oxygen absorbers. You'll find everything from granola to chicken packaged in these large cans that are great for families or multiple meals.

But for sheer freeze-dried foodie fodder (say that ten times fast) nobody beats Backpacker's Pantry. They offer treats like Kathmandu curry, hatch green chili mac and cheese, Cuban coconut red beans and rice, and how about a little dark chocolate cheesecake or crème brulée to elevate your disaster dining? You can buy individual meals or case packs to create your own mix and match menu. They also have plenty of vegetarian and vegan options.

Pressure Canners

For the best of the best in pressure canners check out the All-American brand. Not only does it not have a gasket that needs replacing, it's built like a battle tank, and comes in a variety of sizes from 10.5 quarts (about $350) to a whopping 41.5 quarts (about $650).

For less-experienced canners with a smaller budget, the Presto is a great choice. It does require a rubber gasket, so be sure you always have an extra or two on hand, and that they are in good condition. The 16-quart Presto runs about $150 and is also great for use in water bath canning.

CLEANING PRODUCTS

Blueland

Blueland is on a mission to help eliminate single-use plastic packaging from everyday cleaning products. Their products are designed as a reusable, refillable system. Forever bottles, shakers, and tins can be refilled with powdered soaps or teeny little tiny tablets so you're not paying shipping costs for heavy (mostly water) cleaners.

The company features seven products: three cleaners, foaming hand soap, powder dish soap, dishwasher tablets, and laundry tablets. All ingredients are cruelty-free and are found on the EPA Safer Chemical Ingredients List. You can find them at *blueland.com*

Brandless

For cleaning products that are super-affordable, no-frills, effective, and come in refillable concentrates, check out the line from the e-commerce company, Brandless. They feature laundry detergent as well as products for cleaning tub and tile, granite and stone, multi-surface, and glass. The entire line is also made in America and Green Seal certified nontoxic.

Their mission is: "By focusing on quality over packaging and people over promotion, we're leading a movement that believes that making better choices should be simple and easy." Check them out at brandless.com.

JAWS

JAWS stands for "Just Add Water System" and it's just that simple. The company is a longtime player in the refillable cleaner business and has saved over forty million bottles from landfills by utilizing non-toxic refill pods of concentrate, reusable bottles, and water right out of your tap.

The full line of rainbow-colored cleaners has products for glass, kitchen, hardwood floor, granite and tile, a daily shower cleaner, foaming bathroom cleaner, multi-purpose cleaner, and a strong disinfectant cleaner. They also have an extra level of safety built into each pod which will only release the cleaner when the pod is in the bottle with the cap screwed on tight. You can find them at jawscleans.com.

Branch Basics

Branch Basics has one nontoxic soap concentrate product that, when combined with water in various quantities, replaces your glass cleaner, hand soap, all-purpose cleaner, and laundry detergent! Talk about a magical clutter buster! You can replace dozens of toxic cleaners with one concentrate that does it all. All you have to do is fill the bottle to the indicator lines with concentrate and water, and you'll end up with product mixed just right for all the different jobs around the house. Learn more at branchbasics.com.

E-BAGS

Mystery Ranch

Mystery Ranch makes fitted bags for men and women that are designed for different body shapes and have proven themselves through years of hard use in both back country and combat applications. Hopefully your needs won't be that great, but overkill is definitely your goal for an evacuation bag.

Tasmanian Tiger

Tasmanian Tiger makes ballistic nylon bags that will pretty much survive being thrown out of an airplane or getting run over by a tank.

KNIVES

Nope, this is not to cut a guy. This is a utility and survival knife. Good quality is the key, so stay away from anything with a stainless steel blade which is brittle, and never carry a Swiss Army knife for the knife part. Feel free to carry one for all the other super cool little tools, but a fixed-blade, full-shank knife is stronger than folding knives.

Folding knives are more convenient, and smaller when folded, so think about which type would serve you best and make the call. Why do you need a knife if it's not for self-defense, you ask? You can use it for a variety of things: scraping wood to make fire-starter material, flash a distress signal, cut a rope or paracord, dig in soft ground, use the butt of the handle to hammer or break glass, chop or cut food, cut through a seat belt, and a thousand other uses. Make sure your knife has a good sheath that can attach to a belt and, if it folds, that it's a locking blade.

Kershaw Blur Folding Knife

This is one of the few models they still make in the USA and is a great go-to pocketknife.

RAT-3 by Ontario Knife Company

This fixed-blade utility knife is worth every penny. I (Bill) own about five of these; one in every kit.

The ESSE 3

This knife has the same blade design as the RAT-3 but better materials and a more ergonomic handle.

Medford Knife and Tool

The Cadillac of knives, each blade is hand-hammered and forged. The quality and workmanship of their blades is top-notch and a Medford will last a lifetime or two.

CLOTHING

Base Layer
Tops and Bottoms

Softness, comfort, and wicking are your watchwords for base layers. And remember to change your base layer at least once a day if it becomes wet from sweating or the weather. If you are going to be walking long distances, wear a spandex-type layer so you don't end up with chafing on your arms, legs, or groin. Wool is a great material, but if you are allergic to wool, go with a wicking synthetic fiber. (Ibex, Patagonia, Smart Wool.)

Socks

Socks should be wool/wool blend if you are not allergic. Even if you have been in the past, it's worth trying out the new no-itch wool and blend ahead of time. Many people with previous wool sensitivity can wear these without problems. Or try wool socks with a synthetic liner so your skin doesn't touch the wool. Other synthetic wicking fibers can be worn by those who simply can't wear wool. Socks are one of the most important clothing items you have so don't go cheap. If you have space in your bag, pack two to three pairs a day minimum. Use foot powder and change them frequently and immediately if they become wet. Socks can be dried with your own body heat by putting them between your outer shell and inner insulating layer. (Darn Tough, Smart Wool.)

Mid-Layer(s)
Mid-Weight Jacket

Splurge on a nice fleece, or wool jacket if you can. This is the piece you will probably wear the most, so quality is everything. (Ibex, Patagonia, Arc'teryx.)

Sweaters/Hoodies

Essential and beloved, sweaters and hoodies should be in your closet and on your body during evacuation. Always go with wool or other natural materials like hemp when possible. (Ibex, Pendleton, Patagonia, Carhartt.)

Shirts

Cotton works for summer and hot temperatures. For colder temperatures choose wool and flannel. (Carhartt, Woolrich, Columbia.)

Pants

Wear sturdy, well-fitting, canvas-type work pants with six pockets. (Duluth Trading Company, Carhartt, Patagonia, Ibex, Columbia.)

T-Shirts

Plan on using two per day. Natural fibers are the way to go for this layer. Change them out when they become wet from perspiration or weather, and dry out the one you just took off as quickly as you can. (Patagonia, Carhartt, Ibex, Smart Wool.)

Outerwear

It's best to get good-quality outerwear if you can. This is the stuff that's really going to matter when you need it. It's hard to put a price on not being wet and cold and miserable while you're already stressed out, but it's high. (Patagonia, Arc'teryx.)

Rain Gear

Raincoats and pants are obvious choices, but rain ponchos are great because they can do double duty as tarps, a solar still, a small tent, or even sleeping bag covers, plus a poncho will cover your pack. Remember that rain gear is waterproof in both directions so it keeps moisture out and it keeps moisture in. Good-quality rain gear will have vents under armpits and in the groin area to allow moisture to escape. If you have unvented rain gear, wear a wool T-shirt and change it out frequently. (Patagonia, Arc'teryx.)

Cold and Wet Shell

Gore-Tex is great as a shell for cold and wet conditions like wet snow or cold rain, and as an outer layer that can be removed easily and dried. Look for Gore-Tex that is reinforced in areas like elbows and knees to extend its life. (Patagonia, Arc'teryx.)

Thin Shell/Wind Breaker

It's always a good idea to make sure this piece has the most water resistance possible, and if you layer it with a lightweight jacket, it will keep you comfortable even in the cold. (Patagonia, Arc'teryx.)

Soft Shells

This type of shell is water-resistant and flexible when layered with other outerwear. It can also be great in cold, dry or cold, damp conditions. (Carhartt, Arc'teryx, Patagonia.)

Parka

This is the outer layer for serious cold. If you're in the northern tier, you'll definitely want a down or polyester-filled parka and a waterproof outer shell so the insulation doesn't get soggy in cold wet environments. Look for ones with a ruff and a deep hood. (Carhartt, Arc'teryx, Patagonia.)

Mittens

In really cold environments mittens are way better than gloves for keeping your hands warm and frostbite-free. They allow your fingers to huddle together and share the warmth! If you have to be working with your hands, just wear a glove liner inside the mitten so you can pull your hand out with the liner on, and do whatever task you need to do. Always get mittens with shells and an extra pair of mitten liners so you can change the liner out if it becomes wet. (Outdoor Research.)

Cold-Weather Gloves

Gloves work pretty well, down to about 20°F. It's always a good idea to own a couple pairs of warm winter gloves, and multiple types of glove liners like wool and fleece. (Outdoor Research.)

Work Gloves

Mechanix brand or Hatch gloves can make all the difference in an emergency environment. You must protect your hands during preparation and cleanup efforts. Most of us don't use our hands for rough stuff, but hands are the most important tools you have and you can't risk putting them out of commission. Get a couple of good pairs that fit you comfortably and will protect you. Mechanix brand gloves have great dexterity and wear-resistance in a flood, earthquake, or other dangerous environments where the risk of cuts and scrapes is high. Hatch makes Kevlar pat-down and anti-knife gloves for law enforcement that are lifesavers and will protect you from just about anything.

Boots/Shoes

Always wear sturdy shoes in an evacuation situation. Sandals, flip-flops, slides, loafers, brogues, canvas sneakers, mules, heels, peep toes, boat shoes, and sling-backs are all a big fat no-go for adults and kids. Pick something that fits well, covers your whole foot with room to wiggle your toes, and can be adjusted for tightness with laces. Ankle support is great too. If you're walking a long distance, Vibram soles fit the bill because they are extremely durable. Boots should be leather or nylon, and if you are in a warm environment they should be vented at the sole to release moisture. If you are facing a wet or flooding environment, wear neoprene esior rubber rain boots and get the tallest ones you can find! Be sure to change your socks frequently. (Merrill, Rocky, Danner, Xtra Tuff, Muck.)

Belt

Get a nylon riggers type or a leather belt with a heavy-duty small buckle —no giant rodeo belt buckles! Leather belts should be oiled periodically. (Wilderness, Carhartt, Duluth Trading Co.)

WEAPONS

Stun Guns

Taser is the only company that makes a dependable, accurate cartridge-fed device that's worth spending the money on and can be trusted as a primary defensive weapon. Their X1 model works beautifully. Keep in mind that with a cartridge-fed taser you need to have a few extra cartridges with you just in case you miss or they brought friends.

Ammunition

For both 12-gauge and .45 ACP a great go-to defense ammo is Hornady Critical Defense. Hornady makes some of the best, most dependable ammunition available and is the gold standard. Check with whomever you buy your ammunition from on specific needs you have and they can direct you to just the right round. Twelve-gauge shotguns have everything from standard bullets to smoke rounds, tear gas/pepper rounds, sponge rounds, bean bags, flares, parachute flares, rock salt, paint, chalk, and that's not even half of them. Like everything involving firearms, take your time with your ammunition choices and follow the manufacturer's safety recommendations.

EMERGENCY CONTACTS

WRITE IN YOUR LOCAL EMERGENCY NUMBERS HERE:

Police: _____

Fire: _____

Ambulance: _____

Disaster: _____

Emergency Services: _____

911:

This number will reach emergency services in the United States, Canada, Mexico, Argentina, Jordan, Palau, Panama, Philippines, and Uruguay. Prank calls or misuse of the number can be considered a crime in most places.

SUICIDE AND CRISIS LIFELINE: Call, text, or chat 988.

Gives access to trained crisis counselors who can help those experiencing suicidal, substance abuse, and/or mental health crises, or any other kind of emotional distress. Think of it as the 911 for mental health.

SUBSTANCE ABUSE AND MENTAL HEALTH SERVICES ADMINISTRATION HELPLINE: Call 1–800–662-HELP (4357)

SAMHSA's national helpline is a free, confidential, 24/7, 365-day-a-year treatment referral and information service in English and Spanish for individuals and families facing mental and/or substance abuse disorders.

SAMHSA'S DISASTER DISTRESS HELPLINE: Call 1-800-985-5990

A 24/7, 365-day-a-year national hotline dedicated to providing immediate crisis counseling for people who are experiencing emotional distress, anxiety, or depression-like symptoms related to any natural or human-caused disaster. This toll-free, multilingual, and confidential crisis counseling and support service is available to all residents of the US and its territories.

VETERANS CRISIS LINE: Call 1-800-273-8255, text 838255

A free, confidential resource for veterans of all ages and circumstances.

ABOUT THE AUTHORS

BILL FULTON

Bill Fulton was raised on a ranch in Montana and from his earliest days he learned how to live off the land and off the grid. His family's ranch provided money and food, and "fun" for him was survival camping with his buddies in the hills and caves outside of town. Yes, he's eaten frogs and mice on a stick, roasted over a fire in a coffee can, and nope, he doesn't recommend it.

He spent eight years in the Army undergoing extensive training in anti-terrorism; weapons and explosives; hazardous materials; public health and safety; emergency management; and law enforcement, and after he left, he owned and operated a military surplus store selling survival equipment and gear, and teaching people how not to die in the Alaska wilderness. Today he runs his own sustainable organic farm in New England where he lives with his wife, two daughters, six goats, twenty-seven chickens, and four peacocks—one of which has an attitude problem.

JEANNE CHILTON DEVON

Jeanne Chilton Devon is an Alaska adventurer, author, and entrepreneur whose landmark retail store sold merchandise that helped people enjoy the great outdoors in a state where modern-day conveniences like electrical outlets, cell service, and "fancy indoor camping" in a cabin are sometimes not available. Living on the Last Frontier, she's experienced a massive volcanic eruption, hundreds of earthquakes, hurricane-force winds, power grid disruption at sub-zero temperatures, and been caught on a boat that lost its propeller in the Gulf of Alaska, a hundred miles from the harbor (hooray for sail power!). In a tiny blip on the map in Interior Alaska—where an avalanche on the one road south means you're cut off from everything, and where when someone says it's forty degrees outside, they could mean above or below zero—she and her husband have a giant freezer full of foraged wild mushrooms, berries, moose, salmon, halibut, and summer vegetables from the garden.

In her other life, she's a *New York Times* bestselling author, a multiple national award-winning blogger, and the recipient of half a dozen Alaska Press Club awards for her writing about environmental issues, Alaska militias, and politics.